I0795468

Literature for Little Bodhisattvas

Contemporary Buddhism

MARK M. ROWE, SERIES EDITOR

Recently published in the series

Morality and Monastic Revival in Post-Mao Tibet
Jane E. Caple

Buddhist Tourism in Asia
Edited by Courtney Bruntz and Brooke Schedneck

Monastic Education in Korea: Teaching Monks about Buddhism in the Modern Age
Uri Kaplan

Buddhism and Business: Merit, Material Wealth, and Morality in the Global Market Economy
Edited by Trine Brox and Elizabeth Williams-Oerberg

Lotus Blossoms and Purple Clouds: Monastic Buddhism in Post-Mao China
Brian J. Nichols

Living with the Vinaya: An Ethnography of Monasticism in Myanmar
Ryosuke Kuramoto

Literature for Little Bodhisattvas: Making Buddhist Families in Modern Taiwan
Natasha Heller

Literature for Little Bodhisattvas

Making Buddhist Families in Modern Taiwan

Natasha Heller

UNIVERSITY OF HAWAI'I PRESS
HONOLULU

Paperback edition 2026

Printed in the United States of America

First printed, 2025

Library of Congress Cataloging-in-Publication Data

Names: Heller, Natasha, author.
Title: Literature for little bodhisattvas : making Buddhist families in modern Taiwan / Natasha Heller.
Description: Honolulu : University of Hawai'i Press, [2025] | Series: Contemporary Buddhism | Includes bibliographical references and index.
Identifiers: LCCN 2024023280 (print) | LCCN 2024023281 (ebook) | ISBN 9780824897642 (hardcover) | ISBN 9798880700417 (epub) | ISBN 9798880700424 (kindle edition) | ISBN 9798880700400 (pdf)
Subjects: LCSH: Buddhism and literature—Taiwan. | Buddhism—Study and teaching (Early childhood) —Taiwan. | Buddhist children—Taiwan.
Classification: LCC BQ1045.T282 H45 2025 (print) | LCC BQ1045.T282 (ebook) | DDC 294.3/4441—dc23/eng/20240805
LC record available at https://lccn.loc.gov/2024023280
LC ebook record available at https://lccn.loc.gov/2024023281

ISBN 9798880700134 (paperback)

Cover art by Chih Wei Hsu

University of Hawai'i Press books are printed on acid-free paper and meet the guidelines for permanence and durability of the Council on Library Resources.

To my parents

Contents

Series Editor's Preface

HOW DO BOOKS WRITTEN FOR CHILDREN AND families picture the Buddha? What can children's literature tell us about the ways Buddhism is propagated away from monasteries and temples? How do children come to learn a tradition? Through a comprehensive investigation of children's Buddhist picture books in contemporary Taiwan, Natasha Heller continues the important project of expanding what scholars consider Buddhist. She convincingly argues that the stories in these books be considered a form of commentarial literature that explains and translates scriptural concepts for contemporary families using Buddhist "characters": Xuanzang becomes a foreign exchange student and a great explorer on par with Captain Cook and Marco Polo; "Everyone's mama," Guanyin, and other cute and friendly bodhisattvas model ideal behavior as everyday companions for children; and "naughty" monks like Rahula and Ikkyū teach children and parents about the creative possibilities in transgressive behavior.

Through these and other wonderful and detailed examples, Heller shows us the iterative strategy of teaching Buddhism in and to families, the affinity work of modern character formation, the gendered work of family Buddhism, and what it all says about Buddhist organizations in contemporary Taiwan. Moving seamlessly between historical texts and philosophical interpretations on the one hand, and contemporary picture books on the other, Heller's erudite textual readings and detailed visual analysis situate the stories solidly in the long history of Buddhist literature and propagation. *Literature for Little Bodhisattvas* shows us the exciting possibilities of a Buddhist studies scholar taking contemporary Buddhism seriously.

Acknowledgments

PORTIONS OF THIS PROJECT AS WELL AS OTHER RESEARCH on picturebooks and religion have been presented at lectures and conferences at Boston University, Duke University, the Harvard Buddhist Studies Forum, Ludwig-Maximilians-Universität, Northwestern University, Rutgers University, University of British Columbia, University of California–Berkeley, University of Virginia, and Yale University. Related papers were given at annual meetings of the American Academy of Religion, the Association for Asian Studies, International Conferences of the Sheng-yen Education Foundation, the Children's Literature Association, the Taiwan Children's Literature Research Association, and the International Symposium for Children's Literature and the Fourth US-China Symposium for Children's Literature at the Cotsen Children's Library of Princeton University. Comments, questions, and discussions at all of these helped me to refine my thinking about Buddhist picturebooks over the many years that I was engaged with this project. Donald S. Lopez, Jr. offered useful feedback on an early draft. Beverly Foulks McGuire and Vanessa Sasson generously read through the manuscript and provided thoughtful comments. A workshop at the University of Lund organized by Paulina Kolata and Gwendolyn Gillson helped me rethink key aspects of my argument. I am grateful, too, to the anonymous readers of the manuscript for their feedback and suggestions, and to series editor Mark Rowe and Stephanie Chun at the University of Hawai'i Press for their support and guidance.

For intellectual comradeship and inspiration I especially thank Heather Blair, Megan Bryson, Natalie Gummer, Elena Valussi, and many others who have provided scholarly companionship over the last several years.

Support I received for my research at both the University of California, Los Angeles, and at the University of Virginia made the present book possible. The College of Arts and Sciences and the East Asia Center at the University of Virginia generously provided a subvention for illustrations, and a Faculty Writing Retreat sponsored by the Provost's Office offered a conducive environment for final revisions. I would like to express my appreciation to the Digital Production Group at the University of Virginia Library. Dharma Drum Mountain, Fo Guang Shan, Grimm Press, Luminary International Buddhist Society, and Tzu Chi Compassion Relief Foundation were generous with images and copyright permissions. I also want to recognize the often-overlooked and anonymous skills and labor that go into book production, both of the picturebooks analyzed within these pages, and this book itself. I would like to acknowledge Wendy Bolton (copy editor), Mai Shaikhanuar-Cota (proofreader), Mardee Melton (cover designer), and especially Gianna Marsella (managing editor).

Jack Chen and Damien Heller-Chen are the best family (along with our cats and hedgehogs) an academic could hope for.

My parents, Lynn and Bobette Heller, provided me with a large collection of children's literature and frequent trips to the library; these early years gave me an abiding love of picturebooks that is reflected in the current project. This book is dedicated to them.

Romanization and Abbreviations

MULTIPLE ROMANIZATION SYSTEMS HAVE BEEN USED IN TAIWAN. For consistency and ease of reading, I have chosen to romanize all Chinese names, titles, and terms using *pinyin,* which is the most common system used in the United States. I have made an exception for Tzu Chi instead of Ciji, as the former is already widely used in English-language sources. Chinese surnames are given first.

References to the Chinese Buddhist canon use the standard abbreviation T for *Taishō shinshū daizōkyō* 大正新修大藏經, edited by Takakusu Junjirō 高楠順次郎 and Watanabe Kaigyoku 渡邊海旭 (Tokyo: Taishō issaikyō kankōkai, 1924–1932), accessed through the Chinese Buddhist Electronic Text Association Chinese Electronic Tripiṭaka.

Introduction

> Bai Juyi asked: "What is the great meaning of the Buddhist teachings?"
> Niaoke said: "Do no evil and pursue all good."
> Bai said: "A three-year-old child could understand *that*."
> Niaoke replied: "Although a three-year-old child may understand it, there are eighty-year-old men who cannot do it."
>
> *The Record of Chan Master Yun'e*

> Q. So the world itself can be viewed as a kind of picture book, as a series of illustrations from which a child will learn?
> A. Yes. For example, if you have two brothers at home, and one of them is a "bigger quantity" and the other is a "smaller quantity," a child immediately knows the difference. That is mathematics. Children can of course be taught such things in the traditional manner. But their joy is always much greater when they make the discovery for themselves.
>
> *Illustrator Mitsumasa Anno in conversation with Leonard S. Marcus*

Why Picturebooks?

This book had its beginnings in a bookstore in Taiwan. The 2011 meeting of the International Association of Buddhist Studies was held at Dharma Drum Buddhist College, on the northern coast of Taiwan. During one break in scholarly presentations, I wandered down to the bookstore that is part of the compound, and there I found myself drawn to the children's books displayed on a far wall. In one of the books that I saw that day, a bodhisattva shows up to help a little boy clean his room, defeating a monster made up of trash along the way. That's not all the bodhisattva does: she also helps him negotiate the problems of noisy neighbors, and to pick up litter from a local park. The bodhisattva guides the little boy to be a helpful member of his family, a good neighbor, and a responsible citizen—all common themes in the type of children's literature that seeks to socialize children into certain kinds of behavior. Here the bodhisattva frames all her activities with the little boy as acts of purification that are a means of creating a sacred Buddhist realm on earth, and so this story explains the salvific work of bodhisattvas for modern children. More importantly, it also shows the little boy having a personal relationship with the bodhisattva, independent of parents or other mediating adults; the bodhisattva supports the child as he learns how to act as a Buddhist within his social world.

That these picturebooks were sitting on a shelf in this Buddhist bookstore signaled a new and ongoing commitment to creating literature for children. Taiwanese picturebooks do not appear until the late twentieth century; they are very much an innovation of contemporary Buddhism. Picturebooks are not lesson plans or textbooks for early education, but their own genre of literature. To create a picturebook takes more effort than a text-only book: not only does it require an author who writes the story, a picturebook needs an illustrator who draws, paints, or collages images to accompany that story. The production process involves multicolor printing, glossy paper, and books in differing sizes. All this is to say that a picturebook is not a trivial effort.

The Buddhism represented by the picturebooks in this store did not align, however, with the Buddhism that was the object of academic inquiry at the conference. There, the vast majority of presentations were on premodern texts, with a predilection for philological or philosophical approaches. Both women and children appeared infrequently as topics of inquiry.[1] There is a long history behind the texts and topics that have been taken up by Buddhist Studies—one that I will not go into here—but suffice it to say that expanding what counts as "Buddhism" in the scholarly realm has often been met with challenges.

Children's literature might be considered by some to be "Bad Buddhism." Writing in the introduction to a special issue of *Journal of Global Buddhism,* Hannah Gould and Melyn McKay describe the risks in studying topics that do not conform to "normative ideals about what Buddhism is and should be." If subjects or communities deviate from these ideals, they may be seen as less worthy of study, and by extension, those who research them as less legitimate scholars. Gould and McKay note that textual sources form the "backbone of normative constructions" about what is properly Buddhist, but that only certain texts count: those in the canon or adjacent to it are readily considered Buddhist, while advertising material for Buddhist shrines are not.[2] Picturebooks are colorful, cute, and often humorous, not necessarily attributes that are associated with Buddhism; these same attributes make them pleasurable to read—and should our objects of study be *fun?* Picturebooks might also be perceived to dumb down Buddhism, attempting to be accessible and choosing simplicity over recondite language. They are not targeted for monks or even adults as a sole audience. To the untrained eye they may seem unsophisticated, and so their readers must be too.

Perhaps no such doubting reader will have even picked up this book, but I wish to state at the outset that the picturebooks studied here are Buddhist, and properly within the domain of Buddhist Studies. They are published by Buddhist organizations, almost always written by Buddhist authors, illustrated in ways that reference Buddhist art traditions, and convey Buddhist teachings even when their subjects are not explicitly Buddhist. Because these books are indisputably Buddhist, they are a legitimate and important source for the academic study of Buddhism. And not just for scholars who happen to be parents of their intended readers—these books show us how Buddhist stories, concepts, and values are translated into new contexts. Their aim is to make Buddhist families, and thereby remake Buddhism.

Picturebooks are worth studying in their own right, as one of the many sources that give us insight into contemporary Buddhism. But the unique attributes of picturebooks—as opposed to texts exclusively for an adult audience—can tutor us as scholars in ways that parallel how they train their target audience of children and their parents. First of all, picturebooks explicitly combine the textual and the visual, while attending to the material form. Given that Buddhist traditions have always drawn on these multiple dimensions, picturebooks are yet another source that allow us to get beyond the text as content and to see it as a materially situated form. Second, picturebooks address multiple audiences (as I will discuss below), and so compel us to consider how Buddhist sources might address different ages, social positions, and family status—and the perspectives that each of these offers. Third, and perhaps most importantly, picturebooks also ask us to pay attention to the act of reading—how it is shaped by material affordances, how it is a part of social relations, and how it relates to the world outside the page. In particular the picturebooks examined here show how reading is in dialogue with social interactions; reading (in the extended meaning of the word) is one mode of being Buddhist.

Buddhist picturebooks are material sources for the study of lived religion. As Robert Orsi explains, lived religion centers "religion as a form of cultural work" that is "situated amid the ordinary concerns of life": "The key questions concern what people *do* with religious idioms, how they use them, what they make of themselves and their worlds with them, and how, in turn, men, women, and children are fundamentally shaped by the worlds they are making as they make these worlds."[3] The picturebooks studied here cluster in the first two decades of the twenty-first century, showing how contemporary Buddhist worlds are made through literature for "little bodhisattvas" (*xiao pusa* 小菩薩, an affectionate term for children). This literature offers us insight on how Buddhism is presented to young readers as part of their social lives: it shares tropes, characters, and values with genres of Buddhist literature intended for adults, and indeed assumes an audience of different ages. Picturebooks show authors and illustrators transforming religious texts (as I will demonstrate in chapters 2 and 3), using religious idioms in contemporary life (chapters 4 and 5), and also making new Buddhist worlds (chapters 6 and 7). Picturebooks are part of the "cultural work" of modern Buddhism, and part of that work is to make Buddhist families.

In my subtitle and throughout this book, I use the word "modern." Although I do so primarily in its everyday meaning, I want to pause at this point to reflect on the more complex history of the term as it relates to Asia and Buddhism. Eric Hayot notes the "retrospective" nature of the term, acknowledging the developments brought about by "European voyages of discovery, the rise of capitalism, the establishment of the modern nation-state system, the Scientific Revolution, and the beginnings of industrialization."[4] Hayot also surveys the problems with asserting "modernity" as an era, and with applying periodization from the European experience to other places. For China, the emergence of modernity is usually located much later than in Europe, in the late nineteenth century or early twentieth century. Chinese modernity was bound up in the confrontation with Western political and military power and the collapse of the Qing dynasty. Culturally, it was connected with the New Culture movement, whose authors wrote in the vernacular (rather than literary Chinese) and who often offered strenuous "critiques of Confucianism, traditional customs and habits, oppression of women, superstition (*mixin*), and the ethical system of ritual (*li*)."[5] Such critiques happened through both the form and the content of literature and art produced in the early decades of the twentieth century.

Buddhism was readily classified as traditional, ritual-bound, and superstitious by critics, feeding into calls for reform: Buddhism had to find ways to be modern. As we will see, in the context of Chinese Buddhism this meant new educational institutions and engagement with science, along with the introduction of media such as periodicals. David L. McMahan, in his field-defining *The Making of Modern Buddhism,* identifies "detraditionalization" and "demythologization" as characteristics of modernist Buddhism. The former means a "shift of orientation from external to internal authority and the associated reorientation from institutional to privatized religion," while the latter refers to how certain elements are stripped of "literal truth-value."[6] Although we see some of this in Taiwanese Buddhism of the late twentieth century, it is also possible to argue for the persistence of what might be termed "tradition" and "myth," as well as for the ongoing importance of institutional religion. As McMahan also observes, the modernization of Buddhism happens "through the heterogeneous adaptation of the discourses and practices of modernity."[7] This characterization points to what has been called elsewhere "uneven modernity." Unevenness is often understood as a by-product of different rates and types of development. For scholars such as Haomin Gong "unevenness is not simply an adjunctive and dispensable dimension" but a defining part of "modern lives."[8] Gong writes about postsocialist China, and Taiwan exhibits different types of uneven modernity. The authors, illustrators, and readers of the books I discuss here do not directly theorize this uneven modernity. Rather what we see reflected is the shared reality of living within the structures—capitalism, nation-state, scientific discourse—identified by Hayot.

In this book I focus on modern Buddhism as a family religion. Very simply, family religion is the religious practices of a biologically or maritally related group of people. It is defined by *who* is engaging in it and by an emphasis on collective or group practice. This group dimension contrasts with the practices and experiences of individuals (emphasized when religion is taken as a mode of self-cultivation). Further, the family is a special type of group, characterized by mutual responsibility between multiple generations and bonds that are closer than those of voluntary associations. A family includes parents and children, at very least, and, as I use the term, assumes bidirectional interactions; family religion is thus both more than religious parenting and the religion of children. Family religion often takes place within the home, but should be distinguished from household religion, which denotes *where* religion is practiced.[9] Cuong Mai, writing about the association of Guanyin 觀音 with fertility in late imperial China, emphasizes that family religion is "practiced separately from established, institutionalized religions."[10] We see this in the case of rites at family tombs and offerings to ancestor altars at homes. But family religion also has continuities with institutions: their world-making is often shaped by the resources provided by religious institutions. I argue that modern family Buddhism in Taiwan is constituted through literature for families, treating the home as the primary site for religious formation through a process of iterative learning that inculcates interpretative strategies to be applied as children grow into moral social actors. Picturebooks are novel in the way that they combine content and form, but they also engage long-standing concerns in Buddhist Studies. In particular, they allow us to think in new ways about literature, education, and families.

Picturebooks enact one form of contemporary Buddhism, allowing us to see the multidimensionality of lay Buddhism, one that includes different stages of life. Because picturebooks necessarily incorporate both adult and child perspectives, we can see how Buddhism intersects with the social life of families and how ethical life takes shape. In the pages of picturebooks, we see how Buddhism is presented developmentally, and how a person becomes a Buddhist. In the production of picturebooks we see the creativity of contemporary Buddhism, in the ways that it combines Buddhist visuality with pop culture, retells old stories, and invents new narratives.

Literature

Buddhist picturebooks are a recent entry in a long history of generic innovation in Chinese religious literature. Buddhists in China began inventing—rather than translating—new texts from the beginning of the religion's transmission. They created scriptures that they gave an Indian backstory, but they also developed new genres of Buddhist texts: apologetic dialogues that mimicked early philosophical texts and the "records of words" (*yulu* 語錄) of the Chan tradition are two examples. Some new genres combined words and images, such as the *bianwen* 變文 and *bianxiang* 變相 found at the Silk Road oasis and Buddhist complex at Dunhuang. These represent narrative moments and places, and when used in a performative context, an audience might listen to a story, participate in rituals, and look at images as part of a single event. This is how Stephen Teiser believes that illustrated scrolls of *The Scripture on the Ten Kings* (*Shiwang jing* 十王經) were used; given low literacy rates in medieval China, "watching pictures" was an important part of religious life.[11] Sutra frontispieces, illustrated scriptures, and precious scrolls (*baojuan* 寶卷) also integrated pictures and text. Frontispieces could be generic preaching scenes, but some also made reference to the content of the scripture more specifically.[12] For example, illustrated versions of scriptures about the monk Mulian 目連 and his visit to purgatory to save his mother are formatted so that pictures of action appear above the text and are sufficient on their own to tell the story. According to Rostislav Berezkin, these illustrations "might have assisted poorly educated or semi-literate readers in deciphering the text or just served an aesthetic purpose." And precious scrolls were illustrated for the enjoyment and edification of the reader; as *baojuan* were often read in the inner, or women's quarters, they might have also served to introduce children to religious stories.[13]

For centuries, then, Buddhists in China have used the combination of words and pictures to make Buddhist scriptures and themes accessible and appealing to varied audiences. How words and images relate has changed based on available technologies of reproduction and printing, and the social contexts in which they were used. As we know from the work of Elizabeth Eisenstein, printing technology alters how ideas circulate, with wide-ranging effects.[14] Likewise the development of improved printing technology in China during the Ming dynasty accelerated the distribution of literature of all sorts and facilitated certain kinds of religious practice, such as the ledgers of merit and demerit (*gongguo ge* 功過格) and other mass-distributed religious texts.[15] Again in the early years of the twentieth century, advances in printing technology made possible Buddhist journals enhanced with graphic design, eye-catching fonts, photographs, and cartoons. The emergence of modern picturebooks (the history of which is discussed in more detail in chapter 1) depended in part on the availability of full-color printing to create a space in which a compelling visual and haptic experience was inseparable from the message.

New types of text can create religious communities. Writing about the emergence of *observationes* (collections of medical case histories) as a disciplinary genre in late sixteenth- and early seventeenth-century Europe, Gianna Pomata has argued that "genres are intrinsically social: contributing to a genre means consciously joining a community."[16] In the context of modern Buddhism, the journals that proliferated in China in the early twentieth century similarly shaped a new understanding of lay Buddhism and created a national community of Buddhists linked through rapidly distributed texts.[17] Picturebooks, as a new and distinct genre of Buddhist literature, prompt the question of what community is being formed through their production and consumption. The answer to the question goes beyond just "children" as an audience: although picturebooks generally are found in libraries and schools as well, Buddhist picturebooks are part of the community of Buddhist families. As with the *observationes,* which circulated "information within communities wider than those identified by school training," Taiwanese Buddhist picturebooks are aligned with organizations but not institutional settings. The community of Buddhist families is a virtual one, brought into being by a shared corpus of literature.

Education

Buddhist picturebooks and other children's literature differ from other kinds of educational efforts in that they emphasize an iterative, rather than step-oriented, process. Buddhist picturebooks intend to teach something—attitudes, practices, concepts—but do so in a way that is very different from modern monastic models, which center on institutional spaces and sequential courses of study. These developed out of early twentieth-century reforms that updated institutional structures and curriculums in response to perceived gaps and weaknesses in the type of education monasteries had traditionally provided. The reformer-monk Taixu 太虛 (1890–1947) was an early and important innovator, establishing schools that offered an alternative model of Buddhist education based in part on Western higher education.[18] Students of these schools spread this model to other locations throughout China, by founding or teaching at new Buddhist academies or through leadership positions at monasteries.[19] Revised course offerings went beyond Buddhist texts and doctrine to include science (biology, psychology) and Western philosophy; foreign languages also were part of the expected course of study.[20] Advocacy for Buddhist education also extended into new areas: educational reformer Jiang Qian 江謙 (1876–1942) promoted the inclusion of Buddhism both in preparatory work for teachers and in elementary classrooms during the 1920s and 1930s. Although unsuccessful, his arguments sought to place Buddhism alongside a modernized Confucianism as a form of self-cultivation that complemented the study of texts.[21]

What we can notice in these developments is how their features overlap with public or state-sponsored education. This is not entirely new: premodern examinations for monks were motivated by the need to prove that monks were competent and capable of making positive contributions to society. In the modern era Buddhist monasteries introduced elements that made them more like secular institutions of higher learning, and Jiang Qian's efforts attempted to insert Buddhism directly into public schooling. This suggests a kind of competition insofar as Buddhists are aware that they may be edged out by, or at least must distinguish themselves from, state-sponsored schools. We see this across East Asia: Thomas Borchert observes that novices in Sipsongpannā are shaped both by village temples and Chinese public schools.[22] Uri Kaplan notes that the Chogye order in Korea has the same "education fever" that is reflected in the intense energy devoted to university exams.[23] Examinations and graded public education both rest on the assumption that there is an end point: the goal is to produce competent citizens or full-fledged monks.

In contemporary Taiwan, Fo Guang Shan provides an example of this sequential, graded education. It has established schools for elementary, junior high school, and senior high school age students, as well as seminaries. The seminaries offer two years of training in Buddhism before an examination for those who are interested in further specialized education.[24] For lay Buddhists, the Buddha's Light International Association (BLIA) has been offering a yearly examination in Buddhist topics since 1990, with different levels ranging from elementary to adult. The tests aimed at young children have relatively little specifically Buddhist content, emphasizing instead proper behavior within the family, pro-social behavior at school and with friends, and good study habits. As Stuart Chandler notes, this academic structure was intended to "counter the characterization of Buddhism as superstitious and anti-intellectual" but runs the risk of being too much like other educational experiences students encounter.[25]

Picturebooks offer a different model of learning. Even as they are targeted for different ages and reading abilities, Buddhist picturebooks do not assume that they should be read in sequence or that there is a measurable way of assessing mastery of the material. Rather, picturebooks represent an iterative training in Buddhist interpretive strategies. What I mean by "iterative" is a looping process of returning to stories and themes, in contrast to a sequential building up of concepts. A picturebook may be encountered more than once, whether by the parent reading to the child, or the child paging through it alone, perhaps just looking at images. The story in its pages might be read first at one age, and returned to when older. The density of information (visual and textual) and the pleasure that is derived from immersive illustrations supports and rewards repetition. This iterative process builds a set of narratives or themes that function as templates for interpreting other texts, or, more importantly, everyday experiences. For example, Xingyun 星雲 (1927–2023), in his *Picturebook Heart Sutra* (chapter 2) tells the story of an old woman using beans to count recitations; the same story appears in a picturebook about Guanyin and in a commentary on the *Heart Sutra* for an adult audience. Through repeated exposure to the story, readers learn to apply its message—the importance of sincere intention—to different contexts. Children (and adults) do not *complete* this iterative education but become ever more skilled interpreters, using repeated narratives to read their experiences in Buddhist ways. The goal is to live as Buddhists, with the family as the social context for this education.

Families

The genre of Buddhist picturebooks creates a community of family Buddhists. Buddhism has most often been studied as the religion of the individual, or of collectives such as lineages or monasteries, but a growing body of literature focuses on the family as a significant social unit of religious community and transmission. Two recent works on Buddhist families—at very different times and places—show how this focus can draw our attention to understudied dimensions of Buddhism. Jessica Starling, in *Guardians of the Buddha's Home: Domestic Religion in Contemporary Jōdo Shinshū*, uses an ethnographic study of temple wives to draw attention to "the integral role of family as the connective tissue of Buddhist communities," especially as families are "instrumental in providing religious education."[26] Starling contrasts the public-facing aspect of the temple with the kitchen, "where the less visible, reproductive labor of the religion takes place."[27] Religious labor and education may not even be flagged as such: when asked if they bring up Buddhist teachings in casual encounters with parishioners, the majority of Starling's informants say that they do not. Although what they do may look like counseling, they also tend not to describe their activities in this way.[28] Yet as one of the primary contact points for the temple, the everyday conversations of temple wives provide models of Buddhist life.

Starling highlights the gap between "prescriptive, philosophical, and textual forms of Buddhism" and how the religion is actually practiced. This gap is reinforced by disciplinary approaches, with those scholars engaged in the study of Buddhist texts most often focusing on premodern sources, while those scholars concerned with lived religion often doing so from an anthropological perspective. Starling points out that gender also figures into this divide, with women often excluded from textual sources and their experiences better captured through ethnographic approaches.[29] This is an example of how disciplinary norms prioritize different objects of study and may overlook important dimensions of Buddhism.

Even within the study of premodern texts, the choice of genre can shape how we understand Buddhism. This is a central argument of Shayne Clarke's *Family Matters in Indian Buddhism,* in which he demonstrates that sutra literature and vinaya texts offer very different perspectives on families within the monastery. Through a careful reading of vinaya texts, Clarke is able to show that families (parents and children, husbands and wives) often entered the monastery together, and that nuns might give birth and nurse children within its walls. Such realities are in contrast to the picture of the Buddhist monk as a solitary renunciant cut off from familial ties that emerges from a selective reading of the scriptural tradition. Rather, Clarke finds Buddhism to offer a "family-friendly monasticism."[30] He also suggests that the field of Buddhist Studies might have developed in different ways had scholars taken vinaya materials into greater account at an earlier point.[31] Like Starling, Clarke concludes that what we can understand of Buddhist families is shaped by what we take as objects of study; the types of texts we read capture different dimensions of Buddhism. I argue here that picturebooks are necessary sources for understanding family Buddhism in Taiwan, and by extension they are an important part of the literature of lay Buddhism, a defining force in the religious landscape of modern Asia.

Picturebooks and family Buddhism also complicate earlier models of childhood education. Texts like *Twenty-Four Exemplars of Filial Piety* (Ershisi xiao 二十四孝) present stories that inculcate values—here, care for one's parents—by offering as models exemplary individuals. They are didactic, with clear lessons. These stories serve as narrative reference points for how to act; allusions to model individuals abound in premodern texts of all sorts. The exemplar tradition is hierarchical, assuming that children need to adapt to adult-approved norms of behavior. As we will see, Buddhist picturebooks provide many models for children, from the great monk Xuanzang 玄奘 (602–664) to other children, all embedded within social relationships. Picturebooks show models not just for children but for parents as well, and encourage imaginative inhabiting of different roles.

How Do Picturebooks Work?

Having explored *why* picturebooks are an important source for understanding Buddhism in contemporary Taiwan, across the three axes of literature, education, and the family, I want now to discuss what a picturebook is and *how* it works. Picturebooks are complicated: they are often treated as a subgenre of children's literature, but there are different types of picturebooks, some of which overlap with other genres of children's literature. Maria Nikolajeva has called picturebooks a "synthetic medium" in which the "overall meaning" is in "the interaction between different communicative means."[32] In this view, picturebooks must have both pictures and text—but how much of each is not always clear. Kristin Hallberg defines picturebooks as having at least one picture on each two-page spread, a fairly broad definition.[33] Other scholars would confine the use of the term "picturebook" to the thirty-two-page format commonly found in Western picturebooks.[34] However capacious or narrow the category of "picturebook" is taken to be, it assumes that both pictures and words play a role in the telling of a story. The pictures are usually taken to describe or represent, while the words do the work of narration.[35] Taiwanese picturebook publisher Hao Guangcai 郝廣才 emphasizes the important functions of illustrations—to direct the reader's gaze, create visual interest, and tell a story apart from that contained in the text.[36] How story and image work together varies, based on the relationship between author and illustrator, and even how the book is produced: if the pictures are added after the text has been written, and the author is no longer involved, they are more likely to serve to expand the textual narrative. There is a spectrum of proportions of words and images, and also a range of ways that they interact.[37] When text and picture are equally important, they can do different kinds of work: one can fill in the gaps left by the other, one can provide a commentary on the other, or they can tell a story from two different perspectives.

Defined by the combination of words and images, picturebooks are most often targeted for young children before they are of reading age or just as they begin to read. Picturebooks are usually designed to be read by parents and children together, and so have a dual audience of adults and children. A child reading *Medicine-Master Buddha's Birthday Present* (discussed in chapter 5), for example, would likely focus on the adventures of a young girl who is the primary character; adult readers might see a message in how her parents' work has disrupted family life. Thinking about how these two audiences differ requires engaging "child" and "adult" as categories, and considering how their meaning has changed over time. In this example, the little girl is independent, and both parents have demanding careers outside the home, reflecting modern ideas of what it means to be a child or adult. Yet "child" and "adult"—and their relation—are not fixed even in the present. The view that distinguishes children from adults through the former's lack of maturity emphasizes the *distance* between adult and child and privileges the natural authority of adults (perhaps they are the primary mediators with buddhas and bodhisattvas). In contrast, the perspective that treats childhood as its own phase of biological and emotional development emphasizes the *continuities* between phases of life—while still assuming children are less developed and, in some ways, deficient. The traditional view of children in China was closer to the latter, deeming children to be marked by "ignorance, helplessness and immaturity" and so in need of instruction and molding by parents and other adults.[38]

In an effort to respond to models that treat the child as lesser or other, Marah Gubar has proposed a "kinship model," asserting "that children and adults are fundamentally akin to one another, even if certain differences or deficiencies routinely attend certain parts of the aging process."[39] This model does not assume that one stage of life is inferior to the other; *both* may have deficiencies as well as strengths, yet share enough that they can speak to each other across their differences. In the example above, we see how children and parents might take different lessons from Medicine-Master Buddha's intervention. The kinship model helps us understand the dual readership of children's books. With models that imply difference or deficiency, a dual readership is a bifurcated readership, with children and adults having parallel experiences. (Some picturebooks are indeed written with this kind of dual readership in mind, and so include puns in the text, or visual references that require advanced cultural knowledge to address literate adult readers.) The kinship model suggests a different kind of dual readership that combines or moves across the perspectives of children and adults. This corresponds to what U. C. Knoepflmacher and Mitzi Myers have called "cross-writing": "a dialogic mix of older and younger voices [that] occurs in texts too often read as univocal."[40] For Knoepflmacher and Myers, the concept of cross-writing allows us to read children's literature with greater sophistication, seeing how "cross-writing of genders and generations can reinforce or challenge existing cultural ideologies."[41] The presence of cross-writing, along with the voices given to children and adults in picturebooks can reveal the cultural models of childhood and adulthood at work.

Both children and adults are constructed through literature that represents these different phases of life, and because picturebooks are meant to be shared, the constructions of children within them act not only on child readers but on adults as well. Picturebooks may show models of childhood that differ from the models of childhood that adults encountered in their own youth (as is likely the case with *Medicine-Master Buddha's Birthday Present*). These new models, in turn, can reshape how adults think about children and their role as parents. In chapter 5 we will see children developing friendships with bodhisattvas and buddhas in this book and others; in the picturebooks considered in chapter 7, children are seen as capable advocates for environmental issues. Outside the narratives themselves, paratextual material such as blurbs, cover copy, and introductions further explain to adults how picturebooks should be understood.[42]

What Do Picturebooks Do?

I propose we call the kind of work that picturebooks do "affinity work." In this book I argue that picturebooks are a literary genre that forges connections to Buddhism that will be developed throughout childhood; they are the material form of a specific kind of domestic religious labor. I derive this expression "affinity work" from the term *yuanfen* 緣分, which might be translated as "predestined relationship" or "fated affinity," and conveys the idea that people are destined to meet. Without diminishing the possibility of destiny, foreordained relationships often come about because two people are working toward similar goals or have shared interests. Affinity work lays the groundwork for later connections, providing the possibility for encounters that feel fated. In chapter 6 I look at several picturebooks depicting family conversations and argue that these interactions do not so much *teach* children about Buddhism as bring it into the space of the family, creating links to Buddhist traditions and institutions. Parents do this alongside the routine activities of homemaking and child-rearing. They also engage in affective labor, those efforts to create certain kinds of positive emotional states within the home.

To understand how affinity work functions *within* Buddhist homes, it is helpful to consider this alongside another form of women's labor, that of kin work (not to be confused with the kinship model discussed above). In her "The Female World of Cards and Holidays: Women, Families, and the Work of Kinship," Micaela di Leonardo introduces "kin work" as distinct from "housework and childcare." Kin work, she writes, refers to "the conception, maintenance, and ritual celebration of cross-household kin ties," which includes communication with other families, and the organization of celebrations. It also encompasses reflection on these ties, leading to decision-making about which ties should be cultivated and which let wither.[43] Di Leonardo points out that thinking about kin work allows us to see how nuclear families are connected to each other, not simply to larger social and economic systems, and that the creation and maintenance of such cross-household ties is labor almost exclusively carried out by women.

Scholars of contemporary Buddhism in the Himalayas and in the People's Republic of China have used similar concepts to explore the work of creating ties within the Buddhist world. Elizabeth Williams-Oerberg has used the term "connectionwork"—a term she takes from the Tibetan *drelwa ('brel ba),* meaning "connections"—to describe "how religious belonging is formed or not formed among the participants and a charismatic religious leader" through the performance of ritual.[44] Williams-Oerberg focuses on how rituals create an emotional and sensorial experience that contributes to "the interrelational recognition of charisma not only by an audience for a leader, but among the audience members."[45] Buddhist rituals generate connections not only during the ritual performance itself, through the liminal, charged affective states it evokes, but also during their preparations, which bind groups together. Something similar is at work in lay Buddhist communities in the People's Republic of China, who, at the direction of the prominent monk Jingkong 淨空 (1927–2022), have been very active in producing and distributing Buddhist literature. Gareth Fisher characterizes these as "collective efforts that created new forms of sociality outside of family and work."[46] Williams-Oerberg's "connectionwork" and the lay labor of organizing observed by Fisher both overlap with the concept of affinity labor that I propose, as they are undertaken by lay Buddhists and have important affective dimensions. However, affinity work is one step removed from ritual sites and charismatic leaders; I understand it as a form of religious work that takes place within the home, alongside other forms of abstract labor.[47]

If we take a step back, we can see that picturebooks themselves are part of affinity work, and indeed they are the material affordances of affinity work. The purchase or acquisition of this children's literature creates connections to Buddhist organizations. Within the home setting, *reading* these books is both part of child care and the affective labor of homemaking, and also generates loose ties that extend outward from the nuclear family. Affinity work is processual but not completist; it aims not for a particular credential or end point in religious development but rather for a deepening nexus of Buddhist meaning created through repeated interactions. This is the iterative process that picturebooks encourage as well, with each re-read thickening associations and meaning-making. The development of these affinities facilitates reading everyday experience through a Buddhist lens, and, eventually, acting in Buddhist ways. That picturebooks have a dual audience allows us to see how affinity work is part of adult formation as well. By creating Buddhist affinities for the family as a whole, caretaking adults also deepen their own sense of connection with Buddhism—and their own ability to interpret the religion for their families.

Insofar as affinity work seeks to make connections over issuing admonitions, it aligns with Gubar's kinship model of the relationship between children and adults. Both children and adults can act in Buddhist ways, as appropriate to their age. As we will see especially in chapter 4 (on "naughty" children), children's literature depicts adults who do not necessarily understand Buddhism or the world *better* than children do. Rather, there is continuity of human experience in which all persons could benefit from repeated engagement with Buddhist sources. This continuity is especially appropriate in a Buddhist context that emphasizes what Lina Verchery has called "ontological continuity,"[48] recognizing that that all sentient beings are alike in being entrapped by the six realms of rebirth. If humans share something important with animals, as we will see in chapter 7, how much more do adults and children share? Picturebooks promote the recognition of these commonalities.

In their material forms, picturebooks elicit bodily and sensory engagement, which make affinity work real. In the way that they ask readers to do something, picturebooks are quite like Buddhist sutras. Charlotte Eubanks describes the common injunctions to readers as "what a sutra wants" and this list for premodern sources typically includes listening (*ting* 聽 or *wen* 聞), accepting (*shou* 受), upholding (*chi* 持), reading (*du* 讀), reciting (*song* 誦), and expounding (*shuo* 說).[49] Through different sensorial modes of engaging with the text—hearing, touching, vocalizing—the sutra is internalized and reproduced. These instructions are embedded within the text, telling readers how they can relate to scripture, and although the reader may only take one of these actions, the multiplicity of possible encounters is part of the potentiality of the sutra and linked to the sacredness of the scripture itself, as both text and object. It is also a different kind of reading, one that is less focused on the acquisition of knowledge and instead invested in the transformation of the reading subject.

Picturebooks likewise prompt readers to a series of encounters with the text that use different senses. A list of a "what a picturebook wants" would include *listening, reading, holding, viewing, touching,* and *sharing.* In the Buddhist picturebooks that I will discuss, readers are asked to *listen* to the words of a bodhisattva spoken by their parent. The phonetic markers next to characters help children to *read* themselves stories drawn from Buddhist scriptures. The books can be thick cardboard for young hands to *hold,* or young readers may *view* glossy illustrations, whose colors and detail—such as of Xuanzang's journey (chapter 2)—create imaginative worlds. The illustrations invite *touch,* through a line of stitching on a monk's robe that invites a reader to follow along, and through games that offer explicit prompts to trace a path for a buddha. The inclusion of prefaces and other guides show that the books are meant to be *shared* by adults and children. What one can do with a picturebook reflects the importance of its material form.

That material form creates a space for the interaction of two (or more) embodied persons. Through reading picturebooks together, parents and children learn to share attention, a skill that has moral and ritual implications. Reading a book together, children learn to follow their parent's gaze, and parents, through "gaze checking," observe what their children are looking at. Both sides learn to coordinate their attention and share their excitement through a structured encounter with the book.[50] Shared reading is also a bodily interaction: not only do children move their hands to turn pages and point at objects, but they also adjust themselves to better attune their experience with that of the parent or caregiver. The adult reader is making the same motions, in a kind of echoing back and forth, as children learn the appropriate actions for reading a book together. Vocalizations—both in the form of words and nonverbal sounds—also play a role. Shared reading thus first teaches children how to pay attention both to the parent who is reading to them and to the object of their shared attention. Then children learn what they can do with that attention, through the questions their parents ask during the reading of the story, and, eventually, through the questions the child asks as well. When children are old enough, the parent guides the child in the development of moral awareness through discussions of the story they read together. The parent also enacts it: from the very beginning, through the call to shared focus, to the open-ended questioning that assumes the child has her own ideas about the story, shared reading plays out an entanglement of two different minds.

Although the literature on shared reading emphasizes what happens to children as they are read to, something is happening to parents as well. This can be on the emotional level, as parents feel positive about reading to their children (at least for the first few times through a story each day). But it can also offer a parent a means to refine their own understanding of other minds, as their children speculate on feelings and reasons in ways that might not be anticipated or understandable to parents. Parents, too, are practicing shared attention in novel ways. Shared reading, as a repeated activity structured by physical objects and bodily interaction, overlaps with other types of family rituals. The act of reading a Buddhist book together is affinity labor, creating affective connections that will continue to develop.

Sharing a Buddhist picturebook is one way to be a Buddhist, and the contents of the books explore what this might mean. They assume that the domestic spaces are legitimate, and indeed important, places for religious education; they depict what Buddhist families could look like in contemporary Taiwan. They show how Buddhist scriptures and exemplars can be reimagined for modern times and so model Buddhist interpretive strategies. They tell stories in which children are capable of understanding Buddhist ideas and of acting autonomously in line with those ideas, even as they still behave in childlike (even problematically so) ways.

My method is to take picturebooks seriously, reading them in the same way that I would read a thirteenth-century Chan portrait or a Ming dynasty temple commemoration. I look for the ways that these picturebooks are in conversation with Buddhist sources and with the broader culture in which they have been produced. (There is, after all, no way to extract Buddhism from the specific times and places in which it is practiced.) To this end, I have spent time in textbook archives, perused parenting magazines, and read picturebooks published by non-Buddhist religious organizations, along with going back to canonical Buddhist sources when they inform the picturebooks in question. I have also drawn strategies and vocabulary from the scholarly study of children's literature and picturebooks and consulted work on child development. Because I want to read these works closely and multidimensionally, each chapter focuses on only a few books.

The first chapter argues that Buddhist picturebooks in Taiwan are the result of three developments: first, the growth of Humanistic Buddhist organizations that are not beholden to the state, and that produce a wide range of media to promote the dharma; second, dramatic changes in family life and parenting that created the audience for picturebooks; and third, the importation of Western picturebooks as a new kind of children's literature in the postwar period. In each of the chapters that follow, I focus on a set of exemplar texts from four major Buddhist organizations, read against a larger corpus of Buddhist picturebooks. The second and third chapters examine how Buddhist literature has been adapted into picturebook form and how these adaptations offer interpretative strategies that can be adopted in everyday life. Chapter 2 argues that Xingyun's *Picturebook Heart Sutra* participates in the commentarial tradition of this scripture, both in text and through illustrations by Giuliano Ferri. I show how *Picturebook Heart Sutra* re-particularizes fables and stories for a Buddhist audience, in contrast to an earlier impulse to universalize Buddhist narratives for a general audience. Further, *Picturebook Heart Sutra* initiates children into the intellectual and affective practice of reading Buddhist texts and commentaries—anticipating that this will be an iterative process—while also teaching them how to read non-Buddhist texts through Buddhist perspectives. Children's literature about Xuanzang (chapter 3) recognizes the monk's popular appeal, reclaiming the monk from his fictional representation and modernizing him in clearly Buddhist ways. Depictions of Xuanzang's journey center Buddhist learning as equal in importance to scientific exploration; the Tang monk is shown to exemplify the qualities necessary for achievement in the twenty-first century. This is another model of Buddhist interpretation, taking a historical figure and re-reading him for relevance to the modern world. Locating positive qualities in Buddhist sources is a way to argue for Buddhism's continued value and importance. The fourth and fifth chapters look at how children themselves are depicted as Buddhists. Through close readings of picturebooks about the Buddha's son Rāhula, Ikkyū Sōjun 一休宗純 (1394–1481), and Shengyan 聖嚴 (1931–2009), I argue that the "naughty little monk" character contrasts with exemplar literature to create a Buddhist path that is accessible and developmental. Imperfect children are shown as capable of change and growth, and their stories encourage empathy toward those who make mistakes. Although the childlike mind is itself valued for its authenticity, these stories also emphasize the iterative process of Buddhist learning: good Buddhists are made—through effort and experience—not born. Chapter 5 traces a shift in the representation of bodhisattvas, from an older model in which the bodhisattva may be immanent in the world but not a part of children's lived experience to a modern one in which the bodhisattva is friendly and approachable. Through both the visual idiom of cuteness and child-centered narratives, these picturebooks show bodhisattvas as companions to children as they develop agency as independent Buddhist persons. The sixth and seventh chapters consider how Buddhism intersects with the social worlds of children. Chapter 6 shows how the picturebooks published by Incense Light (Xiangguang 香光) treat the home as a site of religious instruction for children, offering an alternative to the space of the temple that is on the one hand traditional in its gender roles but on the other innovative in centering natural parenting as the model for child-rearing. I further argue that cross-writing—including both younger and older voices—makes these books as much for adult readers as they are for children, thereby authorizing parents to act as Buddhist teachers for their children. Finally, through picturebooks about science, Buddhist authors and publishers prepare children to be ethical actors in their world. This means acquiring scientific knowledge in a Buddhist way, which requires making empathetic connections between the reader and nonhuman life, from dust mites to trees. Focusing on picturebooks from the Tzu Chi Foundation, chapter 7 shows how they extend their Buddhist understanding of medicine and environmental stewardship to young readers. As the topics of these books move from the external world of the natural and human environment to the health and morality of the body of the child, they grow more Buddhist in emphasis. Taken as a whole, this body of children's literature demonstrates how Buddhist traditions can be remade in new genres, and, using the interpretive strategies presented in these new genres, how children and adults can understand being Buddhist in the modern world.

PART I

Books

1

Inventing Buddhist Children's Literature

BUDDHIST PICTUREBOOKS MAY SEEM to be a surprisingly recent phenomenon—yet the conditions that make them possible were not in place until late in the twentieth century. Picturebooks represent a view of childhood and family life that has emerged slowly over the twentieth century, and *religious* picturebooks also rely on organizational structures for their production. In this chapter I briefly chart three separate historical strands that come together in the appearance of Buddhist picturebooks in the late twentieth century. The first is that of the growth of Taiwanese institutions that identify themselves with Humanistic Buddhism. Building on earlier reform movements, these institutions focus on what Buddhism can contribute to society as a whole and were able to expand their missions as government oversight of religion relaxed in the late twentieth century. The second strand is the history of families and parenting, which in Taiwan as elsewhere has been shaped by economic growth and sociopolitical changes. Smaller, wealthier families have greater resources to devote to individual children. Some of these resources might go to the purchase of children's literature, the third historical strand that this chapter will take up. Over the twentieth century picturebooks emerged as a specific subgenre of children's literature influenced by transnational encounters. For these three strands, changes and reforms that started in the early 1900s had a considerable influence on later developments. Since the present work is not intended to be a history of any of these developments, I will provide only thumbnail sketches of these earlier trends. Rather, I will show why the emergence of Buddhist picturebooks in the 1990s and 2000s happened when it did.

Humanistic Buddhism in Taiwan

The decades around the turn of the twentieth century were ones of profound political and intellectual ferment, leading to changes that would shape modern Asia. The Buddhist reform movement in early twentieth-century China faced criticism that religion as a whole was not prepared to meet the challenges of the times. The various Buddhist responses—new types of publishing, reformed institutions, dialogues with science—were ways of reasserting Buddhism's relevance for everyday life in its modern forms.[1] There emerged a shorthand for this idea: Buddhism of the human realm (*renjian fojiao* 人間佛教), often translated as "Humanistic Buddhism." This idea is most closely associated with the reformer-monk Taixu. Taixu advocated for Buddhism's role in improving society, drawing on Christian models and political reformers such as Kang Youwei 康有為 (1858–1927) and Liang Qichao 梁啟超 (1873–1929) as well as Buddhist sources. He saw Buddhism not as a tradition in retreat from society, or overly focused on realms outside of this world, but active in the world.[2] Bodhisattvas, as manifestations of compassionate action, were for Taixu not distant figures but ideals that humans themselves could strive to realize.[3] Similarly, Taixu reconceptualized the Pure Land not as an otherworldly paradise belonging to a distant Buddha, but as a utopic state that could be actualized on earth.[4] Taixu was not the only person arguing for reform along these lines: in Taiwan Zhengfeng 證峰 (1903–1934, lay name Lin Qiuwu 林秋梧) promoted the idea of a Pure Land or Buddhist paradise in this world.[5] However, many key Buddhist figures in Taiwan can trace a lineage to Taixu, primarily through his disciple Yinshun 印順 (1906–2005), who was influential in the spiritual careers of Shengyan, Zhengyan 證嚴 (b. 1937), and Xingyun.

As a hallmark of modern Buddhism, the idea of "Humanistic Buddhism" has been incorporated into the self-identity of many Buddhist organizations in Taiwan in varied interpretations.[6] However, for the middle decades of the twentieth century, Buddhism there was constrained by government limitations on religious activities, part of a wider swath of social controls instituted by the Guomindang 國民黨 (GMD) after their retreat to and recolonization of Taiwan. Buddhism had the advantage of being an approved religion, unlike other practices that were banned or regarded with suspicion.[7] The Buddhist Association of the Republic of China (Zhongguo Fojiao hui 中國佛教會, henceforth BAROC) served as the umbrella organization for Buddhist activities.[8] Under the direction of Dongchu 東初 (1908–1977), BAROC guaranteed to the government that members were legitimate and acted to police members' discourse, especially any hints of Communism.[9] Leaders of BAROC believed that the organization could best serve Buddhism by aligning itself with the government. Throughout the period of martial law,

Buddhist groups were careful to avoid politics, although some strategically praised the GMD.

The end of the twentieth century brought significant change: The lifting of martial law in 1987 and rapid economic development in the 1990s facilitated the growth and development of Buddhist organizations.[10] BAROC's control, deeply tied to GMD dominance, diminished during this period, opening space for others. BAROC leaders were almost exclusively male monastics who had arrived in Taiwan in the later 1940s, and the organization was increasingly sidelined in a changing political and religious landscape. New groups were well poised to adapt to this more open environment, and lay Buddhists were often a significant force.[11] With a focus on working for the benefit of society, Humanistic Buddhism provided a mode of engagement that could avoid explicit political entanglements or confrontations with the government.[12] This period also saw the indigenization of Buddhism on Taiwan (*bentu hua* 本土化), and the development of Buddhist media enterprises such as television stations and newspapers.[13] Following the end of GMD rule, and the reckoning with the atrocities of martial law, people had more space to develop a distinct Taiwanese identity—an identity that has only grown in importance as Taiwanese democratic traditions have strengthened, increasing the cultural distance from the People's Republic of China.[14] Buddhist organizations navigate Taiwanese identity—for example, Tzu Chi's founder Zhengyan regularly speaks in Taiwanese—but also see their work as part of global Buddhism, forging international connections and engaging in NGO diplomacy. Many Buddhist organizations have branches or engage in activities in the People's Republic of China, and so are more likely to identify as "Chinese."[15]

A handful of organizations dominate contemporary Taiwanese Buddhism—and, as we will see over the course of this book, also dominate children's book publishing in Buddhism. The Buddhist Compassion Relief Tzu Chi Foundation (Fojiao ciji jijin hui 佛教慈濟基金會), was founded the earliest, in 1966. It was established by the nun Zhengyan, who grew up in Taiwan during the period of Japanese colonial rule and studied with Taixu's disciple Yinshun.[16] Zhengyan's orientation toward social engagement was influenced by Christian missionaries, whom she observed caring for Taiwan's marginalized populations.[17] Initially the organization relied on small donations and the sale of handicrafts, and women volunteers formed the core of early Tzu Chi members. The next organization to be founded was Fo Guang Shan 佛光山 in 1967, under the leadership of Xingyun. The large primary campus in the southern city of Gaoxiong now includes a monastery, temple buildings, a university, a museum, and a memorial hall.[18] Fo Guang Shan has branches in Taiwan and internationally. Fagushan 法鼓山, known in English as Dharma Drum Mountain, was formally founded by Shengyan in 1989, but grew out of two earlier Buddhist institutions in Taiwan: the Chung-Hwa Institute of Buddhist Culture, focused on scholarship and publishing, and Nongchan Monastery 農禪寺, located in the northern part of Taibei.[19] Both were established by Dongchu, a student of Taixu who had risen to prominence in the Buddhist institutions of Shanghai and Jiangsu before fleeing to Taiwan in the late 1940s; Dongchu also headed BAROC. Shengyan was Dongchu's chief disciple and was named his heir. When he established Dharma Drum Mountain, it incorporated the two earlier institutions. A fourth Buddhist organization, Zhongtai Shan 中台山, was founded in 1987 by Weijue 惟覺 (1928–2016), and is headquartered in Puli 埔里 township in central Taiwan.[20] In 1996 Zhongtai was at the center of a public relations disaster in which young people who had attended a Zhongtai camp were ordained without parental permission.[21] For this and other reasons, Zhongtai now has a lower profile, especially in terms of mass media. Another major Buddhist organization, Xiangguang or Incense Light, was founded in its current form in the 1970s. An order of nuns, it has focused in particular on developing programs for adult education in Buddhism. The following chapters on their picturebooks will explore more dimensions of these organizations' missions. However, the landscape of Buddhist temples, associations, and organizations in contemporary Taiwan extends well beyond this brief survey; Buddhist identity happens in different ways and at different intensities.[22]

As wealthy, well-developed institutions, Tzu Chi, Fo Guang Shan, and Dharma Drum all have large media footprints.[23] They produce journals, radio programs, television shows, websites, and YouTube channels in addition to publishing books. These different media confirm a commitment to reaching multiple audiences in varied ways—and attest to a considerable need for content-generation. Children, too, have been targeted not just with the picturebooks but with cartoons and television shows. Much of this media is intended to be consumed by individuals or families, in contrast to public religious sites and shared activities, such as rituals at temples. As a television plays a dharma talk in the living room, it becomes part of daily life. The media enterprises of the major Buddhist organizations in Taiwan bring Humanistic Buddhism into the "human realm" of private homes.

Models for Parenting

Modernity changed Chinese ideas of childhood, and the parent-child dynamic in the early twenty-first century is significantly different than it was a century ago. Looking globally, scholars have argued that changes in the economic status of children, a result of industrialization, led to redefining their role in families and consequently society more broadly. Viviana Zelizer's *Pricing the Priceless Child: The Changing Social Value of Children* is a foundational work in this area: Zelizer shows that, following restrictions on child labor and mandates for education in the nineteenth and early twentieth centuries, childhood became more recognizable as a stage of life. Further, the value of children shifted from the physical work they could perform for the family to emotional and affective labor.[24] The impact of these changes can be seen in other domains, such as children's literature, which moved "away from didactic and religious instruction and towards works written for children's enjoyment as much as for their edification."[25]

Looking to China, changes in how childhood was understood were part of a larger refiguring of the family. Nationhood was intertwined with new ideals for the domestic sphere: for reformers and policymakers, a modern nation was only possible if families too were modern. A modern family was a *xiao jiating* 小家庭, a conjugal or nuclear family consisting of a married couple and their children, not the *da jiazu* 大家族, the "great clan" or "big family" that had typified the ideal family in imperial China.[26] The responsibility for transforming families fell to women, from fetal education to creating a healthy, happy home environment.[27] The health and moral training of children was called "family education" (*jiating jiaoyu* 家庭教育) and contributed to the creation of good citizens.[28] The family was not a private unit but existed within a moral economy that linked the individual to the state.

The modern child was shaped not just by home life but also by new approaches to schooling. In particular, character development, which had always been a part of a child's upbringing, was carried out in new ways. After the fall of the imperial government, moral education took on new urgency and new meaning: The educational reforms of 1923 replaced self-cultivation with civics and inculcated a new "citizen-morality" through textbooks that taught students how China had developed, how outside forces had taken advantage of its natural resources, and how one could be patriotic. Civics instruction focused first on family, then school, community, and country.[29] What children learned in schools was brought back to families, and children also had access to new journals aimed at them, supplementing what they learned in school. For example, letter-writing manuals aimed at children guided them in proper etiquette and social relations but also equipped them to assist less well-educated members of their family or neighborhood.[30] With greater attention to education and publications for them, children developed new domains of knowledge that gave them agency within their homes and communities.

The changes in family structure and culture in Republican China provide the backdrop for modernizing families in Taiwan, but families there were also shaped by the postwar experience of aid from the United States and other globalizing forces. During their colonial rule of Taiwan, Japan's primary intervention in family life was to institute public schooling, meaning that the Chinese family system continued largely unchanged.[31] Looking at the history of parenting in Taiwan, Pei-Chia Lan notes the period of United States aid (1951–1965) was characterized by treating children and childhood as "the target of public health governance," focusing on family planning, infant mortality, and corporal punishment.[32] Efforts by the United States to reduce the number of children in each family were effective, and the introduction of birth control also gave women greater control over family planning. Consequently, the average number of children in a family dropped from 4 in 1965 to 2.9 in 1985, and then to roughly 1 in 2010.[33] Beyond size, families changed in other ways. As early as the 1960s, conjugal families were the norm.[34] Parents (primarily mothers) found themselves caught up in shifting standards, trying to raise their children in ways that had advantages for the existing family and social structures when those very structures were in the process of changing.[35] The latter half of the twentieth century was a period of rapid economic development, accelerating the transformation of families. Instead of farming or small family-owned industries, which kept the family together in economic endeavors, one or more members of the family was likely to be working outside the household. This in turn altered the pattern of daily life within the household.

Public schooling has made education accessible to all, but, along with the need for long hours studying, has reduced the time children spend with their parents, especially mothers.[36] Schooling also means that children are exposed to ideas and values that may be different from those of their parents. Children may also learn more—and differently—than their parents did, resulting in an "educational generation gap."[37] Because many parents wanted a greater say in how their children spend their time at school, the Humanistic Education Foundation (Renben jiaoyu jijinhui 人本教育基金會) was established in 1987 to give voice to those who found the education system too rigid. The foundation played a key role in advocating for pedagogy that centered on creativity and emotional well-being. Led by "cultural elites" with experience living outside of Taiwan and in global networks, the Humanistic Education Foundation also produced publications aimed at transforming parent-child relations.[38]

Due to demographic shifts, the families that purchase the children's literature discussed in this book are more likely to live in cities. Urbanization has led to living arrangements that continue to favor conjugal families over extended ones, even though grandparents still play a role in child-rearing.[39] Families may also be part of transnational networks, through relatives or through work and education. More women have entered the workforce, and families are more likely to have expendable income that might be spent on children even as they spend fewer hours together.

Middle-class Taiwanese families, like middle-class families globally, have time and money to devote to their children. How they devote those resources is shaped by the future they imagine for their children and their own conceptualization of childhood.

In their approaches to child-rearing Taiwanese parents show a mix of "individualistic" values (such as independence and school achievement) and "collectivist" values (which include obedience, respect, and good behavior).[40] Many contemporary Taiwanese parents look back on their own childhoods as a time of academic pressure and authoritarian parental discipline. They want to offer their own offspring a different kind of childhood, one that is innocent, fun, and happy. Pei-Chia Lan characterizes parents of this type as proponents of "natural growth": they are more permissive, they want to shield their children from too much academic pressure, and they want to provide opportunities for play and engagement with the world.[41] At the other end of the parenting spectrum, according to Lan, are those families organized around raising children who will be competitive in a global market, and want to see them acquire the skills they will need in order to thrive in an imagined arena of transnational competition. This leads to "global pathway consumption" in the form of "international school, overseas camps, and enrichment programs."[42] In this type of family, time management is an urgent issue: children move from school to extracurricular activities, and even time at home needs to be structured for practice and homework. Mothers take on the majority of this family labor, often giving up their careers or scaling back work commitments, so as to manage their children's activities. Fathers may have jobs that require frequent transnational travel, which fuels the desire for global competitiveness and provides connections to transnational networks.[43] There are, of course, many families that fall in the middle of this spectrum, pulled in both directions—appreciating that natural development approaches provide a space for childhood, but also recognizing the importance of global competitiveness. Working-class parents, too, are aware of these different types of intensive parenting practices. To provide more for their children they may take on additional work, but that reduces time the family spends together. Without the resources to devote to extracurricular activities, academic achievement increases in importance, although this is in tension with a more natural approach to child-rearing. Working-class parents may then see themselves as falling short, both of middle-class goals and of their own parents, who are remembered as exercising more effective discipline.[44] In short, families of all types face difficult decisions about how to allocate time and money, and their beliefs about parenting shape their priorities. These child-rearing beliefs may come in part from religious traditions that provide community values.[45] We will see such values expressed in picturebooks.

Picturebooks in Taiwan

As in other places, the picturebooks and other children's literature published in late twentieth and early twenty-first-century Taiwan reflect the changing meaning of childhood over the twentieth century and are part of a longer history of educating children. Facilitated by the growth of print culture, the primers of the Ming and Qing dynasty represent the first shift toward modern children's literature. Many rewrote historical stories in rhyming verse, providing a way for students to gain literacy as well as learn history.[46] Other texts focused on the proper forms of social relationships, ritual behavior, moral cultivation, and the importance of studying.[47] One of the most popular illustrated texts read by children in late imperial China and into the modern era was the *Twenty-four Exemplars of Filial Piety*. This text was well suited for illustration, as there was a story associated with each of the twenty-four exemplars. Like other texts for children, *Twenty-four Exemplars of Filial Piety* incorporates social relations and moral teachings, but also offers children models for their own behavior.[48] However, illustrated texts were probably the exception rather than the norm, and within the context of schooling, illustrations came in for some suspicion: As Minjie Chen notes, Lu Xun 魯迅 (1881–1936) recalls that his teacher punished students who read books with pictures. He and his classmates were all eager consumers of illustrated books, enjoying *Twenty-four Exemplars of Filial Piety* and Buddhist tales of karmic retribution.[49]

By the early twentieth century, Chinese educators were incorporating new ideas about childhood and learning from the West. Childhood, according to Western educators and thinkers such as Friedrich Fröbel (1782–1852), John Dewey (1859–1952), and Maria Montessori (1870–1952), should be protected as a special time. Children learned in ways that were different from adults, and effective teaching capitalized on their natural impulses and development. For many Chinese reformers, a child's instinct for play could be harnessed for educational ends.[50] The use of pictures in learning materials for children reflected these ideas: children would be drawn in by the entertainment value of the images, with learning to follow.[51] New ideas about childhood also led to arguments for new types of literature for children. Instead of didactic texts that sought to create little Confucians, the essayist Zhou Zuoren 周作人 (1885–1967) advocated for fairy tales, integrating them into a description of childhood development in four stages. The creation of these stages also made the child into "a proper subject of adult observation, description, instruction, and discipline."[52] The selection of appropriate books was part of parents' attending to and supporting the ongoing development of their children.

Many in Republican China saw children's literature as a means to nurture citizens for a new nation. Emer O'Sullivan has noted that the education of children is seen as particularly important in times of cultural transition; this was certainly true for Zhou Zuoren and his circle. Not only did Zhou divide childhood into stages with distinct needs and capabilities, he argued that childhood should not be seen as a less important stage of life than adulthood.[53] Many Chinese intellectuals came to believe that, in the words of one scholar, a "civilized and advanced society values childhood and develops children's literature" whereas traditional society did not; having a modern nation meant understanding childhood in specific ways.[54] Children, then, were a way to create that modern nation. For author and translator Guo Moruo 郭沫若 (1892–1978), children had not yet been corrupted by older traditions, and so their development could be shaped by new ideals. Journalist and publisher Ye Shengtao 葉聖陶 (1894–1988) and author Bing Xin 冰心 (1900–1999) likewise both treated childhood as a time of innocence and purity.[55] These early decades of optimism and idealism about childhood and the emergence of a new, modern, democratic Chinese nation ended with the Sino-Japanese War and the civil war that followed World War II. Yet how early twentieth-century thinkers had imagined the role of children's literature in the context of nationhood would continue to have profound effects on education and literature. Not only were these authors and intellectuals exploring how children might play a role in a new society, but they were also reevaluating how childhood should be understood, seeing in this phase of life new kinds of potentiality.

Turning to Taiwan, modern children's literature was first shaped by the period of Japanese colonial rule, which treated it both as a subject for collecting and research and as a site for cultural transformation. Throughout the period of Japanese colonial rule (1895–1945), a major priority was assimilation (*tonghua* 同化) or Japanization (*kōminka* 皇民化) of the Taiwanese population through language, education, and media. Schools, and the textbooks used within them, were a primary way to advance this cultural project.[56] At the same time, a small number of Japanese scholars took an interest in children's culture in Taiwan: Nishioka Hideo 西岡英夫 (1879–?) wrote about children's stories (*tonghua* 童話) in Taiwan. Starting in 1917, Yoshikawa Seima 吉川精馬 published magazines for children, under a series of different titles, and these included simple illustrations.[57] The 1920s saw an explosion of interest in children's rhymes (*tongyao* 童謠), written by both adults and children; these were promoted in schools and published in various periodicals.[58] According to scholar Qiu Gerong 邱各容, the decade of the 1930s was a "golden age" of children's literature during Japanese colonial rule yet little of this literature was published in Chinese due to the language policies of the time.[59] Therefore, literary scholar

Lin Wenbao 林文寶 uses 1945 as a starting date in his analysis of children's literature in Taiwan.[60]

After 1949, Guomingdang rule brought an emphasis on learning standardized Chinese or Mandarin (*guoyu* 國語). Publishing houses, newspapers, and magazines promoted *guoyu* through works for children, and the government supported these efforts, establishing a prize for children's literature in 1957. Official organizations published literature that aligned with government language policy and sought to transmit traditional Chinese culture. Popular organizations and publishers produced works that reflected Japanese influence, but also took up Taiwanese themes. Overall, children's literature of this era—which lasts until 1963 in Lin Wenbao's periodization—consisted primarily of retellings of popular stories or older works with moral lessons for children.[61]

During the 1960s, the translation of American children's books into Chinese marked an important new stage in Taiwanese children's literature. This development was made possible by the Editorial Task Force for Children's Books (Ertong duwu bianji xiaozu 兒童讀物編輯小組), formed in 1964. Associated with the Department of Education, and with the support of the United Nations Children's Fund, the Editorial Task Force aimed to produce and distribute children's books to schools. Through UNICEF, American authors and experts played a major role in shaping the tradition of children's literature in Taiwan. In 1965 Helen R. Sattley (d. 1999) and Munro Leaf (1905–1976) visited Taiwan, giving lectures and visiting schools. Andrea Mei-ying Wu has written of the significance of this tour: Munro Leaf, author of the classic *The Story of Ferdinand,* gave "chalk talks" where he "demonstrated a simple and comical style of drawing" of the sort that he used in his *Can Be Fun* series as a way of adding humor to didactic works.[62] Sattley's involvement included promoting books about Asia for children through the American Library Association. In lectures to Taiwanese audiences, Sattley, who was both a professor of library science and the director of school libraries in the city of New York, spoke of the importance of stories that reflect children's lived experience, and that exposed them to diverse peoples and cultures as a way of forming them as citizens.[63]

Given the involvement of American scholars, and the centrality of translated children's books, the publication of children's literature during this era was a transcultural practice.[64] The work of the Editorial Task Force was innovative in the types of material it produced, which in turn transformed the possibilities for children's books in Taiwan. These include picturebooks that told stories specific to Taiwan, such as *The Old Cobbler and the Dog* (*Laoxiejiang he gou* 老鞋匠和狗, 1969), which features stray dogs, alley shops, and military veterans in a narrative with a clear social message. Another example of late 1960s innovation, *Little Basketball Dada* (*Xiao lanqiu dada* 小籃球達達, 1968) tells a story about social roles through the personification of a basketball.[65] Historian of children's literature Hong Wenqiong 洪文瓊 has observed that Editorial Task Force books were "far more revolutionary and innovative, whether it is in terms of format, layout, printing, writing, or illustrations."[66] These books focused on three themes—literature, health, and science—later adding arts and social sciences, and were placed in public schools, where they had the greatest potential to influence literacy and education.[67] Teachers integrated the books into the curriculum, and schools promoted reading.[68]

Although Taiwan continued to import much of its children's literature, there were also efforts to promote Taiwanese authors. In 1974, the Hong Chien-chuan Children's Literature Prize (Hong Jianquan ertong wenxue chuangzuo jiang 洪建全兒童文學創作獎) was founded; it was given annually until 1992. The purpose of the prize was to encourage higher-quality reading material for children, and to support authors of children's literature.[69] The 1980s and 1990s saw continued growth in children's literature, as well as new scholarly and publishing organizations. During this period, the Hsin Yi Foundation—established with the express purpose of promoting picturebooks—both published extensively and gave awards for children's literature.[70] Another major influence on the development of picturebooks was Hao Guangcai, who founded Grimm Press (Gelin wenhua chubanshe 格林文化出版社) in 1993. Hao sought out collaborations with non-Taiwanese artists, and Grimm books attracted international attention. Taiwanese authors and illustrators also participated in the annual Bologna Children's Book Fair, earning recognition through the prizes awarded there.[71] By 1997, the largest sector for new titles in Taiwanese publishing was children's literature.[72] This development has continued, with diverse and robust offerings in picturebooks and literature for older children. However, as of the late 2010s non-Taiwanese works still dominated: in 2017 roughly 80 percent of picturebooks were imported or translated, with the remainder local productions.[73]

Picturebooks connect with the changing forms of parenting discussed in the previous section through guides for parents. There is a robust literature aimed at parents that talks about both the merits of picturebooks, and the value of shared reading. For time reading together to be well spent—more important because there's so much less of it—parents need instruction.[74] Some guides are general in their approach, promoting parent-child reading and suggesting how to select appropriate literature. Others provide explicit instruction on how to read specific books with children. *Little Treasures Listen to Stories* (*Baobao ting gushi* 寶寶聽故事) is an example of a guide that offers detailed guidance, starting from the premise that reading is multisensory and that any interaction with a book can be considered reading. The book instructs parents on how to interpret both text and illustration, as well as their relationship, and offers over a dozen pages of strategies to keep children engaged, such as melodic, rhythmic reading, the use of props, and so forth.[75] Supplementing printed guides, parents may even attend classes to learn different strategies for reading together.[76] Reading together also opens the path for conversations on difficult topics and moral development, another area that parenting discourse treats as a source of anxiety. Reading picturebooks fosters togetherness not simply through reading but also through the discussions that follow, and so children's literature is deeply entwined with Taiwanese parenting discourse.[77]

Antecedents for Buddhist Picturebooks

The emergence of Buddhist children's books as a recognizable category was shaped by the development of educational outreach to lay Buddhists as part of the modernizing movements in the first decades of the twentieth century discussed earlier in this chapter. As an important example, the writings of Chen Hailiang 陳海量 (1910–1983) instructed lay Buddhists on how to live their daily lives—from family budgets to morning and evening lessons—how to spread Buddhism through music, and how to hold Buddhicized weddings.[78] Chen advanced the idea of a Buddhist family in his *Essentials of Studying Buddhism at Home* (*Zaijia xuefo yaodian* 在家學佛要典), which includes texts and commentaries that he identified as important for lay Buddhists, and also a "reader" (*duben* 讀本) for parents to use with children. This reader is divided into seven levels, with the first level using three-character phrasings like the *Three-Character Classic* (*Sanzi jing* 三字經), which was a standard text for early learning in late imperial China. This first level emphasizes that children should be respectful to their parents and to the Three Treasures, along with other polite and kind behavior. Being a good Buddhist means reciting sutras and the Buddha's name, but also being vegetarian and being compassionate to animals. The next six levels repeat these themes, gradually shifting the proportion of basic morality to Buddhist content: by the seventh level, children are learning core Buddhist concepts and the religion's history in China.[79] At the end of the reader, Chen adds a note in which he stresses that parents should not leave their children's education entirely to teachers and schools, but should view it as their own primary responsibility, linking the child's formation to the Buddhist practices of their parents. Chen also recognizes that mothers have a larger role in their children's upbringing because they spend more time with them; an illustration a few pages later depicts an elegant woman holding a rosary, as two sturdy children bow before her (Figure 1.1).[80] Her fashionable *qipao* and voguish hairstyle position her as a modern woman who is also a good Buddhist mother.

FIGURE 1.1. Illustration from *Essentials of Studying Buddhism at Home,* first published by Daxiong Fenxuntuan 大雄奮迅團 in 1943.

There were also adaptations of and innovations in Buddhist literature that expanded the ways that the tradition might be presented to lay audiences; these are forerunners to the emergence of Buddhist literature aimed more explicitly at children. For example, the short tales of the *Scripture of One Hundred Analogies* (*Baiyu jing* 百喻經) proved popular in the development of modern literary culture in the early years of the twentieth century; in the late twentieth century Fo Guang Shan would adapt these for children, as we will see in the next chapter.[81] Another important example of early modern Buddhist literature is *Collected Illustrations for Protecting Life* (*Husheng huaji* 護生畫集) by Feng Zikai 豐子愷 (1898–1975). A publication with considerable impact in the twentieth century, *Collected Illustrations for Protecting Life* was a series of books with illustrations that bridged woodblock prints and cartoons.[82] Feng was an accomplished artist, trained under Li Shutong 李叔同, later known by the monastic name Hongyi 弘一 (1880–1942); Feng made the first collection in honor of his teacher's fiftieth birthday.[83] Feng focused on the treatment of living beings, including animals, insects, and plants in his illustrations, which, along with clever titles and short anecdotes, prompt people to reflect on their habits, most especially that of eating meat. These are themes that are closely connected to Buddhism, if not exclusive to it. Feng's illustration style was modern and distinctly his own, yet also informed by earlier traditions.[84] Feng wrote six volumes altogether, and various combinations and selections of these have been published continuously since 1928, with never more than a few years' gap between dates of publication.[85] The frequency and scope of distribution—Shanghai, Hong Kong, Singapore, Taibei, Taizhong—attest to its significant appeal. *Collected Illustrations for Protecting Life* has had an enduring influence, especially in the combination of traditional art techniques and modern themes.

Buddhist Picturebooks

Buddhist picturebooks in Taiwan developed subsequently to that of children's literature more generally, facilitated both by the rapid growth of this publishing sector and by the easing of limitations on religious activities after the lifting of martial law in 1987. Hong Wenqiong writes that there are select examples in the late 1970s and 1980s, but that the majority of Buddhist picturebooks have been published from the 1990s until the present.[86] The first Buddhist organization to produce books for children was the Ci'en Youth Education Foundation (full name, Fojiao Cien yuyou jijinhui 佛教慈恩育幼基金會), founded by the monk Kaizheng 開證 (1925–2001) in Gaoxiong in 1978.[87] Hong Wenqiong himself served as the editor for their publications and helped to organize a series of research conferences on Buddhist children's literature. Although Ci'en also published a children's magazine, their major output was a series of twenty books under the title Ci'en Buddhist Children's Collection (Ci'en fojiao ertong congshu 慈恩佛教兒童叢書) (Figure 1.2). All but two of the books were authored by Lin Shimin 林世敏 (b. 1944), a Buddhist layman with a journalism degree and teaching experience. Also from Gaoxiong, Lin had been instrumental in encouraging Kaizheng's turn to children's educational materials.[88] The series covered bodhisattvas, eminent Buddhist figures of China, the life of Śākyamuni, the ten disciples of the Buddha, five volumes of *Journey to the West,* stories of relics, and Buddhist fables (*yuyan* 寓言), fairy tales (*tonghua*), and children's poetry. Ci'en engaged leading artists for the artwork, some of which is in color. Although illustrated, the books in this series are not true picturebooks, as text dominates and the reading level is that of elementary school students. However, the topics and themes taken up in the Ci'en Buddhist Children's Collection return in children's literature published by other Buddhist organizations.

There are only a handful of books that fall between the Ci'en series and Fo Guang Shan's publication of the *Illustrated Scripture of One Hundred Analogies* (Baiyujing tuhuashu 百喻經圖畫書) in 1995, which marks the beginning of more regular and substantial children's publishing from the major organizations.[89] Two books serve as a representative of this interim

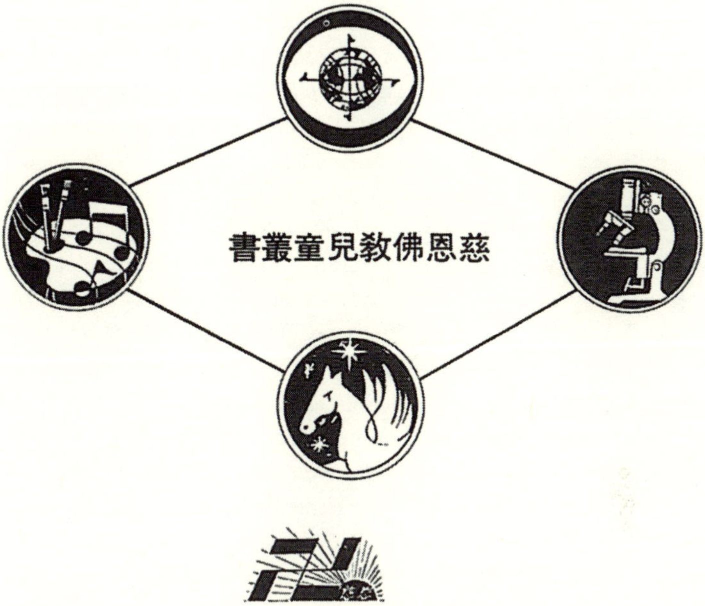

FIGURE 1.2. Logo of Ci'en Buddhist Children's Collection.

period. First, *The Nine-Colored Deer* (*Jiuse lu* 九色鹿), published in 1988 by Puyin 普音, is one of many contemporary versions of this *jātaka* tale. The other book from this period is *Everyone's Mama* (*Dajia de mama* 大家的媽媽), published by a forerunner of the Dharma Drum organization; this story of the bodhisattva Guanyin will be discussed in chapter 5.

Beyond their subject matter, Buddhist children's books have several characteristics that distinguish them from most commercial children's books. Hong Wenqiong identifies three: First, they are sold by the organizations themselves, and are not usually available in mainstream bookstores. Second, Buddhist children's books are more likely to include English translations, and often are tied to other media such as ebooks or compact discs with recordings of the books being read aloud. Third, although commercially published children's books will usually indicate the intended age of the reader, Buddhist publishers tend not to do this, and indeed many of their publications do not seem to be entirely for children.[90] This makes the issues of dual audience and cross-writing yet more salient for Buddhist picturebooks. Although Buddhist picturebooks are produced and purchased primarily within the closed system of religious organizations, they are not consumed in isolation from other materials for children. Because their authors and illustrators are almost always Taiwanese, Buddhist offerings are part of the roughly 20 percent of picturebooks that are written within the country. The high proportion of imported or translated picturebooks mean that many of the stories children encounter do not include characters who look like them or share their life experiences. Commercial children's book publishers in Taiwan also consider how to market their books to a global audience, which makes universal topics such as friendship, family, and the environment more popular than those that are recognizably Taiwanese.[91] Buddhist children's books contribute to the landscape of picturebooks both by offering readers depictions of Taiwanese (or more generally Asian) characters, and by representing an important dimension of Taiwanese culture. In this sense they are more reflective of life in Taiwan than many other books for young children.

Picturebooks need both producers and consumers, and the advent of Buddhist picturebooks in Taiwan is a distinctly late twentieth-century phenomenon. Buddhist authors and publishers had long been experimenting with different genres and formats, and modernizing movements continued to do so. Providing literature for children became more important as childhood emerged as a discrete time of life with developmental stages. Beginning in the 1960s and 1970s in Taiwan, creative children's literature—modeled first on American examples—sought to entertain as much as educate. When Buddhist groups expanded their media enterprises in the 1990s and 2000s, they also included print materials for young children, influenced by the broader field of children's books. As we will now see, these have both adapted canonical sources and offered new types of Buddhist stories. In Buddhist picturebooks, religious tradition animates, and is animated in, everyday life.

2

Once I Have Heard a Story

LET'S IMAGINE A CHILD OPENING A PICTUREBOOK, and seeing a craggy mountainscape, populated by a lone monk leading a train of donkeys. Flip the page and monks sit in meditation scattered across rocky outcrops—is the monk from the first page perhaps among them?—illumined by a sun glowing in a rosy sky. Turn the page again and suddenly the reader is taken to a storm-tossed sea, and then, on the next page, washes up well inland, on a grassy field strewn with flowers, children running across it. Later illustrations take us to a royal palace and a field of grain; with soft edges and intense colors, there is a dreamlike quality to them. What kind of story is this, with such disparate settings? It isn't a story—it is a sutra. Or, as I will argue, it is a *commentary* on sutra that uses stories to explain the scripture's core concepts.

Sutras are not child-friendly. That children should be reading Buddhist sutras, even when adapted for them, is not an obvious conclusion. There are many reasons why they wouldn't: the Mahāyāna scriptures most popular in Chinese Buddhism (such as the *Diamond Sutra,* the *Lotus Sutra,* and the *Vimalakīrti Sūtra*) do not offer action-filled plots, or characters and settings that would necessarily resonate with young readers. Further, *reading* a scripture—as opposed to recitation or copying—was not always the most important way to interact with a Buddhist sutra. To imagine children as young readers of canonical Buddhist texts is to think about those children as having certain kinds of skills, potentials, and interests; the selection of which texts they should be reading, and how, further refines how children are conceived. But such adaptations are not only about children: through their interpretive strategies they present a model of Buddhist reading that can be extended to other circumstances, both textual and lived.

This chapter will focus on the *Picturebook Heart Sutra* (*Huiben xinjing* 繪本心經), written by Xingyun, the founder of Fo Guang Shan, as a case study of how a modern picturebook relates to the commentarial tradition and how young Buddhists are taught to use texts. The *Heart Sutra* (*Xinjing* 心經) is an important text both doctrinally and devotionally; its contents are a concise treatment of Buddhist ontology, and its brevity lends itself to recitation and copying. However, with little narrative structure and no real characters, the *Heart Sutra* is an especially counterintuitive choice for young readers. To make it approachable, *Picturebook Heart Sutra* functions as a commentary on the original text, using metaphors, stories, and illustration to explain philosophical concepts. This multifaceted commentary argues for the *Heart Sutra* as a way of understanding the world through a Buddhist lens.

The Commentarial Context

The *Heart Sutra* is a foundational text for Buddhism in China, and the history of the text and its commentaries in China demonstrates why Xingyun would find it a natural choice for reinterpretation as a children's book. It is a succinct expression of Perfection of Wisdom (Prajñāpāramitā) thought, roughly a page long; the original text is included on the final page of *Picturebook Heart Sutra*. It records the speech of the bodhisattva Avalokiteśvara, here called Guanzizai 觀自在, instead of the more common Guanshiyin 觀世音 or Guanyin, reflecting how the famed monk Xuanzang translated the name. Having Avalokiteśvara as the primary speaker is unusual. This is the only Prajñāpāramitā scripture in which this bodhisattva appears, suggesting that the text was written at a point at which the cult of Avalokiteśvara was already well developed.[1] The bodhisattva, from within his practice of the perfection of wisdom, perceives that the five aggregates (*yun* 蘊, Skt. *skandha*) are empty; he then explains this emptiness to Śāriputra, one of the disciples of the Buddha. Understanding emptiness is the perfection of wisdom, and what allows the bodhisattvas to attain an unobstructed mind. The scripture ends with a mantra.

This concise text contains a series of difficult concepts, the first of which is the perfection of wisdom. This is the highest of the six perfections (*du* 度 or *boluomi* 波羅蜜; Skt. *pāramitā*), or the practices of effort, meditation, and wisdom. Next, there are the five aggregates, a way of describing the different elements that make up human existence: form (*se* 色), sensory reception (*shou* 受), ideation (*xiang* 想), impulse (*xing* 行), and consciousness (*shi* 識).[2] Without having reached emptiness, the central concept of the text, the reader has already encountered two sets of concepts that would require a relatively high degree of prior knowledge to be comprehensible. The core of the scripture consists of the identity of form with emptiness, which then applies, by extension, to the other aggregates. As we will see, this is knowledge that readers can use to understand emptiness in the world around them.

Xingyun's *Picturebook Heart Sutra* is part of the robust commentarial tradition that emerged around the *Heart Sutra*. As John McRae puts it, "The elegant brevity and multivalent profundity of the text have made it a favorite subject of commentators from the middle of the seventh century up until the present day, and there is no other single text . . . that has been interpreted by such, a long and virtually unbroken list of illustrious authorities."[3] To note a few of the important Chinese commentaries, the earliest is by Kuiji 窺基 (632–682), who treated the *Heart Sutra* as an "extensive, wide-ranging debate between Yogācāra and Madhyamaka."[4] Kuiji devotes a significant amount of space to a discussion of practice, based on the first line of the scripture in which Guanzizai (Avalokiteśvara) is described as practicing (*xing* 行) the perfection of wisdom.[5] A few decades later, Fazang 法藏 (643–712), the third patriarch of the Huayan 華嚴 school, wrote a commentary in which he sought to explain how meditation and the bodhisattva ideal relates to the theme of the scripture.[6] There are two clusters of Chan commentaries on the *Heart Sutra,* according to McRae, one dating from the Tang and Song dynasties, and another from the late Ming and Qing dynasties. The first series is characterized by the use of Chan terminology in the interpretation of the scripture, and also by the use of the "rhetoric" and "phraseology" of encounter dialogue. Some use Chan-style verses; others add capping phrases like those found in *gong'an* anthologies.[7] The late Ming and Qing Chan commentaries pick up on themes popular in their time, such as the unity of the three teachings (of Buddhism, Confucianism, and Lao-Zhuang Daoism).[8] Modern exegesis of the *Heart Sutra* continues with commentaries by prominent figures in the history of modern Chinese Buddhism, including Taixu, Hongyi, and Shengyan.[9] What these various commentaries show in aggregate is that the *Heart Sutra* is open to interpretation by different strands of Buddhist thought and practice, and adapt the scripture to particular intellectual circumstances. Xingyun innovates in the *Picturebook Heart Sutra* and elsewhere, integrating Buddhist storytelling with the commentarial tradition of this scripture.

Explaining the Text

Xingyun's work on the *Heart Sutra* is extensive, including several books, lecture videos, and web content. He sees this text as the linchpin of Buddhist teachings, and his preface for adults in *Picturebook Heart Sutra* frames it as such. He writes that the Buddha spent twenty-two years of his forty-nine-year career preaching wisdom (*prajñā, banruo* 般若), the core theme of the *Heart Sutra.* Opening the text for children, Xingyun emphasizes the historical context: "The *Heart Sutra* was translated by the great teacher Xuanzang of the Tang dynasty." In the next two sentences Xingyun describes Xuanzang's background, his status as a translator, and his journey to retrieve scriptures; Xingyun then positions the *Heart Sutra* within Prajñāpāramitā thought and its centrality to the Buddha's teaching.[10] The *Heart Sutra* has traditionally been taken as a translation by Xuanzang, and Xingyun is quick to link the scripture to preaching of the Buddha. The following page expands on this, as Xingyun explains that the content of the scripture is a result of a dialogue between Avalokiteśvara and the disciple Śāriputra that took place when the two were gathered with the Buddha, other bodhisattvas, and hundreds of disciples at Vulture Peak. These details are not in the scripture and point to its complicated history. Jan Nattier's pioneering work on the *Heart Sutra* has shown that the text is very likely not a translation from a preexisting Sanskrit text. Further, the scripture is not included in Xuanzang's compendium of Prajñāpāramitā translations, suggesting that his name was added after the fact. Nattier concludes that the *Heart Sutra* is an extract from the *Great Sutra on the Perfection of Wisdom* (*Mohe banruo boluomi jing* 摩訶般若波羅蜜經, T. 8, no. 223), translated by Kumārajīva 鳩摩羅什 (344–413); this extract was later edited, possibly by Xuanzang. Even if he was not the editor, Xuanzang "was responsible for the widespread popularity of the *sutra* in China, and in all probability for its initial circulation."[11]

We do not see this level of detail in a children's book, of course, but Xingyun's focus on the scripture's connection to Xuanzang is a first signal to readers that *Picturebook Heart Sutra* should be understood as a commentary on an important scripture, as this is a way of situating the text within Buddhist literature. He proceeds with the glossing and textual explication that defines the commentarial tradition. The next page turns to the central concepts of the text (so identified by Xingyun), through a paraphrase of the scripture itself. Here, Guanzizai as a character says "All the suffering of the world is because everyone does not understand the principle that 'form is not different than emptiness, and emptiness is not different than form.'"[12] Xingyun then glosses form (*se* 色) as "being" or existence (*you* 有) and emptiness (*kong* 空) as "nothingness" (*wu* 無); he explains their relationship through the metaphor of moving waves and the still ocean. They share a fundamental nature and cannot be separated, yet manifest in different ways. Xingyun here draws on a very long tradition of using water and waves to explain relationships in Chinese Buddhism. In the first of two basic formulations of this metaphor, the mind or consciousness is the object of comparison. In the second formulation, the relationship between waves and water is an explanation for phenomenal reality as an expression of an ultimate principle.[13] This latter use of the metaphor points to the inherent buddha-ness of all things, expressed through the things and activities of the world. While a sophisticated intellectual history informs Xingyun's choices, it also points to the place of the *Picturebook Heart Sutra* in an iterative model of Buddhist education: given the pervasiveness of this metaphor, readers are likely to encounter it again, deepening and complicating their understanding.

This is true too of the several additional metaphors that Xingyung introduces to explain different dimensions of emptiness, drawing on the six metaphors of illusoriness in the *Diamond Sutra* and the ten examples of the emptiness of dependent existence in the *Vimalakīrti Sūtra*.[14] In particular, he wants to convey that emptiness (*kong*) is the basis of all other things: "Actually emptiness contains the limitless, and true emptiness produces all existence." Xingyun elaborates on what counts as existence, listing the parts and qualities of a flower, and the activities of a dog as examples. But in the same way that a flower will drop its petals, all existence will eventually disappear, to later take on another illusory form: "This is like the clouds in the sky that take on different forms when blown by the wind. After a while they disappear, and then arise again."[15] The water and waves metaphor points to the inseparability of emptiness and form, while that of clouds emphasizes the ephemerality and illusoriness of existence. As with canonical treatments, Xingyun's supplementary metaphors illustrate different aspects of the core concept.

Xingyun continues exploring this relationship between form and emptiness on the next page, with yet another analogy, to making fire from wood. Paraphrasing, the wood "actually exists" but if one cuts it apart, there's no fire to be found. When one drills the wood to kindle fire, however, the fire is real. Xingyun:

> This is to say, that the wood originally has no fire but produces fire is just as existence (*you*) is produced from emptiness. The fire comes from wood, and can be seen in wood, and this is seeing emptiness in the midst of existence. Thus we can see that all things are both empty and existent; they are identical in their original form, and it is only through the gathering and dispersal of causes and conditions that they have different variations.[16]

This analogy is the least immediate for young readers—unlike water and waves, or clouds in the sky, both of which modern children are reasonably likely to have observed, they are unlikely to have firsthand experience of making a fire by drilling wood. Xingyun has shifted from the *Heart Sutra*'s terminology, replacing form (*se*) with existence (*you*). Above, he had glossed form as existence, and emptiness as nothingness (*wu*); he has now merged these pairs together. Further, the relationship between still water and waves is not the same as that between wood and fire, as fire is different than wood and can be obtained in ways that do not involve wood. This analogy works to explain the sudden appearance of phenomena, but also introduces new terms, such as “causes and conditions” (*yinyuan* 因緣). These early pages introduce several important Buddhist terms, but do not explore their implications. This instead will happen through the stories Xingyun tells: parables extend metaphors and show their application.

Illustration as Commentary

As we saw in the opening lines of the chapter, the illustrations are rich and compelling on their own—but they do not form a coherent whole and cannot be understood without the text. This differentiates them from many picturebooks, whose illustrations retell the narrative and can stand on their own. The illustrations in *Picturebook Heart Sutra* participate in the work of the textual commentary, expanding on key themes even when not directly illustrating them. The illustrator is Giuliano Ferri, an Italian artist with international status and a long list of books to his credit. The first illustration features a monk riding a white horse, while wearing a backpack that ends in a sunshade. This latter feature would help viewers familiar with how Xuanzang is commonly depicted as a pilgrim to identify him (as we will see in the next chapter). The donkeys behind him are equipped with baskets to carry sutra scrolls; they diminish in size across as they disappear around curves in the road. Ferri echoes a long tradition of Chinese landscape painting with this illustration; it is possible to see hints of Mi Youren's (米友仁, 1074–1151) style of mountains within clouds. But this is not just incorporating Chinese modes of depicting landscapes—Ferri plays with the forms of the peaks and the absence implied by the mist so as to echo the theme of these opening pages. Forms and emptiness are bound together in this illustration, balanced on a diagonal axis that cuts across two pages. The following page also depicts mountain peaks and mist: here the Buddha preaches on Vulture Peak, accompanied by Guanzizai and with an audience of monks. Each of the monks sits in meditation on a separate peak, as clouds flow between them. On the right-hand page, beneath the block of text, the mist has melded with water, preparing the reader for Xingyun's analogy using water and waves. Two illustrations accompany his explanation: occupying the entire right page, an enormous wave swoops diagonally upward, carrying with it a boat at the mercy of the wind and waves (see Plate 1). A smaller illustration below the text on the left page shows the boat on calmer seas. The drama of the waves is a visual commentary on Xingyun's comparison—the form of the waves may be inseparable from the water, but it is a dangerous manifestation. One might see here echoes of metaphors in which the mind is likened to agitated waves. These first three illustrations reinforce the interrelation between form and emptiness explained through words.

The next two illustrations train the reader in seeing visual patterns. In the first illustration, opposite Xingyun's explanation of emptiness and transitoriness through flowers, dogs, and clouds, Ferri has depicted a round grassy hill strewn with flowers, over which a dog chases three children. In the sky, cloud doubles of the dog and children repeat the pursuit. On the following page, the dog—now with a juicy cut of meat in his mouth—pauses on a bridge to gaze at his reflection in the water below (illustrating a fable to be discussed in the following section). The arc of the bridge echoes the curve of the hill on the previous page, while the illusory part of the image (cloud forms, reflection) has been transposed from sky to water, and top to bottom.

Ferri's illustrations associate images with concepts, and so function in similar way to textual metaphors. Thinking about the illusoriness and transience of the world can bring to mind a floating bubble, a wave ebbing away, or a cloud shaped like a dog; in turn these phenomena (in visual or textual form) can be reminders of the ultimate emptiness of the world. Both images and metaphors are effective because they are simple and easily recalled. *Picturebook Heart Sutra* begins with metaphors as an explanatory commentary on the concepts of the original scripture. In the latter half of the picturebook Xingyun tells five stories to illustrate these concepts. Like metaphors, these stories help make the concepts vivid and memorable. Their narrative form also shows how these concepts might be applied in various situations.

Fables and Stories

Xingyun's use of stories as a form of commentary particularizes them, repurposing what might be universal stories to serve as exegesis for the *Heart Sutra*. This is the reverse of what we often find in children's literature, especially fairy tales or fables, which is to take a story from a specific location or tradition and show how it can carry a universal message or be used in a new context. *Jātaka* tales, for example, have been a popular means of Buddhist pedagogy, and a form of entertainment. Naomi Appleton has argued that the lack of specific locations or names makes *jātakas* amenable to adaptation in different times and places across Asia.[17] Appleton also connects the indeterminate qualities of *jātakas* to Bruno Bettelheim's assertions that the "vagueness" of fairy tales meant that they could "resonate" with everyone.[18] Adaptations of *jātaka* tales for children have also been popular in the West, perhaps because they seem to parallel Aesop's fables and fairy tales.[19] Writing about *jātaka* tales in an American context, Karen Derris points out that these stories are sharable across generations, with simple messages about moral choices in behavior and the consequences of such choices.[20] In contrast to this type of universalizing, Xingyun employs stories as a means to particularize Buddhist ideas. A comparison with an earlier Fo Guang Shan adaptation of Buddhist scripture makes clear how his approach differs.

The *Illustrated Scripture of One Hundred Analogies* published in 1995 is an early example of how adaptation and illustration could use Buddhist scripture as source material for children's literature. The *Scripture of One Hundred Analogies* is amenable to being treated as literature or entertainment for the young to begin with, as we learn from the preface to the series written by popular author Zheng Shiyan 鄭石岩 (b. 1945). Zheng praises the stories as "entirely without a sermonizing tone, without rigid conclusions, they are simply lively stories." Therefore he believes both children (here, *xiao pengyou* 小朋友) and adults can benefit from these stories, emphasizing that, like picturebooks, the scripture has a dual audience.[21] Zheng emphasizes the *story* quality of the *Scripture of One Hundred Analogies,* downplaying any Buddhist "sermonizing" that might be present.

In their illustrated version published in 1995 Fo Guang Shan further tailors the *Scripture of One Hundred Analogies* for young readers through character development, the addition of illustrations, and by changing the lessons the stories are meant to impart. For the *Illustrated Scripture of One Hundred Analogies,* Fo Guang Shan editors selected forty of the parables, publishing them in twenty volumes. An interesting feature of this set is that there is not a single illustrator, or unified approach to adapting the stories visually. Some use a modern, cartoonish style intended to accentuate the humor of the story; other illustration styles evoke folk art such as papercutting. The varied illustration styles are visual means to argue for the scripture's adaptability and applicability: these stories can appear, literally, in different forms. However, the variation and multivolume format also diminishes the sense of the scripture as a text with a single message.

Illustrated Scripture of One Hundred Analogies speaks to late twentieth-century character education beyond their Chinese Buddhist context. For example, "I Only Want to Build the Third Floor" is a story about a foolish man who, hoping to match his friend's impressive home, wants to build just the third story of a house. The unnamed characters of the original are given the names Mr. Summer 夏先生 and Mr. Winter 冬先生, and their opposing personalities, reinforced through the illustrations, become part of the story. Mr. Winter is a pessimist, and combined with his foolishness, he will never be satisfied (see Plate 2). The setting too is generically modern: the house at the center of the story could be anywhere, with arched windows hung with curtains, a red-tiled roof, and a brightly colored interior.[22] All the characters are drawn in near-caricature that adds to the humor of the story, with lots of patterns and details (such as a dog sleeping in a construction site) that add visual interest. The Buddhist moral at the end of the original story has been removed, universalizing it to a story about misguided desires.

Other stories are depicted in places that are clearly not in East Asia as a way of suggesting universal applicability. The text of "Cattle Thieves" (Touniu de ren 偷牛的人) does not specify a location, but the illustrator, Cao Junyan 曹俊彥, sets it in a village that might be the Middle East, Central Asia, Russia, or a kind of fairy-tale space that is an amalgamation of other places. Another way that these stories can be universalized is by making the characters into animals. A number of the stories feature animals to begin with, and others lend themselves to being rewritten in this way. As Lucile Desblache points out, the use of animals in fables tends "to iron out any difference within species or individuals, ruling out particularism: bears, wolves, insects, imaginary beasts and so on were equalized in so far as they became tools of analogy or satire."[23] Removing particularism in stories from the *Scripture of One Hundred Analogies* helps them to function not as Buddhist lessons but more generally as literature for character formation. The editors and adapters of Fo Guang Shan's *Illustrated Scripture of One Hundred Analogies* do not explicitly label these stories fables, although other modern adaptations of this scripture did so.[24] They highlight in this adaptation the qualities that the scripture shares with fable literature—uncomplicated stories that could take place anywhere, with messages applicable to any audience. Their simplicity and accessibility mean that fables also have utility in explaining philosophical concepts, as we will see in the case of the *Heart Sutra*.

Like the *Illustrated Scripture of One Hundred Analogies*, the transformation of the *Heart Sutra* into picturebook form reflects Xingyun's commitment to widening the audience for Buddhist teachings. They relate to their source texts in different ways, because their projects have different aims. The *Illustrated Scripture of One Hundred Analogies* is a translation, aiming not to explicate the text but to rewrite it for a new audience. Translation entails interpretation, so the new stories show one way of understanding the original text. That original text, however, has been reduced to an appendix. As I have begun to argue, *Picturebook Heart Sutra* is a commentary, and as such maintains a much closer relation to the original text—from the purported translator to Guanzizai as its addressee. What connects the two is the use of stories. Xingyun, however, uses universal stories to illustrate specifically Buddhist ideas.

Commentary through Stories

Xingyun takes this approach when he writes for adult audiences as well. Stories are a means to connect the *Heart Sutra* to everyday life, which is its special function:

> What kind of scripture is the *Heart of the Perfection of Wisdom?* The *Amitābha Sūtra* is a scripture that describes the extraordinary adornments of Amitābha's land of extreme happiness; the *Vimalakīrti Sūtra* is a scripture that expounds the bodhisattva path of Mahāyāna through the achievements realized by the layman Vimalakīrti; what the *Heart of the Perfection of Wisdom Sutra* explains is the most personal and vital concern for everyone—if you want to understand yourself, you should use the *Heart of the Perfection of Wisdom.*[25]

A section of one of his books on this scripture is titled "Reading the *Heart Sutra* Through Stories" (Touguo gushi du Xinjing 透過故事讀心經). Here is how Xingyun uses stories in this context: as is typical in commentaries, he begins with a word or phrase from the scriptures and briefly explains it. Xingyun then tells one or more stories to help illumine the meaning of that phrase. These stories may be drawn from other Buddhist sutras, from Chan stories (including those that originate outside the tradition), or his own experiences, along with various contemporary anecdotes. After telling a humorous anecdote to illustrate *zizai* 自在 (a component of the bodhisattva Guanzizai's name), Xingyun explains what it means for his audience: "If you are at ease with yourself, you will affirm yourself, this is true effort. If you are not able to affirm yourself, and need external affirmation, then you have to use other people's interests as your own interests and use other people's glory as your own."[26] Unlike more scholastic or philosophically oriented commentaries, Xingyun is not interested in pinning down a proper Buddhist definition for the term *zizai* or contextualizing it within Buddhist doctrine; rather, he wants to show how it can be applied. This is the same approach that he uses in *Picturebook Heart Sutra,* choosing stories and themes that he believes are appropriate to a younger audience. The stories may be more memorable than the words of the scripture, and so are a powerful way to convey the text's meaning.

Even though Xingyun's picturebook adaptation does not take a traditional approach, we should understand it as a form of commentary in both words and images. We have seen how he explains the scripture's opening with a series of metaphors to clarify key concepts. Xingyun does not repeat the text of the scripture in its entirety—a common strategy in commentaries—but rather takes the bodhisattva's assertion of the identity of form and emptiness as a jumping-off point for stories that illustrate the implications of this statement; these stories take up the majority of the pages.

The first story is a retelling of one of Aesop's fables (identified as such in the text) interpreted through the terminology of the *Heart Sutra.* Xingyun prefaces the story by noting that attachment to existence (*you,* instead of *se*) is the cause of suffering. In the fable, a dog, carrying a hunk of meat, sees its reflection in a stream (Plate 3). The dog mistakes it for another dog, opens his mouth in a misguided attempt to snatch the reflected-dog's meat, and thereby loses his own meat. Xingyun explains that worldly phenomena are like the reflections in the water, which we mistakenly take for real, giving rise to disputes; this makes us like the greedy dog who ended up losing what he had.[27] The dog's stolen steak is a stand-in for all worldly things, which are ultimately illusory in nature.

Xingyun places *Picturebook Heart Sutra* into the long history of adapting Aesop's fables for children but makes it a tool for Buddhist commentary. Little is known of Aesop (ca. 620–564 BCE), the storyteller whose name became attached to a growing set of fables, and they were not written down until roughly three centuries after his death. Jesuit missionaries to China translated some of these fables to use in teaching Christian morality: Matteo Ricci (1552–1610) and Didacus de Pantoja (1571–1618) both included a selection of stories in their works; Nicolaus Trigault (1577–1628) with Zhang Geng 張賡 (1570–?) translated thirty-eight stories into Chinese.[28] Since medieval times, publications of Aesop's fables have included illustrations, and it continues to be a popular inspiration for picturebooks, including an adaptation by Giuliano Ferri. For the fable included in *Picturebook Heart Sutra,* Ferri follows typical depictions. The appearance of the dog ranges from cute to somewhat menacing, but it is almost always shown on a small bridge over a stream, from which the canine is afforded a good view of the reflection below. There is more continuity between Ferri's illustration and the visual history of Aesop's fables than there is with Xingyun's interpretation. Traditionally the moral is that greed leads to loss, while Xingyun emphasizes the illusoriness of the thing sought. Xingyun takes a fable from the global literary tradition and "Buddhicizes" it in order to explain the *Heart Sutra*.

The next story that Xingyun tells is the parable of the blind men and the elephant, and again he takes a universal story and particularizes it through the *Heart Sutra*. This parable exists in many versions (Hindu, Jain, Buddhist) originating from the Indian subcontinent. Here, Xingyun uses it to explain that although "the true principle of emptiness" is unitary in nature, people perceive it in different ways. Xingyun elaborates, "If people perceive a problem based on their presuppositions, then no matter how they look at it, it will not be easy for them to see the heart of the matter." This serves as a segue to his retelling of the parable, set in an unnamed kingdom in the past, with the blind men asking the king to touch the elephant he has received as a birthday present. The first takes the trunk to be a snake; the second mistakes the tusk for a spear; the third believes the ear to be a fan; the fourth hypothesizes that the elephant's leg is a tree trunk. The last two blind men feel the side of the elephant and its tail and believe it to be a wall or a rope, respectively. All six men cling to their point of view, and the sighted king, amused at their ridiculous disputation, tells the crowd not to be like the blind men, attached to one's own limited perspective. Xingyun's concluding remark is that it is only with the "eye of wisdom" (*zhihui de yan* 智慧的眼) that one can see the true form of the elephant.[29] By showing how this story can be read in a *Heart Sutra* way, Xingyun is providing the interpretive tools to see the elephant in other contexts.

The core message of this story is that our perception of the world is limited and faulty, but what that has to do with emptiness is not made explicit in Xingyun's commentary. Again, the illustrations do significant work here: in the illustration accompanying the first page of the parable, an elephant is adorned with a tapestry blanket and houdah with curtains drawn in at each pillar. Along with a tasseled cap that matches the blanket, these convey that the elephant belongs to someone important. The blind men who feel different parts of the elephant are depicted with eyes closed, and each in a different style of dress with a corresponding cap. Tied around one of the elephant's front legs is a rope that trails off the bottom of the page; the animal is fettered. It stands next to a bamboo forest, from which rays of light emerge, landing primarily on the empty houdah. There's a lushness to this illustration that makes it enjoyable to look at, but it also supplements the text. For example, that the blind men are in costumes indicating different places of origin offers a visual representation of presuppositions or limited perspectives. More subtle is the interplay between the houdah and the bamboo. Bamboo has an empty center, and thus may be read as a symbol of emptiness.[30] The beams of light emanating from the bamboo represent wisdom or understanding; they fall on the vacant houdah, an empty mind. The following page brings us to a depiction of the king, who stands between two pillars, two other pillars flanking them. With his hands extended upward and downward to form a diagonal, he conveys his dominion over this realm, and in particular over the men squabbling about what the elephant is. The four pillars echo the supports of the houdah on the previous page, so similar spaces have moved from vacant to occupied. Ye Jingyi argues that the king symbolizes sagacity or awakening; he has the "eye of wisdom" described by Xingyun.[31] Reading these two illustrations as a series, we see that illumination that comes from emptiness (bamboo, light, houdah) leads to wisdom (the king).

By opening with these stories, Xingyun shows how the *Heart Sutra* can be used to understand non-Buddhist narratives, an interpretative strategy that can be extended to other contexts. The first two stories he uses originate outside of China, and have been retold in many formats, including in picturebooks. It is possible that young readers would have encountered these stories in other books, or told by teachers or parents, with slightly different moral conclusions. Three more tales are recounted in *Picturebook Heart Sutra,* all with Chinese sources and less well known. For Xingyun, the link between the blind men and the elephant and the next story he tells is the fallibility or limitations of the senses. With only the sense of touch applied to one part of the elephant, the blind men reach the wrong conclusions. Likewise, in our everyday experience people get into arguments based on what they have personally seen and heard, but "really our senses of sight, hearing, smell, taste, touch, and consciousness often deceive us; if everything we know comes from illusory, unreal phenomena, then it is easy to diverge from what's real."[32]

To illustrate our mistaken assumptions about what is real, Xingyun tells a story about a little boy who steps on something as he walks home one evening. It makes a noise that he thinks sounds like the croak of a frog, and the boy assumes that he's killed the animal. When he gets home, he is too upset to eat his dinner. After confessing what he's done to his mother, she suggests that they go back to the field, whereupon they discover that what he stepped on was actually an eggplant. All the boy's anxieties disappear in an instant. Xingyun here adapts an anecdote from the sermons of the Song dynasty Chan monk Qingyuan Foyan 清遠佛眼 (1067–1120), which has a monk as the central character in the story.[33] There, stepping on a frog at night has greater significance: the monk was renown as a vinaya master, meaning that he especially would be expected to keep the precept of no killing. The frog did not emit a sound, but rather the monk mistook the sensation of the seeds for frog eggs—meaning that he believed he not only killed a frog but all her offspring as well. That night, the monk dreamt of a hundred frogs appearing to demand his own life, a common trope in tales about retribution for killing animals. Having the frog be full of eggs not only adds to the misdeed of stepping on it, but also intensifies the sensory experience. In Foyan's version, when the vinaya expert realizes his error in the morning, he understands that world is nonexistent (*wufa* 無法). Foyan doesn't come right out and say it, but it seems that the vinaya master has had something like an awakening experience; Foyan concludes by asking whether we can know if it was really an eggplant or a frog.

Xingyun's explanation of this story focuses on the senses, and how the *Heart Sutra* treats them as empty in both matter (*wuzhi* 物質) and spirit (*jingshen* 精神). Rather than the philosophical question of Foyan's version, the story becomes a simple misunderstanding brought about by trusting too quickly in one's senses. Changing the character from a monk to a little boy gives young readers a focalization point. It also allows Xingyun to introduce another character, the boy's mother, who guides him to reconsider what he has experienced. Although the mother is one of only two women in the

Picturebook Heart Sutra, and this is the only family unit depicted, the exchange between parent and child provides a model of how similar conversations might happen in the reader's own family.[34] Stepping on an eggplant might be unlikely, but mishearing or mis-seeing is a common experience for all ages. The mother is attentive to her son, and helps him to resolve his doubts and disquiet. Although the Buddhist conclusion is outside the frame of the story, this is an example of affinity work—how affective connections within the family unit can lead to later engagement with Buddhism.

The domestic setting continues on the following page, which accompanies the next anecdote Xingyun uses to illustrate the concepts of the *Heart Sutra*. Here an elderly woman is depicted sitting in a small house or pavilion next to a serene pond; an eye-catching owl is perched on its roof.[35] Before readers get to the anecdote that accompanies this image, Xingyun introduces a new metaphor, glossing the term *prajñā* (wisdom):

> We can compare *prajñā* to a mirror. No matter whether someone is fat or thin, beautiful or ugly, one only needs to look into the mirror of *prajñā* to see one's original true face. Disciples of the Buddha typically recite scriptures, worship the Buddha, listen to the Buddhist teachings, and do all sorts of meritorious deeds in order to polish the mirror within the mind.[36]

The mirror is another common metaphor in Chinese Buddhism, used to represent the unobstructed true mind, equivalent to inherent buddha-nature; readers are likely to encounter the mirror metaphor in other Buddhist texts. As the first line tells us, the mirror does not reflect external appearances, but one's true, ultimate nature. Yet the mirror may not always be perfectly reflective, hence the need for Buddhist effort.

The concepts of mind and effort are linked in the story Xingyun tells next: an old woman recites a mantra every day, using a pint of beans to count her recitations. After many years of this practice, the beans come to move by themselves, jumping from one pile to the other each time she utters the mantra. There is, however, a problem: The old woman believes that she is reciting the mantra associated with Guanyin, "oṃ maṇi padme hūṃ," but has gotten the last syllable wrong. What she is reciting is the equivalent to "oṃ maṇi padme *cow*."[37] One day a Buddhist teacher visits her village, and lodges for the night with the old woman. He overhears her recitation and points out her error in an unkind way. The granny diligently tries to correct herself, but she's recited the mantra so long with the mistaken syllable that when she tries to change it, she cannot concentrate or make her mouth produce the right sounds. Moreover, the beans cease spontaneously counting themselves. With this Xingyun concludes the story and turns to the moral:

"The great wisdom of *prajñāpāramitā* is hidden deep within our minds, we just have to clear away miscellaneous thoughts, concentrate our intentions, and we'll be able to break through troubles and the obstructions of our thinking minds. No matter 'oṃ maṇi padme hūṃ' or 'oṃ maṇi padme cow,' it just matters whether our thoughts are focused."[38] Xingyun here implies—but doesn't state explicitly—that the old granny should go back to (or did go back to) her original way of reciting the mantra, because what matters is her intention and concentration in carrying out the act. Through the previous story, readers learned that the senses cannot be trusted; now Xingyun shows that the mind is the source of wisdom. He also subtly makes the point that perfection in ritual actions is not necessary. Tolerance of imperfection points to a developmental approach to Buddhist learning, a theme that returns in books about naughty children (see chapter 4).

Commentaries on the *Heart Sutra* invariably discuss the mantra with which it concludes, and of course the scripture itself is recited. The old woman recites a different mantra, but the inclusion of the story is a way to signal the importance of mantras for understanding the *Heart Sutra*. As with the story of the eggplant, Xingyun did not invent this anecdote. According to Ye Jingyi, the story comes from a collection of Nan Huaijin's writings on Guanyin. Nan Huaijin 南懷瑾 (1918–2012) was a Buddhist layman shaped through three years in meditation on Mount Emei 峨眉山 and study in Tibet. Xingyun and Nan collaborated on a book that included commentaries of the *Heart Sutra*. Nan's version gives the woman a longer backstory and differs in some other details, but also concludes with the monk realizing he was wrong—because sincere intention is what matters—and returning to tell the old woman that she can recite the mantra however she likes.[39] A condensed version of the story is also included in the section on Guanyin in Fo Guang Shan's *Four Great Bodhisattvas* (*Si da pusa* 四大菩薩). Here Guanyin observes the old granny at her counting, noting the error in her pronunciation alongside the spontaneous jumping of the beans. Even the beans, readers are told, "feel the sincerity of the old granny" and Guanyin herself is moved by this.[40] The same story can be placed in different interpretive contexts—for both children and adults—but Xingyun's use of the old granny's recitations in *Picturebook Heart Sutra* is framed so that it serves as commentary to that text. The repeated use of the story is also part of the development of a repertoire of images and stories that can be used to interpret both Buddhist ideas and real-life experiences.

Xingyun tells one more story, launching into it without preamble on the following page. It concerns an unnamed Jin 金 dynasty (1115–1234) Chan master who has a fondness for orchids. When he has to make a trip, he charges a disciple with taking care of the orchids that he's planted at the temple. The disciple accidentally knocks over the stand and all the orchids are destroyed. He confesses as soon as the Chan master returns, entreating his teacher not to be angry. The Chan master replied, "I planted orchids because they are fragrant and elegant-looking; I planted orchids to enjoy them and to offer them to the Buddha, not to get angry about!" The illustrations play on the chaos, both physical and mental, created when the orchids were knocked over. On the left-hand page, accompanying the text, the disciple stands with his hands raised and mouth open as pots of orchids tumble around the edges of the page. On the facing page, the pots have come to earth and their smashed remains are shown surrounding the disciple and the Chan master, the former kneeling contritely and the latter leaning on a staff with one hand extended forward. Both monks are depicted in saffron robes with one shoulder bare, and so Ferri suggests a location other than China. This is a popular story, but its origins are not clear: no Jin dynasty Chan master matches the one described.[41] Xingyun does not tie the story explicitly to the *Heart Sutra,* and it parallels that of Aesop's greedy dog: forms are ultimately empty, and so attachment to them should be avoided. The Chan master manifests this when he does not get angry about the smashed orchids. As with the granny, imperfection and error are expected and tolerated. (Indeed—and thinking of picturebooks' dual audiences—we might wonder if this story is intended to be a reminder to parents to react appropriately to household mishaps.)

The final two pages are dedicated to a summary offered both through the illustration and text (Plate 4). Ferri returns here to the visual themes of water and mountains that we saw in the early pages of the book: Orange-tinted mountain peaks in a body of placid water echo the mountains on which the Buddha and his disciples gathered earlier. Trees resembling those depicted in Xuanzang's journey soften the landscape, and beams of light shine in from the right, a reminder of the use of light in the tale of the blind men and the elephant. A sailboat reminds readers of the relationship between the water and the waves; three boys sit with a contented dog, gazing at the five blind men who lead each other down an island path. To the right, the mother has her arm around her son on a promontory. In front of them, the old woman kneels in profile, watching her beans jump. Closest to the reader, the young disciple holds up an orchid in offering. Xingyun's concluding thoughts are offered in a brief paragraph: "After we recognize the connection between 'emptiness' and 'existence,' and apply them in our own lives, 'emptiness' is a way of stressing tolerance, and 'existence' refers to creativity. When a mind of tolerance exerts itself in creating, this is putting into practice the great wisdom of the *Heart Sutra.*"[42] Although the concept of tolerance follows naturally from stories just told—it is the emptiness of the orchids that allows the Chan master to take in stride his student's mistake—individual creativity is not much in evidence. The illustration clarifies Xingyun's assertion: the stories themselves are acts of creativity that emerge from an understanding of emptiness.

To interpret the *Heart Sutra* for young readers, Xingyun draws on a number of different sources, including a non-Buddhist fable, and explains how they illuminate concepts such as form, emptiness, and wisdom. This establishes a familiarity with a scripture they will likely encounter again when older. Likewise, the stories he tells will appear in other materials, building a looping model of Buddhist education that anticipates ongoing learning over different life stages. His metaphors and stories provide a visual, concrete way of understanding conceptual relationships. They also offer a model for interpretation, showing how stories can provide insight into philosophical concepts. We have seen that Xingyun endorses applying the concepts of emptiness and existence in lived experience, and the stories he uses are examples of how to do just that. By offering *Heart Sutra*–inflected readings of familiar narratives (or narratives that will reappear in other places), Xingyun shows how emptiness and existence can be used to interpret different kinds of stories. Starting with a globally known fable demonstrates that this interpretive strategy is not limited to Buddhist material. Through *Picturebook Heart Sutra,* Xingyun offers a Buddhist method of reading with wide application.

Frames for Reading

Picturebook Heart Sutra is both a Buddhist text and children's book in a crowded marketplace and can be read in both contexts. As we have seen, the strategies used here are seen elsewhere in Fo Guang Shan's publications: Xingyun also employs stories as explanatory devices in works for adults. Specific narratives and concepts in *Picturebook Heart Sutra* also reappear in other Fo Guang Shan sources. *Picturebook Heart Sutra* reflects Xingyun's long-standing commitment to lay Buddhist education, and education for children. Yet *Picturebook Heart Sutra* is not just a Fo Guang Shan work. Published in collaboration with a commercial press, the paratexts of *Picturebook Heart Sutra* also argue that it teaches important skills and imparts cultural knowledge.

As the founder of Fo Guang Shan, Xingyun's personal career is reflected in that institution's cultural agenda.[43] Born Li Guoshen 李國深 in Zhejiang, his family entrusted him to a monastery in a time of distress; he was ordained at the age of fourteen. Following the end of the war of resistance against Japan (known also as the Second Sino-Japanese War), Xingyun began attending Jiaoshan Buddhist Academy 焦山佛學院, whose instructors included many who had been influenced by the Buddhist reform movement. Not long after his graduation, he fled to Taiwan with a small group of like-minded monks. Forced to start over with no connections, Xingyun first took charge of a small temple in northeastern Taiwan. There he engaged in various endeavors to spread Buddhism to the local population, starting with the foundation of groups to recite the name of the Buddha. Xingyun also emerged as a popular lecturer and experimented with ways to expand the audience for Buddhism, an approach that he continued. Xingyun declined to work with BAROC during his early career, and instead chose to establish strong connections with lay elites. Richard Madsen has argued that he was able to capitalize on his "network of supporters" during the early phase of Taiwan's economic rise in the late 1960s to build his own Buddhist institution, eschewing the established system of monastic leadership.[44]

From the very beginnings of his monastic life, Xingyun considered children and young people as an integral part of the audience for Buddhist teachings. After his graduation in 1947, Xingyun became the principal of the White Pagoda Primary School (Baita xiaoxue 白塔小學), affiliated with Jiaoshan Buddhist Academy. During this period, he produced a periodical that gained an active readership among young people (*qingnian* 青年).[45] These types of efforts introduced innovations such as a youth choir and writing classes for young people and extended to remedial classes for middle school and high school students. Still quite young, Xingyun showed a good understanding of children and a willingness to spend time with them. He developed more classes for children, as young as preschool age, and these evolved into weekly Buddhist programs. Xingyun borrowed a practice from Christian Sunday schools, and promised children treats for attending (including a bun called "Buddha's hand"), an effective enticement in rural Taiwan during the late 1950s. His child-oriented teaching included telling stories from the *Scripture of One Hundred Analogies*. Classes introduced children to Buddhism but also attracted the interest of parents through the positive effects on children's behavior, reflected in the saying that "children who study Buddhism don't go bad."[46] Building on these early efforts, Fo Guang Shan counts children's classes, Sunday school, and preschool education as among its "fifty firsts in Buddhism."[47] *Picturebook Heart Sutra* brings Fo Guang Shan's educational efforts for young Buddhists into the space of the family home.

Picturebook Heart Sutra can also be understood as an innovative form of Buddhist literature, a key concern of Fo Guang Shan. Fo Guang Shan is engaged in the creation of a new canon that will include modern scholarly features such as punctuation and paragraph breaks (not part of premodern canons) as well as indices, introductions, and other supplementary materials.[48] Further, Xingyun advocated for expanding the Buddhist canon to include "the literary works of contemporary Buddhists, comics, photographs, engravings, architectural models, music, musical scores for Buddhist chanting, even audio recordings, [and] information stored on computers."[49] This enlarged conception of what counts as Buddhist literature legitimates picturebooks and other children's literature. Fo Guang Shan also publishes paperback editions of Buddhist classics, and contemporary scriptural commentary. This encompasses not only works that are labeled explanations or interpretations but also lectures based on core scriptures or important doctrinal texts. These texts aim to make the Buddhist textual tradition accessible to a general audience. Manga and picturebooks have the same goals, but for younger readers. All these projects around Buddhist literature endeavor to make it more modern and approachable.

Xingyun's method presents *Picturebook Heart Sutra* as a text that has practical utility in daily life through the application of philosophical concepts. The commercial publisher's paratextual apparatus frames this utility in the language of emotional intelligence. *Picturebook Heart Sutra* was initially published by Grimm—one of Taiwan's most successful children's presses—in collaboration with Xianghai 香海, a Buddhist press dedicated to Xingyun's works.[50] With a dual audience, and on shelves competing with a wide range of works, the publisher must make the case for the value of this book to parents or other caregivers who will be purchasing it. The value of *Picturebook Heart Sutra* is first positioned by the copy on the back cover. There, a question appears in large red type: "Why should children read the *Heart Sutra?*" This is followed by four more questions: "Why is it easy for some people to be happy, while others get angry at every turn? Why do some people choose to face challenges, while others run away? Why do some people appreciate others, while some people are always jealous of others? Why are some people generous by nature, while others care about every penny?" The answer to these questions, the back copy poses, lies in differences in the "heart" (*xin* 心), which is then equated to "EQ," emotional intelligence. This term was coined in the United States in the late 1980s, as part of an expansion of what counted as intelligence.[51] Identifying "emotional intelligence" as a distinct domain signals that understanding emotional nuance in social situations is as important as the skills and facts learned from books. As presented here, the "effectiveness" of *Picturebook Heart Sutra* lies in its ability to teach qualities that contribute to success and happiness in life. The *Heart Sutra* is important not as a Buddhist text—which is never mentioned on the cover copy—but as part of a modern character-building education.

Yet from Xingyun's standpoint the *Heart Sutra* is character education. Read from the perspective of EQ, we can see similar themes in Xingyun's introduction, which argues for Buddhism's utility in daily life. He opens by echoing a concern expressed in much adult writing about children's books: modern children are exposed to ever-increasing amounts of information, but not all of it benefits their development. Buddhist scriptures could fulfill that role, but Xingyun writes that most people think of Buddhist scriptures as deep, difficult to understand, and so keep them at a reverent distance. This creates challenges for spreading the Buddhist teachings, and Xingyun says his approach to these challenges has been to lecture on the scriptures in a way that makes them easy to understand so that people can identify Buddhism (*fofa* 佛法) in their daily life, and put it into practice there. Xingyun does not use terms like EQ, but does say that he hopes understanding the concepts of the *Heart Sutra* will lead children to have the "correct outlook on life" and will not lose their way amid the many changes of real life.[52] By situating the *Heart Sutra* as the solution to contemporary problems—too much information, and a constantly changing environment—Xingyun brings this work into the modern discourse of child-rearing that focuses on how best to prepare children for a world seen as full of challenges. Through its paratexts, the *Picturebook Heart Sutra* recontextualizes a complex work of Buddhist philosophy within modern character formation.

Thinking of *Picturebook Heart Sutra* in the context of affinity work, we can see two processes happening—one internal, and one external. Within the pages of the picturebook Xingyun tells stories that depict affinities being developed: between the mother and her young son, between the senior monk and the clumsy novice, and even perhaps between the granny and her beans. The adults in these stories are drawing on Buddhist teachings, either explicity or implicitly, and so show how those lessons might be more broadly applied. Although this is not its primary aim, *Picturebook Heart Sutra* is modeling affinity work. Externally, the connection to EQ allows parents to fit this picturebook into overarching schemas of child development, and to give them a Buddhist inflection. Affective connections lead to a Buddhist "outlook on life."

Grimm later repackaged *Picturebook Heart Sutra* to place it within the Chinese commentarial tradition more broadly. Eleven years after *Picturebook Heart Sutra* was first published, in 2020 Grimm issued it again as part of a three-book series. The content of this new edition is the same (save for the updated photograph of illustrator Giuliano Ferri) leaving the cover to do the work of integrating it into the new series alongside books on Confucianism and Daoism. The cover illustration replaces the starry sky that formerly served as the background with white space, also used in the upper half of the other two covers. Instead of a little boy sitting by the edge of a pond contemplating a lotus flower, a small statue of a buddha tilts its head and brings a finger to its lips in an expression of curiosity or thoughtfulness. Whereas the cover of the 2009 book read (top to bottom): "Master Xingyun, *Picturebook Heart Sutra,* illustrated by Zhuliannuo," the 2020 edition changes the title to *Guanzizai,* and adds "Understanding the *Heart Sutra* from childhood" above it. This latter language is paralleled in the other two books in the series, which claim that they will lead to understanding (*dong* 懂) Confucius and Zhuangzi "from childhood" (*cong xiao* 從小); the two titles are *Kongzi Speaks* and *Zhuangzi Dreams*. Most significantly, Guanzizai / Avalokiteśvara is made equivalent to Confucius and Zhuangzi, and serves as the representative Buddhist for the three teachings (*sanjiao* 三教) of this series. Guanzizai's status here is dependent on the *Heart Sutra* as a classic text parallel to the *Analects* or *Zhuangzi*. Although Confucius and Zhuangzi become a panda and a bear, respectively, no such transformation happens for the bodhisattva. Guanzizai is the speaker but does not play the same role in Xingyun's interpretation that Confucius and Zhuangzi do in their eponymous texts; the bodhisattva is not an active character in the stories Xingyun recounts and in fact is depicted only once.

The back covers of each book provide more context as to why this particular classic has been chosen. That for *Guanzizai* is identical to the earlier version, positioning the text as supporting emotional intelligence. For *Zhuangzi Speaks*, the emphasis is on the uniqueness of this generation of children: they are materially fortunate, but face great challenges, namely the depletion of the earth's resources. Reading *Zhuangzi Speaks* will teach them about the relations between humans and nature, humans and mind, and among humans. Taking a more complex approach, the back cover of *Kongzi Speaks* offers a series of questions and answers, beginning with "What is our most important classic (*jingdian* 經典)?" The answer, naturally, is the *Lunyu* 論語, and the second question asks why, if the *Lunyu* is so excellent, its teachings are not better reflected in the personality and character of its readers. The answer to this question lies in the "method of study" (*xuexi fangfa* 學習方法): when children simply recite the text, there is no means for them to understand it. Recitation of texts was integral to children's education in premodern China, and is also a core part of the system outlined in the contemporary "reciting the Classics" (*dujing* 讀經) movement.[53] But not only is the *Lunyu*'s lack of impact a matter of method, the text itself does not include "stories and examples to explain the principles. Not only will children not understand, but without a teacher to explain, even adults will find it difficult to understand."[54] The next question the back cover copy poses and answers is how to read in a way that will be useful. Using stories to explain the ideas of the text is a means not only to attract the interest of children, but along with illustrations these stories serve as a "new commentary" (*xin quanshi* 新詮釋) on Confucius's teachings. The final question and answer explain why understanding Confucius is important for children: it provides them with a "compass" that can guide them throughout their lives. Condensed on the back cover of this book are ideas about the importance of classic texts and their accessibility to different audiences. This picturebook, with its addition of stories of illustrations to make the text accessible, is described as part of a *commentarial* tradition. In the case of adaptations or interpretations of classic texts, children's literature is not outside the tradition, but a special subcategory of commentary.

The divergent treatment of Guanzizai, Confucius, and Zhuangzi signal to us that these books are, on one level, different. However, all three books use anecdotes or short tales to illustrate philosophical concepts. As we have seen, key concepts in the *Picturebook Heart Sutra* are illustrated through words and images. In *Zhuangzi Speaks,* some of the core concepts are naturalness (*ziran* 自然) and usefulness (*yong* 用). *Kongzi Speaks* not only explores vices and virtues, but performance of teaching—how to tell a story, and give examples to illustrate a principle (*daoli* 道理). Comparing their use of stories, we can appreciate Xingyun's choice of tales—from Aesop to anonymous Chan masters—that allows the *Picturebook Heart Sutra* to be taken up in this new non-Buddhist context even while offering a Buddhist method of interpretation. The three books acknowledge, without making explicit, three different intellectual traditions: Buddhism, Confucianism, and Daoism. This three-book series can be read as a picturebook entry in the discourse of "the unity of the three teachings" (*sanjiao heyi* 三教合一), which treats the three teachings as sharing themes and goals while retaining their own defining characteristics. They offer three different ways of reading stories through virtues or philosophical concepts.

Formative Circles of the *Heart Sutra*

Joshua Landy has argued for thinking about some fiction as "formative": These are "texts whose function it is to fine-tune our mental capacities." "Formative fictions" provide the reader with "skills" and "know-how" through a process that Landy calls the "formative circle." One's "cognitive capacity" allows for engagement with a formative text, which in turn "fine-tunes" that cognitive capacity.[55] Although the *Heart Sutra* may serve as a formative text for adult Buddhists, its concepts are likely beyond the cognitive capacity of most children. Xingyun's *Picturebook Heart Sutra* makes the scripture into a formative text for younger or more inexperienced readers through stories, and those stories provide skills for reading the concepts of illusoriness, emptiness, and so forth into other narratives and circumstances. Embedding it within affinity work enhances *Picturebook Heart Sutra* as a formative text, creating affective connections alongside cognitive ones.

Both for adults and for children, Xingyun uses his commentaries on the *Heart Sutra* to make the text applicable to everyday life through stories. In contrast with the *Illustrated Scripture of One Hundred Analogies,* which stripped away Buddhist morals in favor of general lessons, the *Picturebook*

Heart Sutra uses the discourse of form and emptiness to show how any story can be read in a distinctly Buddhist way. Where the *Illustrated Scripture of One Hundred Analogies* universalizes, the *Picturebook Heart Sutra* particularizes. In the art for the *Picturebook Heart Sutra,* Giuliano Ferri supplements Xingyun's text by illustrating the balance between form and emptiness through the use of contrasts and empty space. The illustrations provide a through line, uniting the disparate stories into a coherent whole by echoing page formats and repeating images, and create a visual commentary on the scripture. *Picturebook Heart Sutra* imagines children as readers of stories, both in text and image, and as interpreters of those stories, able to abstract from them lessons and to apply them in their world. It also prepares them to encounter the *Heart Sutra,* its metaphors, and Xingyun's explanatory stories again, as they will do in other Fo Guang Shan materials. These repeated, iterative encounters both form affinities with Buddhist materials, and deepen and expand readers'—both child and adult—understanding.

3

Modernizing Xuanzang

HE IS TOLD HOW DANGEROUS THE TREK WILL BE. He is told he will die. He is nearly shot by a guard, as he sneaks past a watch tower—an arrow, released from the guard's hand in the upper-right of the double-page spread, whizzes past the young monk's startled face in the lower-left corner, its fletching a blur. The desert he needs to cross will challenge him with quicksand, strong winds, and demonic apparitions; yellow swirls almost obliterate the monk and his horse in the illustration. He spills his water bag, then his horse collapses, and he does too: he lies sprawled with hands outstretched in desperation, one holding a rosary.[1] And this is only the first stage of his journey! But this young monk is determined, sustained both by his faith and the help of other Buddhists. His pilgrimage will be recorded in the chronicles of his time; he will be the stuff of legends.

The pilgrim-monk Xuanzang is one of the most exciting figures in Buddhist history, and authors of children's literature have recognized his wide-ranging appeal. His story is epic, meaning that no picturebook could touch on more than a few brief episodes of his life. Xuanzang is not only a religious eminence but also a cultural hero, the kind of dynamic figure that can serve, properly framed, as a model for modern children. Which events from his life are selected, and how they are represented, illumines what Xuanzang means for both commercial authors and modern Buddhist organizations. In the previous chapter we saw that *Picturebook Heart Sutra* could be packaged alongside books presenting Confucian and Daoist ideas, and that Buddhist picturebooks do not exist in isolation. Alongside of picturebooks published by other religious organizations, there are many commercial picturebooks that treat gods, goddesses, temples, legends, and religious practices. Buddhist figures, too, are not the sole domain of religious publications, especially when they are culturally and historically important. In non-Buddhist contexts, Xuanzang's biography has been mined for entertainment and secularized in textbooks.

Modern Buddhist children's literature reclaims Xuanzang from these treatments, emphasizing that the traits that make him an exemplar are Buddhist in nature and origin, even as they downplay the miraculous elements of his biography. Some Buddhist authors and publishers place Xuanzang among a group of eminent monks, updating traditional modes of monastic biography. Dharma Drum goes further, proposing a new way of categorizing and narrating the lives of monks in order to argue for Buddhism's relevance in the modern world. This chapter traces the pilgrim-monk's depictions in picturebooks from both commercial and Buddhist publishers, showing the emergence of a Xuanzang who can serve as a model for twenty-first-century children. In such presentations, the Tang monk exemplifies curiosity about the world, perseverance in the face of challenges, and the importance of vow-making as an expression of personal commitment.

The Promise and Problem of Xuanzang

Authors of modern biographies of Xuanzang—for both children and adults—draw on historical sources that recorded the lives of monks to promote Buddhism. The first such collection of monastic biographies was put together by Baochang 寶唱 (fl. early 6th c.) as *Biographies of Famous Monks* (*Mingseng zhuan* 名僧傳); now extant only in fragments, this collection was an important source for *Biographies of Eminent Monks* (*Gaoseng zhuan* 高僧傳) compiled by Huijiao 慧皎 (497–554). Huijiao's work drew on secular biographical writing to establish a set of conventions for monastic biographies: First, he aimed not to be comprehensive or representative but included monks worthy of emulation.[2] Second, Huijiao classified monks by areas of expertise, and third, he compared multiple accounts in the interest of establishing historical facts.[3] Huijiao's format and approach were followed in subsequent collections of monastic biographies, the Tang dynasty *Further Biographies of Eminent Monks* (*Xu gaoseng zhuan* 續高僧傳) and *Biographies of Eminent Monks Compiled in the Song Dynasty* (*Song gaoseng zhuan* 宋高僧傳). Biographies of monks were also compiled as part of the development of a particular tradition or lineage, as in the Chan "Transmission of the Lamp" records (*chuandeng lu* 傳燈錄). Biographies often open by stating the secular surname, family background, and hometown of the monk, a practice from nonreligious biographies that serves both to anchor the monk in a time and place and to establish his social standing. Monastic biographies, not surprisingly, focus on those aspects of a monk's life that make them suitable as *Buddhist* exemplars. This is apparent in the categories by which the collections are organized, but also in what makes its way into the biography.

As one of the most prominent monks of his time, with a life narrative considerably more dramatic than even most monks deemed famous, Xuanzang's biography is correspondingly complex. Very briefly, Xuanzang was an erudite Tang dynasty monk who found wanting the translations of Buddhist texts available to him. In order to collect texts and study in the Buddha's homeland, Xuanzang set off, like the pilgrim-monk Faxian 法顯 (338–423) before him, on a pilgrimage to India. After a journey lasting seventeen years, he returned to the Tang with hundreds of texts; he then spent the rest of his life working to translate these texts. Xuanzang wrote an account of his travels, *The Record of the Western Regions of the Great Tang* (*Da Tang xiyu ji* 大唐西域記, T. 2087). The compiler of *Further Biographies of Eminent Monks,* Daoxuan 道宣 (596–667), also wrote a biography of Xuanzang, most likely in the late 640s. Early editions of Daoxuan's work were preserved at temples in Japan, while the biography of Xuanzang included in *Further Biographies of Eminent Monks* as it appears in the Taishō canon reflects additions and revisions through the 660s.[4] There is also a stand-alone biography of Xuanzang, the *Biography of the Tripiṭaka Master of the Great Ci'en Monastery* (*Da Ci'en si sanzang fashi zhuan* 大慈恩寺三藏法師傳, T. 2053), attributed to Huili 慧立 (615–ca. 677) and enlarged by Yancong 彥悰 (fl. mid 7th c.). Drawing on state historical sources in addition to Buddhist ones, Jeffrey Kotyk has concluded that "Xuanzang's own travelogue and Daoxuan's biography of him paint Xuanzang as a considerably humbler figure" and that "Daoxuan's account is generally in accord with most of the state accounts." Written while Xuanzang was alive, Daoxuan would have been unlikely to exaggerate aspects of the monk's life and influence.[5]

Each of these several works presents a different slant on Xuanzang's life and travels. For example, Max Deeg has argued that Xuanzang emphasized "motifs and legends" that featured Buddhist kings as a means to "educate the emperor," while such episodes are absent from *Biography of the Tripiṭaka Master.*[6] Yancong, in *Biography of the Tripiṭaka Master,* has the monk stealing across the frontier, and surviving a solo trek across the desert through miracles.[7] Deeg points out that Yancong's embroidered account of Xuanzang's journey was often confused with Xuanzang's own *Record of the Western Regions.*

Beginning with *Biography of the Tripiṭaka Master,* the mythologization of Xuanzang's life commenced only a few years after the monk's death. By the Song dynasty, the Buddhist dimension of the fictionalized accounts of his journey was just one among many elements that interested readers and hearers.[8] The legends and supernatural elaborations coalesced in the Ming novel *The Journey to the West* (*Xiyou ji* 西遊記), attributed to Wu Cheng'en 吳承恩 (ca. 1500–ca. 1582). Here, Tripiṭaka (the character loosely based on

Xuanzang) is a young and hapless monk who has the monkey-king Sun Wukong 孫悟空, the human-pig hybrid Zhu Bajie 豬八戒, and the general Sha Wujing 沙悟淨 as companions and protectors on his journey. Sun Wukong is as central to the story as Tripiṭaka is; the sidelining of the monk plus the fantastical, supernatural nature of the narrative make *The Journey to the West* a work that is at odds with how many modern Buddhists want to present themselves.

For Xuanzang to represent modern China and modern Buddhism, his narrative must be reclaimed from superstition and fiction—a challenge extending from the early years of the twentieth century until now. The 1935 children's book *Xuanzang,* published in Shanghai by Ertong shuju (Children's Press) articulates this problem:

> We children all call Xuanzang the "Tang monk," a name that comes from *The Journey to the West.* Is there a child who does not know about the Tang monk from *The Journey to the West,* who went to India in search of scriptures, along with Sun Wukong, Zhu Bajie, and Sha Wujing? But *The Journey to the West* is a mythical tale, and what is written there is an imaginary story. This book is the *true* story of the Tang monk, Xuanzang.[9]

Recouping Xuanzang as a Buddhist monk means demythologizing him while retaining the excitement of his story against a backdrop of the continued popularity of *The Journey to the West.* Books offering retellings of parts of *The Journey to the West,* are numerous, aimed at many different levels of readers. There are also cartoon adaptations, television shows, movies, and so on—the internationally popular Japanese franchise *Dragonball* had its initial inspiration in *The Journey to the West.*[10] In short, it is difficult to imagine a child growing up in a Chinese cultural sphere without being aware, in some fashion, of Xuanzang.[11]

Picturing Xuanzang

The range of visual images historically associated with Xuanzang provides modern illustrators with models for emphasizing different aspects of the monk; most settle on an iconography of itinerancy that supports narratives of travel and exploration. From the twelfth century onward, Xuanzang was represented not only through texts, but also in painting, prints, and sculptures.

Dorothy Wong has distinguished four ways that Xuanzang was represented: as a "teacher and translator," as the "founder of a Buddhist sect," as a "pious pilgrim," and as a "witness to and recipient of supernatural help."[12]

Visual representations of the monk tend to emphasize one of his roles. For example, during the Kamakura period (1185–1333) picture scrolls depicted him as the founder of the Faxiang 法相 (J. Hossō) school. In these scrolls, the difficulty of travel was downplayed in favor of showing the monk's interactions with the regional rulers he encountered. Xuanzang's visits to sacred sites associated with the Buddha are depicted, as is his time at the Buddhist university of Nālandā. Illustrations show people lining the streets of the capital as Xuanzang returns with boxes of sutras, and him later translating those texts. Wong argues that the Kamakura picture scrolls of Xuanzang were part of the Hossō school's glorification of their founder, common among Japanese schools of Buddhism at that time. In this context, it was important to show Xuanzang's connection with Indian lineages and his relationships with the emperor and other rulers.[13]

Perhaps the most recognizable visual representation of Xuanzang is as an itinerant monk; the most reproduced image of him is almost certainly the Kamakura painting in the Tokyo National Museum. Images of this sort typically show Xuanzang with a large pack of sutra rolls on his back, with an incense censor suspended from the pack to hang above his head. With his mouth slightly open, this painting is sometimes described as depicting the monk reciting the *Heart Sutra*.[14] The Kamakura painting likely draws on Song dynasty models, and it circulated back to China in the early twentieth century. In 1933 two stele were carved and placed in the Stele Forest (Beilin 碑林) in Xi'an 西安; both used Kamakura paintings of Xuanzang as their model, and the Japanese renderings of the pilgrim have been very influential in modern Chinese representations of the Tang monk.[15]

Depicted in motion as a seeker of scriptures, Xuanzang is one of many itinerant figures in Buddhism, including performers of transformation texts (*bianwen*), and other historical personages who were known for pilgrimages.[16] Haewon Kim has argued that a key feature of these images is that the figures they depict are *in motion*. Monks walk for a variety of reasons, but for all of them, motion separates them from static icons, "apart from the mundane world." Portraying monks as walking, Kim argues, "underscores their position and role in the world of sentient beings."[17] As we will see, the Kamakura-era image of Xuanzang as an itinerant monk—burdened with texts, but in motion—would become the most significant way of representing him in Taiwanese children's literature.

Secularizing Xuanzang

Outside of religious contexts, Xuanzang is unquestionably the most popular Buddhist monk, presented as a hero of Chinese history.[18] This extends to public schooling, where Xuanzang is found in history textbooks as part of discussions of the development of Buddhism in China, where he is treated as a representative monk of the Tang dynasty. Xuanzang's role goes beyond just historical figure, however; he is also held up as a model for children of a modern nation. For example, in the textbook *Life and Ethics* (*Shenghuo yu lunli* 生活與倫理) dating from 1975, Xuanzang appears in the fourth grade text exemplifying perseverance (*youheng* 有恆).[19] He is included in subsequent revisions and printings through 1998. This last example frames the story by asking students if they have ever heard of *Journey to the West* (*Xiyou ji*), just like the 1935 children's book mentioned earlier in this chapter (textbooks too have to recoup Xuanzang from popular culture and superstition). Then, the very first line of the story offers a modern take on Xuanzang: not only is he labeled an eminent monk (*gaoseng* 高僧) but he is also called a "foreign exchange student" (*liu xuesheng* 留學生).[20] The textbook gives a standard account of Xuanzang's journey to India in search of the scriptures, including the hardships he endured along the way, followed by his return trip to China and nearly two decades of work translating scriptures. Students are meant to understand that he is doubly persevering, both in regard to physical obstacles and also in his scholarly efforts. Following the narrative, students are given discussion questions that ask them to identify *how* the monk persevered. The questions then pivot to the students' own experiences overcoming difficulty, followed by two activities to reinforce the lesson's themes. The textbook transforms Xuanzang's religious devotion into the modern virtue of "perseverance." Xuanzang is thus pedagogically important both for historical reasons—as a key figure of the Tang dynasty—and for what he can do for modern character formation. Perseverance is a quality that children can cultivate in emulation of him.

A secular picturebook similarly decenters Xuanzang's religious motivations in order to frame him as a brave explorer. *A Pilgrimage of Ten Thousand Miles* (*Wanli qujing lu* 萬里取經路) was published by Grimm Press in 1999 as part of a series titled "Four Great Explorers" (Si da tanxianjia 四大探險家). The other three explorers are Marco Polo (ca. 1254–1324), James Cook (1728–1779), and Robert Falcon Scott (1868–1912). All three men had motivations to explore far different from those of Xuanzang. Marco Polo's travels began as part of his family's mercantile enterprise. James Cook's explorations are tied to British colonial expansion, as he was the first European to map Australia's eastern coastline, which he claimed, under the name "New South Wales" for Great Britain. Robert Falcon Scott led scientific expeditions to Antarctica and was in the second party to reach the South Pole. As the only non-European among the four men chosen as subjects, Xuanzang's inclusion makes a claim that China produced great explorers too.[21] All four books are illustrated by Robert Ingpen, an Australian artist in his first of several collaborations with Grimm Press. Grimm frequently makes use of non-Taiwanese illustrators, and Ingpen's unified visual style that further links the four men as global figures.

In *A Pilgrimage of Ten Thousand Miles* the great monk's journey is both religious research and cultural exploration. Author Lin Qingxuan 林清玄 (1953–2019) treats Xuanzang's exploration as exceptional in Chinese history, resulting in the expansion of a religion. Considering the context of the series overall, religious understanding is here treated as equal to scientific knowledge as a legitimate motivation for exploration. Summing up the monk's contributions, Lin writes: "Not only was Xuanzang a great religious figure, translator, and man of letters, he was also the most outstanding traveler in Chinese history. His travels to India not only expanded the horizons of Chinese people, but also opened their eyes to wisdom (*huiyan* 慧眼)." Note that Xuanzang is twice identified as representing China, claiming him as a national figure not a just a Buddhist one. By using the Buddhist term *huiyan*, which refers to religious discernment, Lin parallels greater understanding of the world with deeper spiritual knowledge. Lin goes on to say that with this "exploration" (*tanxian* 探險) Xuanzang resolved doubts and disagreements within Buddhism, and facilitated its spread to Korea, Japan, and the rest of Asia.[22]

Lin also presents the Tang monk as curious about the world and interested in more than Buddhism. Xuanzang is described as visiting various teachers—one of whom is also depicted in the illustrations—but also intrigued by regional customs. As he traveled, he "paid attention to the unusual traditions and different customs of each place, recording the buildings and landscape. In this way, the long journey became his classroom—if he went somewhere, he studied that place."[23] Following this general characterization of Xuanzang's interests, Lin includes an anecdote that involves a local custom of throwing flower rings onto a statue of a bodhisattva. Xuanzang successfully throws his flower garland onto the statue, confirming that his wishes will come true, all of which relate to his own Buddhist mission. As Lin tells it, Xuangzang's story moves back and forth between exploration and religious commitment.

Lin Qingxuan's background allows him to thread more religious dimensions through this story of explorations. A prominent Taiwanese literary figure, in the late twentieth century Lin became known for intertwining his own experiences with Buddhist themes; the resulting books sold incredibly well. Paul Farrelly characterizes Lin's work as "easy to read and making the familiar teachings of Buddhism relevant to contemporary readers," which, in the years of economic growth following the lifting of martial law, met a "growing interest in self-based and commercially distributed spiritual solutions."[24] Lin brought his experience popularizing Buddhism to his retelling of Xuanzang's story.

One example of this is the pine tree that frames the account of Xuanzang's journey. In *A Pilgrimage of Ten Thousand Miles* the tree reflects two key religious dimensions: the importance of making vows and the miraculous response of nature to spiritually advanced people. The first illustration in the story shows a young monk sitting amid tall yellow grasses, his head resting on one hand as he leans over his crossed legs (Plate 5). We can't see his face, or where his gaze is directed, but only a few feet away from him is a scraggly pine tree, with a temple beyond. The text sets the scene:

> In the third year of the Zhenguan era of the Tang dynasty (629), Xuanzang lifted his head to look at the gorgeous colors of the rosy clouds, using his hand to stroke the small pine in front of the temple. With emotion, he said, "Tomorrow, I'm going to distant India in search of scriptures; if you'll miss me, grow towards the west. Wait until I'm headed home, and then grow eastward. We will certainly meet again!"[25]

The final pages of the book show Xuanzang in his traveling costume beneath the same tree, which has grown taller and filled out, with a pronounced bend to mark the start of Xuanzang's journey westward. The tree as his only companion at the beginning and end of his travels emphasizes the solitary nature of the monk's quest. This pine is not an invention of Lin Qingxuan; identified as the "rubbing the top of the head pine" (*moding song* 摩頂松) in a note below the illustration, it appears by this name in the Song dynasty Buddhist chronicle, *A Complete Chronicle of the Buddhist Patriarchs* (*Fozu tongji* 佛祖統紀) by Zhipan 志磐 (ca. 1220–1275). Lin's version is a modernization of what Xuanzang is reported to have said to the tree.[26] The tree is akin to other kinds of natural resonances we see reflecting the holiness of Buddhist figures. Like appearances of strange light or fragrant aromas at the death of prominent monks, the tree's altered growth indicates that there is something exceptional about Xuanzang. His intention, too, is special, and before he undertakes his journey he makes a vow (here, *lishi* 立誓) before a statue of the Buddha: "As long as I still have breath in my body, I must bring the scriptures back to the central plains. If I am unable to retrieve the scriptures, then bury my bones in the yellow sand!"[27] As we will see in stories about Xuanzang from Buddhist publishers, his vow-making is a key part of the story.

Robert Ingpen's moody and romantic illustrations reinforce the exceptional nature of Xuanzang's journey and his mission of cultural exploration. The end pages set the stage: they feature a map of Asia with Xuanzang's routes to and from India marked. The standard depiction of Xuanzang as an itinerant, wearing pilgrim's sandals and with a backpack filled with sutra scrolls, hovers over southwestern China and much of Southeast Asia. The illustrations in the body of the book generally center on Xuanzang, with other figures and the scenery often drawn in less detail, or in darker colors. This serves to emphasize the independence of Xuanzang's mission, similar to how the illustration of the tree highlighted the monk's solitude. Ingpen includes careful illustrations of Indian Buddhist art and architecture, as well as the cityscape of Chang'an, as a means of indicating Xuanzang's cultural encounters. Throughout Xuanzang appears to be quite young, and in several illustrations seems to still have the kind of roundness that disappears with full maturity. Xuanzang began his journey when he was in his mid-twenties and would have been in his early forties when he returned. Ingpen's illustrations downplay the aging process, and Xuanzang seems to be roughly the same age at the beginning and at the end. The monk's youthfulness is emphasized visually, which makes his achievements all the more extraordinary. *A Pilgrimage of Ten Thousand Miles* portrays Xuanzang as an inquisitive explorer of the world, worthy of admiration.

Reclaiming Xuanzang as a Great Monk

Secularizing treatments of Xuanzang do not entirely eliminate the religious dimensions of his life, but they are subordinated to the theme of exploration. To position Xuanzang as one of the "greats" is a strategy shared by Buddhist publishers as well, but they place him among eminent monks rather than famous explorers. Nearly forty years apart, two biographies of Xuanzang for children share key themes: his elite status as an eminent monk, the importance of his contributions for Buddhism, and his commitment to his mission, expressed through vows. These biographies were produced by Ci'en Publishing—which, as discussed in chapter 1, was one of the first presses to offer Buddhist materials designed for children—and Fo Guang Shan. For both Ci'en and Fo Guang Shan, the pilgrim-monk is grouped with other figures of historical importance for Chinese Buddhism.

Ci'en Publishing includes Xuanzang in their two-book set titled *China's Great Monks* (*Zhongguo weida de chujiaren* 中國偉大的出家人, 1980). Intended for older readers, text dominates most pages, with single color illustrations approximately every other page, and, less frequently, multicolor illustrations. Given Ci'en Publishing's role in shaping Buddhist children's literature, these biographies are important background for later picturebook adaptations. The first volume includes missionary and thaumaturge Fotudeng 佛圖澄 (233–349), commentator and cataloger Daoan 道安 (312–385), author and apologist Huiyuan 慧遠 (334–416), the pilgrim Faxian, the famed translator Kumārajīva, meditation master Bodhidharma 菩提達摩 (d. ca. 535), and the exegete Zhiyi 智顗 (539–598)—all monks who might be described as instrumental to Buddhism's establishment in China.

The second volume begins with two monks of the Tang dynasty—Xuanzang and Chan patriarch Huineng 慧能 (638–713)—then jumps to Xuyun 虛雲 (1840–1959), Hongyi, and Taixu of the Republican period. The table of contents thus is an argument about Chinese Buddhist history and its modern forms: the most important figures were those that established the religion in medieval China, or those that sought to revive the tradition in the early twentieth century.[28] Lin Shimin, the author of both volumes, writes in the introduction that monks were selected based on their contributions to Buddhism, their significance in Buddhist history, and their influence in later ages.[29]

Lin Shimin emphasizes Xuanzang's childhood behavior as an indicator of the monk's innate virtue; this part of his biography is elided in the Fo Guang Shan and Dharma Drum books discussed below. An anecdote from the monk's childhood is used to demonstrate his filiality:

> Xuanzang was very filial to his father and mother, and one day, when he was eight years old, he was sitting next to his father, listening to the *Classic of Filial Piety*. When his father reached the line "When Confucius lectured on the way of filiality, Zengzi immediately stood up from his seat," Xuanzang also immediately arose and stood respectfully.[30]
>
> His father thought this was strange, and asked him, "Why did you stand up?"
>
> Xuanzang said, "When Zengzi heard his teacher discuss the principles of filial obedience, he promptly stood up in order to show his respect. I am presently listening to your instructions, so how could I not stand up?"
>
> When his father heard Xuanzang's words, he happily rubbed the child's little head, saying: "What a good child! In the future, you will certainly be a person without compare!"[31]

This passage closely follows the *Biography of the Tripiṭaka Master,* elaborating the conversation. The Huili/Yancong biography takes the exchange between father and son as evidence of Xuanzang's early intelligence, going on to describe his love for the sages of the past, ability to understand the Classics, and lack of interest in associating with children of his age.[32] This account of Xuanzang's precocity is not in the Tang dynasty *Further Biographies of Eminent Monks,* suggesting that it is part of the mythmaking around the monk. It indicates that Xuanzang was always exceptional—that he was born this way.[33] With this story, the authors integrate elements of the exemplar tradition into a Buddhist biography. Importantly, Xuanzang is shown to be a filial son before he was an eminent monk, linking Confucian values with Buddhist achievements. Exemplars provide models of how to behave in the world and ideals to aspire to, even if not always realistic. In the Buddhist tradition, it is eminent monks, both past and present, who best fulfill this role.

The anecdote about Xuanzang's childhood filiality reads differently, depending on whether one takes the perspective of an adult or a child. An adult might read it with detachment, perhaps thinking of their own childhood, or their children. On the other hand, a child might be expected to see such exemplary acts as providing a model for their own behavior. For example, in primers in late imperial China, students were also exposed to tales of precocious or exceptional children. Their intellectual achievements were intended to inspire children to similar efforts, and their moral behavior showed "the ideal child" as "equipped with adult Confucian virtues at a very early age."[34] By including Xuanzang's respect for his father, the Ci'en biography of Xuanzang for young readers continues a tradition of holding up exceptional children as models to emulate. (As we will see in the next chapter, more recent Buddhist works often turn from these ideas of the ideal child.)

The seriousness of Xuanzang's undertaking established, Lin Shimin selects a series of episodes to tell the story of Xuanzang's journey: the beginning of his travels across the desert and his meeting with the king of Gaochang 高昌; weeping underneath the bodhi tree; the great debate at Kānyakubja (Ch. Qunücheng 曲女城); and his return home to translate. For Lin, Xuanzang's importance rests with his translations. After summarizing the shortcomings Xuanzang saw in the Chinese Buddhist scriptures of his time, Lin writes that the monk was determined to personally go to India, in order to "look at Buddhist scriptures in their original language, to bring them back to the China, then translate them into the Chinese language, so that every Chinese person would be able to understand them."[35] The use of *Zhongguo* 中國 three times in two lines drives home Xuanzang's contribution to his homeland. The concluding lines of the biography make a similar point: "He personally translated over 1,300 fascicles of Buddhist scriptures, which will forever be a part of the treasury of Chinese culture and will be worshipped and praised by generation after generation of the descendants of Yan Di and Huang Di."[36] Yan Di 炎帝 and Huang Di 黃帝 are mythical rulers that are considered the ancestors of Han people with no connection to Buddhism. Lin echoes school textbooks and *A Pilgrimage of Ten Thousand Miles* in treating Xuanzang as an exemplar of Chinese civilization, not merely an exceptional monk.

In the Ci'en biography, illustrator Luo Qingyun 羅清雲 (1934–1995) emphasizes Xuanzang as a pilgrim but also his encounters with rulers. The cover image for the volume is a modernized version of the monk as itinerant: Xuanzang is shown with his traveling pack, leaning forward as if into the wind. A rosary is draped from his right wrist, and a protector-deity hovers above him. A smaller itinerant image that is a closer copy of the Kamakura painting appears on the first page of the text. The only color image appears early in the story, showing Xuanzang meeting the king of Gaochang, who leans slightly backward with hands in front him, making the monk the dominant figure. Two images emphasize Xuanzang in front of groups: an illustration of the debate at Kānyakubja shows him facing a crowd of monks with a variety of expressions (skeptical, puzzled, pleased) while the final image shows a group of people bowing down to a haloed image of Xuanzang hovering in air, depicting their reaction after the monk's death. Although limited in number, the selection and emphasis of these illustrations suggest a parallel with the Japanese picture scrolls of Xuanzang as the founder of a school or lineage of Buddhism. These depictions of the monk demonstrate his connections with India, scholarly eminence, and reverent reception. Here, these illustrations tell a story of Xuanzang as a "great monk" of China.

Turning to Fo Guang Shan, their picturebook treatment of Xuanzang highlights his role as the founder of the Faxiang school. *An Illustrated Book of the Founders of the Eight Schools* (*Bazong zushi tuwenshu* 八宗祖師圖文書, 2017) is in a series titled "Fairy Tale Manga Collection," (Tonghua manhua congshu 通話漫畫叢書).[37] The size and length of the books place them as picturebooks, as does the ratio of text to illustration. Despite the series title, they are not manga in format, in that the story is not told through sequential panels, and there are no speech bubbles. However, the illustration style borrows from the tradition of graphic novels or cartoon, with human figures outlined in black and colored in. The Chinese characters are not accompanied by pronunciations and the text is written at a higher level than the monastic biographies by Ci'en Publishing discussed above. This suggests an audience older than that of most picturebooks.

The two-book set covers the founding figures of the eight schools or lineages of Chinese Buddhism: Huiyuan (Pure Land), Bodhidharma (Chan), Zhiyi (Tiantai), Jizang 吉藏 (549–623, Sanlun), Daoxuan (Vinaya), Xuanzang (Faxiang), Śubhakarasiṃha (Shanwuwei 善無畏, 637–735, Esoteric), and Fazang (Huayan).[38] These same figures are memorialized in a series of statues in a modern style at the Fo Guang Shan Memorial Hall, and thus the books also tie to an important site in Taiwanese Buddhism. Shi Miao Guang writes that these statues are part of an artistic program designed to educate and inspire, and that "each piece becomes a stop for school excursions where students are able to learn . . . by forms of visual connection and storytelling."[39] These books about monks are part of a larger multimedia educational endeavor for Fo Guang Shan: some readers may be reminded of a past visit, or find the books' messages reinforced by a future one. Reading stories of the monks at home connects to—and creates affinities with—their representations at Buddhist sites.

Fo Guang Shan's vision of Xuanzang is distinguished by his feats of daring bravery. For the series as a whole, the cover and promotional material emphasize the resistance that each monk faced, and the sacrifices that they made.[40] This theme is apparent from the opening pages of Xuanzang's biography, which offers the basic biographical facts of his birth and entrance into the monastic order. We then meet the monk in a marketplace as he prepares for his journey and learn of his vow: "I would rather die going to the West than live in the East."[41] As we will see, vows like this are an important part of Xuanzang's pilgrimage. The next pages narrate an encounter with bandits—one of many that punctuated his journey—that proves Xuanzang's commitment and bravery. Xuanzang is traveling down the Ganges River on a crowded boat when pirates charge from the forest and force them to land, whereupon the passengers are stripped of their valuables. The leader of the pirates approaches the monk and announces that he is perfect for the sacrifice they need to make. Xuanzang, unafraid, responds that since killing is a sin, it could be of no use to sacrifice people as offerings to the gods. He urges the pirates to give up their swords and pursue the good. They are persuaded, and Xuanzang hears their confession.[42]

This dramatic episode is given a central place in his biography so as to emphasize not only the monk's bravery and perseverance, but his conversion of non-Buddhists. Whether by virtue of its significance or its expected appeal to young audiences, the pirate encounter takes up the largest amount of space, displacing Xuanzang's departure from his homeland and his struggles crossing the desert. This dramatic episode also happens before he has visited any Buddhist sites. Xuanzang is defined as a Buddhist by how he acts in this moment, rather than his connection to the religion's earlier Indian history. The illustrations reinforce this by depicting the pirates as possessed by demonic forces: wraithlike figures with black skulls and open mouths mark their appearance from the forest, and one appears behind the chief pirate in his encounter with Xuanzang. Their bloodthirstiness is visualized through red drops on the page. The comparative violence of these images corroborates the older readership suggested by other elements. Throughout this episode, Xuanzang is shown standing calmly with hands raised in front of him (Plate 6). Contrasting with the pirate-chief's wide, crazed eyes, Xuanzang's are closed. When the pirates confess, they mimic his posture, revealing that Xuanzang's demeanor and behavior have obvious effects on others.

Fo Guang Shan editors leave out supernatural elements found in premodern sources in favor of emphasizing Xuanzang's personal charisma. The Tang dynasty *Biography of the Tripiṭaka Master* tells this story with extended dialogue and in great detail, including the fact that the human offering was intended to be for the goddess Durgā. Both this version and

Xuanzang's biography in *Further Biographies of Eminent Monks* have the monk get quite a bit closer to being sacrificed. As he prepares for his fate on the sacrificial altar he meditates on Maitreya Buddha. Then a strong wind arises, blowing sand and creating waves so strong that boats are overturned, suggesting a causal connection with his meditative practices. Xuanzang's fellow passengers tell the pirates that this is a sign that they should not kill the monk, and they are finally convinced.[43] The Fo Guang Shan biography omits Xuanzang's contemplation and what appears to be the supernatural response of the wind. With the otherworldly elements stripped away Xuanzang instead relies on his own powers of persuasion.

Following the encounter with the pirates, Fo Guang Shan's biography describes what Xuanzang studied with Śīlabhadra (Ch. Jiexian 戒賢, 529–645) at Nālandā, and highlights his success at the debate at Kānyakubja, which won him great renown throughout India. The concluding page of the biography summarizes Xuanzang's translation work after he returned to the Tang, listing titles and numbers of scrolls; his focus on consciousness-only texts is what made him the founder of the Faxiang school. Accompanying this final page is an illustration of Xuanzang as a bearded, elderly man, a stark contrast with the first depiction of the monk as a very youthful pilgrim. Along with mention of how long different parts of his career lasted—five years at Nālandā, the journey of seventeen years, nineteen years translating—the biography conveys the sense of a long life dedicated to understanding and propagating Buddhism.

Although there are significant differences in the narratives themselves, Ci'en Publishing and Fo Guang Shan both place Xuanzang within groupings of monks, either as a "great" exemplar of Chinese Buddhism or as a founder of a school. Both emphasize Xuanzang's translation work and attempt to signal the long span of his career, from youth to old age. These retellings participate in the long tradition of monastic biographies, presenting the Tang monk as a brave and important scholar, while excising supernatural elements.

Making Vows

Vows are central to retellings of Xuanzang's story, even as other narrative elements vary. In the Ci'en biography, as with *The Pilgrimage of A Thousand Miles,* before Xuanzang sets off on his journey, he swears an oath to heaven (*dui tian fashi* 對天發誓): "In order to bring back Buddhist scriptures and spread the Buddhist teachings, I will not begrudge sacrificing my life in order to complete this mission."[44] Likewise, in the Fo Guang Shan biography Xuanzang says that he would rather die than abandon his quest. This reflects the historical sources: In both primary biographies of Xuanzang, the monk takes oaths at various points in his journey. These moments accentuate his determination, and also imply that supernatural forces may be acting to protect his mission. The use of oaths or vows has a long history that links personal connections, legal contexts, and religion. In early China, historian Mark Edward Lewis writes, an oath was "a solemn statement that invoked the spirits as witnesses to bind a man to act in a certain manner."[45] Oaths were used in this way when legal disputes were heard in temples, committing all parties to tell the truth; oaths or vows were also taken to promise certain actions if deities interceded on the vower's behalf.[46] They are a significant, if not always prominent, part of Chinese religious culture. In Buddhism taking the precepts and the bodhisattva vow are institutionalized examples. Xuanzang's vows are different, in that they are of his own devising rather than written or prompted by others. They are also not social: although others might witness them, his vows represent Xuanzang's commitment to himself regarding a future course of action. As philosopher Kyle Fruh points out, a vow is deeply connected to one's identity: "Taking a vow is an especially formidable or solemn way of bringing a commitment into a central place in one's own self-understanding."[47] Vows establish a connection with a future self. Centering Xuanzang's vows is another means of elevating the importance of the monk's character and minimizing any supernatural support. Xuanzang declared that he would carry out the pilgrimage, and he did, despite the obstacles he encountered. Linking intention and action, some form of making vows or swearing oaths is a part of all the children's book adaptations of Xuanzang's story, and it emerges as an even more significant theme in the Dharma Drum biography of Xuanzang.

A Modern Model with Global Skills

The Dharma Drum picturebook adaptation of Xuanzang's life shows how monks can be adapted as models of modern virtues. This biography of the Tang monk appears in a twenty-six-book series covering 130 important figures of Buddhism, a scope much larger than the two projects just considered. Significant here will be the contextualization of Xuanzang as model of a character trait deemed important for success in the contemporary world.

To better understand the work that this series of books undertakes, it is helpful to see it in the context of Dharma Drum's efforts toward social transformation through education. Dharma Drum Culture (Fagu wenhua 法鼓文化) is the media wing of Dharma Drum Mountain (Fagu shan), one of the major Buddhist organizations in Taiwan. Founded by Shengyan, Dharma Drum Mountain's primary base in Jinshan has grown to include temples, monastery dormitories, and colleges. Having received a doctorate from Rishhō University in Japan and having established Buddhist centers in the

United States, Shengyan exemplified the transnational nature of Taiwanese Buddhism. His view of Buddhist education was informed by his study of and commitment to Chan practice. In particular, Shengyan taught that one's state of mind is the foundation for other kinds of social and environmental transformations.[48]

In the tradition of Humanistic Buddhism, Dharma Drum Mountain focuses on improving this world with the ultimate goal of transforming it into a Pure Land. Education plays an important role in this mission, as reflected in its considerable investment in scholarly activities. The Chung-Hwa Institute of Buddhist Studies, the Dharma Drum Sangha University, and Dharma Drum Buddhist College support Buddhist scholarship, and collectively the three institutions provide training for ordained monks and nuns as well as laypeople who want a Buddhist education. Their educational mission has two other dimensions: The first is "Education through Caring Services" (*guanhuai jiaoyu* 關懷教育), which includes end-of-life care and disaster relief. The second is "Education through Public Outreach" (*puhua jiaoyu* 普化教育), which encompasses Chan meditation classes and retreats, print and audiovisual media, and youth groups. Their children's books fall in the category of "Education through Public Outreach." For these two educational missions, we should note that, unlike formal education, they are less sequential and define education broadly.

Xuanzang's biography appears in the first volume of *Code Words of the Great Teachers, A to Z* (*Dashi mima* 大師密碼 A–Z). From the title alone, it is clear that this series has multiple goals: it aims to improve English vocabulary while also introducing stories about some of the most notable monks in Buddhist history. Writing in a preface to the series, Hao Guangcai—head of the prominent Grimm Press—puts the Dharma Drum series in the context of other literature for children, and earlier biographical sources. He writes that "traditional biographies not only are didactic in their stories, but their printing and illustration [styles] are also stagnant," all defects that *Code Words of the Great Teachers* aims to correct. Hao observes that other kinds of contemporary literature compete for children's attention. He does not name this competition, but asserts that learning about "real, unmagical lives" of the 130 great teachers is better for children "than giving them 130 magic wands."[49] Here we can note that the first book in the Harry Potter series was translated in mid-2000, and by the time the translation of the third book was published, it set records for the size of the initial print run.[50] Monks, it would seem, are meant to provide alternatives to Harry Potter characters as models for children.

The *Code Words of the Great Teachers* series is intended to build character and teach language skills through Buddhist content. For each of the twenty-six volumes, five monks are paired with a word beginning with that letter of the English alphabet (except for X—there are not five words beginning with *x* that would pertain to Buddhism, and so they use *ex* words instead). The stories are also bilingual, appearing in both Chinese and English, and the language-learning objectives of the books are supported through vocabulary lists at the end of each book. Although there are illustrations on almost every single page, the text is denser than picturebooks, and the intended audience is young readers with a fair amount of facility in both languages—or an adult who can guide them. Given that Dharma Drum is an international organization, they may also serve bilingual diaspora communities.[51] The language-learning dimension of the series reflects the interest in having materials for children serve multiple purposes—they should be entertaining but also educational, impart Buddhist ideas but also support academic aims. A key part of academic competitiveness for Taiwanese children is English-language learning, and there is anxiety, both within the government and within individual families, about how to do this effectively.[52] The books in this series promote learning English, placing it alongside Buddhist character cultivation.

Associated with the letter A, Xuanzang is given pride of place in the company of the Buddha, Ikkyū, Zhiyi, and Ananda. These figures are more important than the "A" vocabulary items with which they are paired—aspiration, agility, altruism, amiable, and adamant. Three of them are founders—of Buddhism, first, and then two schools of Buddhism (Zhiyi and Xuanzang). Xuanzang is the final biography in the volume, chosen to exemplify "adamant" or *jianqiang* 堅強. The title of Xuanzang's story describes him as both "adamant" and "unyielding" (*buqu* 不屈): "The Adamant and Unyielding Explorer" (Jianqiang buqu de tanxianjia 堅強不屈的探險家).[53] A brief overview of each figure is given in the "little dossier" (*xiao dang'an* 小檔案) on the introductory page for each story. Here, Xuanzang's connection with the term *jianqiang* is explained as follows: "He did not fear the arduousness of travel, setting off alone from Chang'an to go to India to study abroad (*liuxue* 留學) and seek the scriptures." Like secular treatments, Xuanzang is framed firstly as an explorer and foreign exchange student. The opening paragraph also wants to distinguish the real monk from his fictional counterpart: "If you have seen Tang Sanzang in *The Journey to the West* and taken him to be very cowardly and indecisive, then you'd be entirely wrong! The *real* Tang Sanzang—the Great Teacher Xuanzang—indeed was an intelligent and courageous, strong-willed, and dauntless person!"[54] This opening line not only corrects the mistaken impression people have from popular culture, but also emphasizes the character traits that define Xuanzang.

Author Zheng Lier 鄭栗兒 tells just a small part of Xuanzang's story to illustrate his character, which distinguishes the Dharma Drum approach from monastic biographies. Although both the Ci'en and Fo Guang Shan biographies begin with the monk's secular surname and birthplace, Zheng instead takes up Xuanzang's story when he was twenty-six, and planning his trip in Chang'an. The opening sentences evoke the sensory experience of the capital: "The sound of the bells on the camels of the Silk Road trade caravan outside Chang'an echoed at a distance with the wind-bells suspended from the pagoda at Dajue Monastery. Called by the bells, Xuanzang lifted his head to the western sky and made a firm promise to himself: 'I surely must go to the West.'"[55] The illustrations show the camel caravan in silhouette, a suspended bell, and Xuanzang seated at the base of a pillar. Although somewhat obscured by his robes, his posture is casual, as he leans on his right hand, his right knee slightly raised. As Xuanzang looks upward, his left hand is slightly raised, middle finger touching the thumb in a variation of the teaching mudra. This informal, but clearly Buddhist, depiction of Xuanzang reflects the dynamism with which he is represented visually throughout the story.

Xuanzang is a monk on the move—on foot, by raft, on horseback. The next page shows him from the knees down, his feet clad in the straw sandals closely associated with pilgrimage. Even in children's books it is unusual to see monks represented only by their bottom half. One foot is captured in midair, as the end of his staff kicks up flecks of dirt. The next two-page spread shows Xuanzang on a raft, and, after an intervening depiction of the monk meeting a local governor, we next see Xuanzang with his forehead pressed against a horse's nose. The horse appears twice more, in a monochrome yellow pictorial spread depicting a desert sandstorm, and with head bowed in fatigue as Xuanzang sprawls exhausted on the opposite page. Next, Xuanzang is shown with a sword against his neck, threatened by the king of Gaochang. There are two more depictions of the monk: one shows him in a colorfully updated version of the Kamakura image, in motion on his way home with a pack of scrolls on his back. Finally, Xuanzang is at work on his translations, with the paper and the fabric of his sleeves blending together in pools of color that spread outward. The influence of these translations is represented by groups of monks examining texts in the margins of both pages. Most of the illustrations of the monk show him in movement—walking, with his horse, on a raft. Recalling Haewon Kim's argument that motion in depictions of itinerant monks was a way of emphasizing the activity of Buddhist figures within this world, Xuanzang is shown as moving through the world, which often presents him with a challenging environment.

The depiction of the horse allows the illustrator to further emphasize the difficulty of Xuanzang's endeavor (Plate 7). No animals at all appear in the Fo Guang Shan picture biography, and the horse in the Ci'en illustration is shown partially, as a mode of transportation, or behind and apart from other figures in a scene. Here the horse is much more of a character, its struggles and emotions mirroring that of a monk. This may be connected to changing attitudes toward animals, but it also reflects an immersion in the world: Xuanzang does not appear as a static figure in different scenes but as one actively interacting even with nonhuman animals. This contrasts especially with the still, meditative depictions of Xuanzang in the Fo Guang Shan biography.

Like the monk, the horse has been updated to reflect positive character traits while being stripped of miraculous elements. As described in "The Adamant and Unyielding Explorer," the horse was given to Xuanzang by an elderly and seasoned traveler of the Silk Road. The horse, too, is aged and experienced in desert travel. The elderly man warns Xuanzang of the dangers of crossing the desert, and how much more difficult the trip will be when traveling alone. This encounter reflects *Biography of the Tripiṭaka Master* as the source text.[56] This is one of the places that shows Yancong's fictionalizing, as a solo crossing of the desert is not realistic; Xuanzang almost certainly traveled with merchant caravans.[57] In the original story, Xuanzang recalls that he had visited a divination expert in Chang'an, who had prophesied that the monk would make his trip on a horse meeting the description of the one the old man was riding. As in other places in the *Biography of the Tripiṭaka Master,* the inclusion of this detail supports a vision of Xuanzang's journey as one facilitated by miracles and divine protection. However, Dharma Drum omits this detail, which helps to focus the reader's attention on the personal qualities that Xuanzang brings to his mission. If Xuanzang's success were fated or secured by otherworldly forces, his own attitudes or behavior would be less important. Given that Dharma Drum here takes Xuanzang as an exemplar of determination—being "adamant"—supernatural elements would detract from that message.

Promises and Persistence

As with the Ci'en and Fo Guang Shan biographies, the reader is both shown and told of Xuangzang's commitment to his journey. His actions show him persevering in the face of adversity—bothersome officials, dangerous travel conditions, obstructionist rulers—and his determination is also expressed in speech, often in the form of vows or oath-taking. As we saw, the second line of the narrative has Xuanzang making a "promise" (*chengnuo* 承諾) to himself that he will go to the West. When Xuanzang meets the old man with the horse, he says, "Even if I die on the road, I won't regret it."[58] Although not marked as a vow or oath—he "states" (*biaoshi* 表示) this intention—it is similar in content to the vows in the other two books, where Xuanzang says he is willing to sacrifice himself on the journey. Here, Xuanzang repeats his vow when he finds himself lost in the desert without water: "He thought to himself, 'I have already vowed that I will never turn back before reaching India, even if it means that I will die on the road to the West.'"[59] Zheng Lier repeats the vow to show how it has come to define Xuanzang's identity.

Vows are performative utterances with their own force, but at times they are accompanied by actions to confirm their seriousness, such as a ritual meal or self-mortification. Xuanzang does so when he is pressed by the king of Gaochang, Qu Wentai 麴文泰, to stay as the imperial preceptor (*guoshi* 國師), and Zheng writes, "he decided to refuse food (*jueshi* 絕食) to express his determination to die rather than yield."[60] In one of the source texts, *Biography of the Tripiṭaka Master,* this vow is explicit: "he vowed not to eat in order to move [the king's] heart" (誓不食以感其心).[61] Xuanzang's character and his adamant nature are expressed in the journey itself, but also in the vows that precede and reinforce it.

We have seen that vows play a role in other adaptations of Xuanzang's life for young readers, but vows also have special significance within Dharma Drum. Daniel Stevenson writes that speaking in terms of vows is characteristic of Shengyan's generation, connected both to an older notion of the bodhisattva vow but with a "socially proactive sense" that enjoins Buddhists to "reach out and shape the world around them."[62] We can see the emphasis on motion as reinforcing the importance of the vow: A vow is like an itinerant monk; it moves through the world, and acts within it. Like affinity work, vows are oriented to the future; indeed affinity work may lay the foundation for later vows.

"The Adamant and Unyielding Explorer" spends no time at all in India, making no mention of sites Xuanzang visited, teachers he studied with, or his vaunted success at debate there. To give some sense of how much this adaptation leaves out, all the events it describes take place in the first of ten fascicles of *Biography of the Tripiṭaka Master.* This is a story about the initial phase of his journey, framed by the facts of Xuanzang's journey. Determination is more important at the beginning, as Xuanzang takes on a large challenge and meets repeatedly with failure and obstacles. When looked at from the perspective of character education, rather than monastic biography, the first part of his journey fits the purpose far better (or more dramatically) than the many years Xuanzang spent in India.

Character Education

Code Words of the Great Teachers, A to Z is in dialogue both with the Buddhist tradition of monastic biographies and with modern character education. For the story of Xuanzang, we have already noted several differences between "The Adamant and Unyielding Explorer" and traditional monastic biographies. Widening our view, the selection of figures for this series reflects both continuations and departures. First, the range of monks included provides a perspective on how the Buddhist world is defined in modern Taiwan. Here as elsewhere, the larger the number of figures selected, the more capacious editors can be in who is included.[63] For example, in *Stories of the Great Monks and Laymen of History* (*Lidai gaoseng jushi de gushi* 歷代高僧居士的故事 published by Heyu 和裕, 2001), the first volume contains the stories of twenty-six monks, in chronological order, and the second volume offers an additional fourteen monks, five nuns, twenty-eight laymen, and nine laywomen.[64] In *Code Words of the Great Teachers,* 71 of the 130 Buddhist figures included are identified as Chinese. Thirty-six are said to be Indian, thirteen are Japanese, and four are Tibetan; the rest are Central Asian, Korean, Persian, or Sri Lankan. Indian monks were important in the early part of Buddhist history in China, while Tibetan and Japanese monks appear centuries later—yet overall the distribution of places of origin reflects something of what we would see in Buddhist biographical collections. There are a few examples of non-monks who are considered "great teachers": Layman Pang is included, as is Buddha's aunt, Mahāprajāpatī. That the figures chosen in *Code Words of the Great Teachers* are primarily male suggests the conservatism of the project, continuing the selection biases of earlier compilations.

The code words revise the categorization practices seen in earlier biographical collections to better align with the values of contemporary parents. In *Biographies of Eminent Monks* and *Continued Biographies of Eminent Monks,* monks and others can be associated with a particular specialization, practice, or quality. Here, however, each figure is assigned their own term, rather than sorted into a broader category; there is a single characteristic that makes each one unique. The code words are a mix of nouns and adjectives—primarily character traits that one should aspire to possess, and qualities that would describe such a person. Many of these overlap with ideals for children, expressed either in children's books or in parenting texts: brave, dutiful, determined, grateful, joyful, optimistic, quick-witted, responsible. About twenty of the words are distinctly Buddhist or religious, including terms like karmic-lesson, loving-kindness, penitent, rebirth, yoga, and Zen.

Shengyan's preface to his series begins with his recollection of reading the stories of great monks as a youth. He then makes two interrelated moves: he translates qualities of historical monks into the vocabulary of contemporary child-rearing, and through this translation he defends the appropriateness of children learning about Buddhism as preparation for participation in modern society. He writes:

> I have pointed out that eminent Buddhist monks must have four main qualities: they perfectly uphold the precepts, they practice diligently, they compassionately work to save all sentient beings,

> and they protect the Buddhist teachings. If we put these qualities in modern terms, they are self-discipline, conscientiousness, magnanimity, and understanding reciprocity—these are qualities of all successful people.[65]

Here, Shengyan recognizes that the way we typically speak of historical monks draws on a vocabulary that is roughly 1,500 years old, as exact or similar phrasing could be found in the first collection of monastic biographies, the sixth-century *Biographies of Eminent Monks* (*Gaoseng zhuan*). Shengyan argues that we can reduce the distance between these monks and ourselves by changing the words we use to refer to their character and behavior. Upholding the precepts, unmistakably monastic in tone, becomes "self-discipline" or "self-regulation" (*zilu* 自律), necessary even for kindergartners. The diligent practice of monks becomes *renzhen* 認真, which can be translated as "conscientious," "serious," or "earnest," and is often heard in expressions of praise for children who are careful and thorough in their studies. In the argot of modern parenting, these first two terms belong to the development of executive function. The salvific endeavor of monks in modern terms can be understood as a generosity of spirit toward all, and their protection of Buddhism is recast in more general terms as understanding the "repayment of a debt" (*huikui* 回饋). One frequent way that this term is used is *huikui shehui* 回饋社會—to repay a debt to society. By drawing these parallels, Shengyan signals that the biographies of monks can be seen as something more than the relics of a dusty past, and that they can be re-read for guidance in the present. Indeed, Shengyan's pairing of terms points to the way in which "self-discipline" and other such terms are not uniquely modern but have roots in Buddhism. Buddhist history thus becomes a source of values for the present.[66]

In Shengyan's preface, casting the personal qualities of historical monks in modern terms is a way to respond to critiques of Buddhism: "Many parents think that studying Buddhism will make their children passive and lacking in competitive spirit. But if we think about the qualities of great teachers, then this is entirely wrong." Shengyan recognizes that parents want competitive, proactive children and wants to assure them that Buddhism supports, rather than obstructs, these objectives. There is one other aspect of the relevance of historical monks that Shengyan feels compelled to address, and that is the means by which they acquired their character or personality traits. These monks were exceptional, but this was nurtured by their environment, "not by chance" or "achieved right from birth."[67] Parents can provide an appropriate environment for developing the same types of positive qualities and doing so—from Shengyan's perspective—includes offering them historical monks as models.

Reading Buddhist Lives

The cultural significance and malleability of Xuanzang's journey means that it continues to be an important source for new stories in the twentieth and twenty-first centuries. Xuanzang's journey has been used as source material for many stories, starting just after his death: Buddhist biographers added details and shaped known events to tell of a quest protected by the deities. Other storytellers elaborated the monk's journey, inventing new elements; the culmination of this creative refashioning was the Ming novel *Journey to the West*. Picturebook treatments of Xuanzang's life continue the long line of interpretations of the monk's religious and cultural significance. They also reclaim Xuanzang from popular treatments of the monk, to reinstate him as a suitable exemplar figure for young readers. The number of picturebooks written about Xuanzang attests to how his lengthy biography provides the raw materials to interpret him in multiple ways that speak to modern times. Some Buddhist books, like those from Ci'en and Foguang, treat Xuanzang as an exemplary religious figure worthy of admiration and historical attention. Along with dozens of other Buddhist figures, Dharma Drum assigns Xuanzang a core trait so that he can serve as a model for contemporary children. Themes of persistence and independence are part of secular retellings of Xuanzang's story; vow-making gives these a religious dimension.

Stories for children consistently emphasize Xuanzang's persistence and determination. Although the purpose of Xuanzang's journey was to acquire Buddhist scriptures and learning, it can be tied to other kinds of journeys more common in modern times, such as travels for exploration of new places and cultures, and study abroad. These character traits are tied to the monk's journey, during which he had to endure the harsh conditions of desert travel and dangers such as bandits. His determination can be framed in different ways so that he can serve as a model in varied contexts. For example, in the pages of a textbook, Xuanzang's persistence exemplifies how students might stay the course in their own studies or persevere through personal challenges. Further, Xuanzang's story shows that the world beyond local borders, however these are defined, is one of possibility and expanded horizons, as long as one does not shy away from a challenge. To go out into the world means acting independently, according to these stories. Xuanzang is usually represented as going it alone, either as someone unwilling to put his companions at risk, or as a solo traveler making his own path. Although at times he receives aid, he is also often in opposition to others. He defies orders to stay within the borders of the Tang empire; he resists the king of Gaochang's demand that he remain there as a teacher; he refuses to be cowed by bandits; he holds his own when debating before less-than-friendly audiences. This is another kind of determination—to continue on when others object—woven into the more straightforward commitment not to give up until he reaches his goal. Vows show that words do something in the world, and that choosing what kind of person one will be is a deliberate act. Persistence can also be treated as an important character trait more broadly, as part of the "code words" that make up a successful young person in the Dharma Drum series.

Shengyan's preface suggests that it may be productive to view new stories about historical figures as acts of translation. For Shengyan, determining which modern words would best match the description of eminent monks provides a way of recognizing their value in contemporary times without altering the core of their biographies. In turn, changing the terminology used to talk about these monks allows them to be used as modern exemplars. Shengyan addresses his claims about the "usability" of these stories to parents, arguing that they need to change how they interpret Buddhist texts and their value. What he proposes, and what is then modeled through *Code Words of the Great Teachers,* is a method of reading Buddhist biographies. The example of Xuanzang shows how to be a Buddhist *person*—but not how to be a Buddhist *kid.* The next chapter will ask how it is possible to be both Buddhist and do the things that kids do.

PART II

Kids

4

Naughty Little Monks

A VERY YOUNG MONK IS SCOLDED by his master for being stupid, because no matter how hard he tries he can't get the mantras to come out right in his daily recitations. He gets knocked upside the head for oversleeping and failing to sound the bell for morning lessons. He's chided for using too much water to wash his face—water that he probably had to haul from where it was collected in rain barrels underneath the eaves. This same young monk sees some elderly people, and says to his master, "Teacher, look at those pitiful old people! They don't know that they are going to die soon!" He's admonished once again.[1]

What do we make of a young monk like this? Is he a problem or unrealized promise? And what do we make of stories about such a young monk? Do we as readers sympathize with the little novice, who is probably just being a kid, trying to do his best? Or should we identify with his teacher, attempting to guide his young charge? This chapter argues that in stories such as this one, readers are meant to engage both the child's viewpoint and the adult's, and that naughtiness and mischief help us to do so by showing us the tension between the two.

Thinking about these perspectives allows us to consider what it means for a child to be a Buddhist and what value childhood holds for Buddhism. Buddhist literature can be adapted for kids without making children the central characters, as in the case of the *Picturebook Heart Sutra* and the various picturebook depictions of the monk Xuanzang. Even when Xuanzang's youthful vigor is emphasized, he is not an immediate model for children; emulating his achievements would be far off in the future for young readers. Yet, broadly speaking, narratives for children are often structured around characters who are themselves children. The imagined readers are expected to identify with young characters, and they serve as focalization points, drawing children into the story and representing a child's-eye perspective. Child characters may exhibit the emotions and knowledge appropriate to a young child, but they also reflect how adults think children *are* or *should be*. Sometimes children are innocent and lovable—but sometimes they are mischievous and even naughty. Stories about naughty children have traditionally been corrective texts, designed to "scare the naughtiness out of naughty children."[2] In picturebooks of this type, rule-breaking, mess-making, and misbehavior is an entertaining but temporary release from adult expectations, with order and emotional harmony restored by the end of the story. Such books use humor to reinforce behavioral expectations while giving vent to the frustrations they may cause; naughty children serve as negative examples. But naughtiness or mischievousness can also capture non-adult viewpoints in a way that the well-mannered child cannot.

With the figure of the naughty or mischievous monk, Buddhist children's literature offers a view of character development that allows for mistakes, and even, in some cases, holds out the child's perspective as wiser and kinder than adult authority. In contrast to the more hagiographical treatment of Xuanzang in the previous chapter—in which great monks are often effectively changeless, exemplars in childhood as well as adulthood—stories of pranks and misbehavior show how an average child is a potential good Buddhist. Considering picturebooks' dual audience, these story lines provide alternative models for child readers, and, in the adult responses to the young protagonists, frameworks for parent-child interactions.

Childhood, in monastic biographies, is almost always treated very briefly, and in ways that reinforce the specialness of the subject and adult ideals of childhood. As Miriam Levering has argued, this reflects the expectation that "the subject did not change over the years." Buddhist biographical writing shares this characteristic with biographical conventions more broadly. Levering elaborates: "There is no interest in portraying qualities that appeared late or contrasts between earlier and later behavior. This focus makes a candid portrayal of childhood almost impossible. Consequently, we get depictions of the subject's childhood and youth that presage only later virtues or accomplishments."[3] Monastic biographies make note of any auspicious signs around the birth, such as dreams the mother had or the presence of a caul. They also point out early behaviors that show an affinity with Buddhism, such as playing at ritual, sitting in meditation posture, or early learning of scriptures. These biographical details demonstrate that the child was always destined to be a monk. Monastic biographies, of course, are written about successes—monks who rose to eminence rather than those who were average or even wayward.[4]

In this view, eminent monks are pious and virtuous by nature, not nurture. For successful monks, their early practice of ritual or precocious sense of propriety (like Xuanzang) connected innate character to later achievement.[5] In *Code Words of the Great Teachers* the representation of monks as children is relatively rare and often reinforces hagiographical conventions. As with older biographical traditions, the monk's mother may have had an unusual dream prior to his conception or birth; the future monk may have shown a special affinity for Buddhism at a very young age; he may have been exceptionally precocious in his learning. Some examples of this kind of quasi-hagiographic detail make their way into these stories. When the future monk Xuyun is born, he is inside a "meatball" (*rouqiu* 肉球), terrifying his mother to death; the infant is rescued by a quick-thinking passerby with a knife.[6] The future translator Dharmarakṣa (239–316) was given a sutra in a foreign language at age eight, inspiring him to study Buddhism.[7] Doctrinal innovator Daosheng 道生 (355–434) is described as "exceptionally intelligent" as a child.[8] The reformer Taixu saw his grandmother light a lamp as a young child, and watching its light spread, he was inspired to try to emulate its effects in his own life.[9]

Recalling Shengyan's caution in his preface about monks being made, not born, we can understand why the fatedness of monastic eminence would be underplayed in stories intended to encourage children. If being a monk or an extraordinary person is predestined, there's little impetus for growth and development. Against a background of precocious, kind children who grow up to be wise clerics, stories about monks as naughty youngsters are transgressive, showing bad behavior by those who are especially expected to always be good. They are fun, but they are also stories about the inherent potential, and what the possibilities of childhood mean for adult-child relationships.

Clémentine Beauvais proposes that "childhood" and "adulthood" can be understood as differing relations to time. The adult has accumulated experiences and knowledge, and in that sense has the advantage of time. Yet children have more time remaining in their lives—time for learning, changing, and growing. Beauvais asks, "What if 'unrealised' time were a stronger currency than 'realised' time? A currency in which the child—therefore—would be richer than the adult; more powerful in some sense."[10] This potentiality, however, depends on the outcome not having been predetermined; if a currency can only be spent in a certain way, it is of little use. A child's power rests in the possibility of growing up into *any kind* of adult. For this reason, the naughty child represents a challenge and an opportunity to the didacticism of children's literature. The good child or the precocious mini-monk will grow up to be a similar adult. There's no narrative tension. But the naughty child generates questions: Will they get caught in their misbehavior? How will adults react? Will the child change for the better? Even if the answer to this last question is almost always affirmative, stories about naughty children explore how “unrealized time” might be used in ways that do not conform to adult expectations,[11] and thereby emphasize the power children have.

This chapter considers three stories of naughty children who grew up to be important monks. Two of these are from the *Code Words of the Great Teachers* series and show contrasting treatment of naughty children: The Buddha’s son Rāhula needs correction, to set aside his childishness so he can become a model monk. Ikkyū’s exploits, in contrast, show the value of a child’s perspective. Both these stories are childhoods imagined by adults. In the third story considered, *Master Shengyan’s Naughty Youth* (*Shengyan Fashi de wanpi tongnian* 聖嚴法師的頑皮童年), Shengyan interweaves his own memories with reflections from his adult vantage point. Memories of childhood allow for “cross-writing” (as theorized by Knoepflmacher and Myers), as the author speaks for both the remembered child’s perspective and the adult’s later interpretation. The adult can reflect on both temporalities, that of unrealized time and accumulated time. In *Master Shengyan’s Naughty Youth,* Shengyan uses autobiography to show childhood, in all its dimensions, as a model for how Buddhists can learn through everyday life.

Rāhula’s Reformation

Rāhula’s childhood stands in contrast to that of his father, the prince Siddhartha. The earliest days of Śakyamuni Buddha are frequently illustrated: his birth, bathing, and first steps, and his coddled life within the palace.[12] He was the perfect child, if he can be said truly to have been a child,[13] but he was not the perfect father. Although accounts differ as to the exact timing in relation to Rāhula’s birth, Siddhartha abandoned his wife and infant son so that he could undertake the spiritual quest that eventually led to his awakening. In Śakyamuni’s life story, the presence of Rāhula proves his virility and his success at the householder life; he renounces his old life from a position of power, having achieved what was expected of him.[14] The care Śakyamuni extended to Rāhula is an afterthought at best, yet the Buddha’s son leaves his mother at age seven to become a novice monk.

The encounters between father and son during Rāhula’s training affirm Śakyamuni’s skill in teaching more than they attest to the parent-child relationship. When Rāhula is centered, rather than treated as a secondary character in his father’s narrative, he is a “model for childhood ordination.”[15] He emerges as an exemplar figure for novices and became an object of special veneration for them. Both the pilgrims Faxian and Xuanzang record that he was so treated in India. Novices carried out rites honoring Rāhula in Japan, likely reflecting practices in China as well.[16]

In the Mūlasarvāstivāda vinaya—one premodern source for stories about Rāhula—the path from seven-year-old renunciant to model monk is not depicted as straightforward. This is in part a function of genre: although hagiographies flatter their subjects, vinaya texts show monks and nuns making mistakes so that they can be corrected.[17] Rāhula is no exception, and the Mūlasarvāstivāda vinaya (and other canonical versions) account of Rāhula's youthful deceit is a story *about* a child but not *for* children. There, Rāhula's story appears as part of instructions about false speech (*wangyu* 妄語):

> At that time, the Buddha was staying in the bamboo grove of Karaṇḍa's garden in Rājagṛha, and the novice Rāhula was in Tapodārāma, just outside the site. Many devoted brahmins and lay people came to call in this place, asking, "Venerable! Where is the World-Honored One now?" If the World-Honored One was in the bamboo grove, Rāhula would say, "He's at Vulture Peak!" If he was on Vulture Peak, then Rāhula would reply, "He's in the bamboo grove.". . . . All these people who wanted to venerate the Buddha would be unable see him. Completely exhausted from their efforts, they would return to where Rāhula was. Then Rāhula would ask them, "Were you able to see the World-Honored One?" and they would respond, "We did not see him." They responded, "Noble one! Why do you frustrate us?" He replied, "Truly, I am frustrated too." But people had their suspicions. A bhikṣu told the Buddha about the situation. After the Buddha heard what he had to say, he took up his robe and bowl early one day, went on begging rounds in Rājagṛha, and returned to his former place to eat. After he had eaten, he went to where Rāhula was staying in Tapodārāma. When Rāhula saw the Buddha coming in the distance, he arranged a seat and prepared a bottle of water and vessel to wash the Buddha's feet. Having washed his own hands and feet, he went out to greet the World-Honored One; collecting his upper robe he said, "Well come, World-Honored One! Please take a seat." Upon reaching the seat, the Buddha sat down and used the bottle of water to wash his feet. After he had poured out the water in the foot-washing bowl, there was still a bit left. He spoke to Rāhula: "Do you see the water that I've discarded on the ground?" Rāhula responded, "Yes, noble one, I see." The Buddha said, "Rāhula, if a bhikṣu intentionally speaks falsehoods without shame or regret, I regard him as a fool who has discarded the way of the śramaṇa." The Buddha tilted the bowl on the ground, and said to Rāhula, "Do you see how this bowl is atilt?" Rāhula said "Yes, noble one, I see." The Buddha spoke, "Rāhula, if

> a bhikṣu intentionally speaks falsehoods without shame or regret, I regard him as a fool who has put askew the way of the śramaṇa." Then the Buddha took the bowl and turned it over on the ground, addressing Rāhula, "Do you see the bowl upside down on the ground?" Rāhula replied, "Yes, noble one, I see." The Buddha said, "Rāhula, if a bhikṣu intentionally speaks falsehoods without shame or regret, I regard him as a fool who has turned over the way of the śramaṇa. Again, Rāhula, it is like a mad elephant-king, who had great strength, tusks like cart axles, was strong and powerful, and was excellent in battle. When he went to the battlefield, he used his four feet, his two tusks, and his whole body—but he curled up his trunk. Rāhúla, in order to protect his own life, this elephant did not use his trunk to attack. The elephant master for the other army thought, 'This elephant-king cherishes his life.' Rāhula, if this elephant-king went into battle with its trunk extended, then the elephant-master would know that this elephant did not begrudge his own life, and that when the two armies met the elephant-king would spare no cruelty. It is like this Rāhula! If a bhikṣu intentionally speaks falsehoods without shame or regret, then there is no evil he would not do!"[18]

It is not hard to sympathize a bit with Rāhula: everyone wants time with *his* father. The Buddha does not directly lecture his son about his misdeeds, instead taking the customary foot-washing as an opportunity to instruct his son on the evil of telling lies in a more oblique way. Anālayo notes that the use of a quotidian object ensures that Rāhula will think about the Buddha's chastisement each time he has occasion to use the foot-washing bowl.[19] The Buddha, as a parent and teacher, forms connections between his teaching and the everyday, facilitating later reinforcement of his lesson to his son. Repetition focusing on different aspects of pouring out the water further strengthens the lesson. If somehow Rāhula has missed the point, the Buddha adds an analogy to a war-elephant. This does not address lying directly, instead making the point that one must cherish some things or risk being without any restraints at all.[20] Rāhula learns his lesson, proving the Buddha's skill in teaching extends even to children. The Buddha is primarily a teacher, as any little boy might be tempted in lies of this type, and there is no fatherliness on display.

This account from the Mūlasarvāstivāda vinaya serves as the basis for the story about Rāhula in *Code Words of the Great Teachers*. For younger readers, Rāhula's story usually appears as one of the Buddha's ten most important disciples. These include Ci'en Publishing's *The Ten Great Disciples* (*Shi da dizi* 十大弟子, 1981) and Fo Guang Shan's *Illustrated*

Explanation of the Ten Great Disciples (*Huashuo shi da dizi* 畫說十大弟子, 1998); in both of these Rāhula is treated as foremost in careful practice of the precepts (*mixing* 密行). In *Code Words of the Great Teachers* Rāhula is paired with the word "honesty" (*chengshi* 誠實). The story has the English title "Whose Kid Is So Naughty!" (translating "Sheijia de xiao haizi zhemme pi" 誰家的小孩子這麼皮). This retelling extends the narrative about Rāhula misleading visitors to the Buddha, adds humor, and tweaks the analogies. When we first see Rāhula, he is crouching amongst bamboo with a sly grin on his face; he's looking at two disgruntled laymen on the opposite page (Plate 8). The text explains how they've just been tricked by Rāhula, who has misinformed them about the Buddha's whereabouts. The laymen are shown in flashback to be exhausted, struggling over hills in hopes of reaching the Buddha. Rāhula is smiling and clearly having fun, even as he carries out his assigned task of sweeping.

The Buddha puts an end to the fun and corrects his son. When the Buddha comes to visit, Rāhula washes his feet and the Buddha compares his son to the dirty water. The Buddha is clearly angry and lectures his son on the importance of keeping the precepts, even though he is only a novice, and a young one at that. Having broken the precepts, he "can't again be pure."[21] In this modern retelling, Rāhula tried to excuse himself by saying that he was just having a little fun. The Buddha cuts him off, asking whether he is worried about breaking the basin. Rāhula says that it is made of iron and cannot easily be broken. The Buddha replies that the bowl can indeed be damaged, just like Rāhula's dignity if he keeps up his bad behavior.

Here Rāhula's response is emotional: he weeps in remorse and says that he will be honest from now on. The Buddha pats him on the head and tells the story of the war-elephant who hides his trunk. (The illustration makes the war-elephant nonthreatening and hardly martial at all; he stands on two legs and his facial expression suggests worry or embarrassment.) The trunk is his weakness, and he dies as soon as he is shot there. Rāhula is instructed to care for his words like the elephant cares for his trunk. In the same way that the water basin could serve as a frequent reminder of the danger of falsehood, Rāhula's own nose ("nose" and "trunk" are both *bi* 鼻) reminds him to take care with his words. The story ends with Rāhula demonstrating what he has learned by giving truthful directions to visitors looking for the Buddha.

Thinking back to the Mūlasarvāstivāda vinaya version, we can see how the story changes when intended for children. In the traditional text, Rāhula is given little to say, and what he does say is strongly repetitious. He relates to the Buddha as a teacher, and the anecdote does not reinforce their familial relation. In "Whose Kid Is So Naughty!" the misbehaving child is revealed as the Buddha's son a few pages in. The narrator also reveals that this is not Rāhula's first time engaging in "mischief" (*e zuoxi* 惡作戲, or "practical jokes" in the facing English translation). He's the Buddha's son, he's been misbehaving, and he's been enjoying it. In this depiction, Rāhula is not a child prodigy of a monk, with an innate aptitude for monastic life, nor does he reflect a special inheritance because of his father. He is a kid who happens to have a famous father. This contrasts with precocious children who are depicted as having from infancy an innate drive toward religious practice.

In the modern retelling for children, Rāhula's emotional reactions shape the story, and center it on the child's experience. From his sly smile on the first page, we see that he enjoys tricking people. He later wonders what his father's silence means and breaks down crying when he is scolded. As Heather Blair has observed with regard to Japanese children's literature, picturebooks present ways to practice emotional learning, including "intuiting how others . . . feel" and how to "communicate feeling in important and compelling ways."[22] Children are intended to identify with Rāhula and the emotions he experiences over the course of the events, moving from misguided happiness at his clever pranks, through anxiety about his father's reaction, and sorrow at having disappointed the Buddha so badly, to a new and different kind of happiness at the end. The final illustration shows him smiling broadly, touching his nose, as he tells the truth; he remembers the lesson about the elephant. Lying, for Rāhula, means more than just breaking the rules: because of his deceptions he is made uncomfortable emotionally, and this prompts his reform. Following the rules is a way of ensuring affective alignment with those around you. "Whose Kid Is So Naughty!" is not a story about the importance of monastic rules but rather about a child's potential to be bad or good, and how that shapes relations with others. Rāhula is a stand-in for any young practical joker needing to learn the value of honesty. Through his experience, the narrative seeks to persuade children even as it shows the possibilities for mischief.

There are adult *and* child characters in Rāhula's story, both in the Mūlasarvāstivāda vinaya version and in the picturebook version. Let's take the adult's perspective for a moment: Should a parent be reading this section of the Mūlasarvāstivāda vinaya and thinking about parenting, they would likely conclude that the Buddha—among his many other talents—offers a model of instructing children that seeks to elicit a reasoned response over simply laying down rules to be obeyed. But picturebooks are not just places for *children* to practice emotional learning, nor is emotional learning a process that is completed at some point. Thus a parent reading "Whose Kid Is So Naughty!" might have several affective reactions. The title points to the way that others notice unruly or disobedient children and wonder who is responsible for them. There's a humorous tension with Rāhula being the son of the Buddha, but no parent wants to hear "Whose kid is *that?*" about their own child. More importantly, Rāhula's tearful reaction gives parent-readers an opportunity to consider the emotional dimension of misbehavior and its correction. The child truly perceived as fun what others found vexing. Silence and scolding are unpleasant, and parents see this through the portrayal of the Buddha's bad son. Rāhula's story is an exercise in perspective taking. Within the story, the child fails to take the perspective of those he is tricking or his father. The reader, too, can occupy different vantage points to think through the actions and responses of both child and parent.

Ikkyū and the Childlike Mind

Rāhula reforms; Ikkyū does not, at least not entirely. The Japanese monk Ikkyū Sōjun was known as an eccentric and iconoclast as an adult. A poet and calligrapher, Ikkyū was supposed to have fathered a child late in life. His relationship to the Zen school was contentious—he tore up his certificate of enlightenment—but he spent the last years of his life working to restore the famed Daitokuji temple, which had been nearly destroyed by a fire.[23] None of this is mentioned in the introduction to Ikkyū's story in *Code Words of the Great Teachers,* which describes him as a straight-talker who fought against injustice, and whose "methods full of fun" helped popularize Buddhism.[24] In contrast to many of the monks included in the series, Ikkyū is included because of his childhood exploits, not for his later contributions. He is associated with the English word "agility," translating *jizhi* 機智, which indicates mental agility or quick-wittedness. As told here, his cheeky behavior as a young monk serves to show up the adults around him.

Ikkyū's childhood became a topic for stories shortly after his death, as Melissa Curley has shown, and these stories continued to grow in popularity. These give his adult qualities an early source. Even when quite young, Ikkyū is depicted as both quick-witted and naughty—traits that are forerunners of the antinomianism that characterized his adult life. By the twentieth century, popular retellings of his life included the Toei animated series *Ikkyū-san,* which first aired in 1975 and ran for seven years. Curley observes that modern versions of key stories from Ikkyū's life tend to diminish his deviousness and downplay conflict when intended for very young audiences.[25] Ikkyū can even serve as a model for good behavior such as helping to clean one's school, as he is shown doing similar tasks in the monastery.[26]

With the Japanese cartoon *Ikkyū-san,* stories of the monk became part of the cultural flows of modern Asia. This animated series aired in the People's Republic of China in the 1980s and was popular throughout Asia. Japanese producers did not actively promote their products for the wider Asian market, and indeed in Taiwan policies that limited Japanese products were in place until 1993.[27] Consumers in Taiwan, Hong Kong, the PRC, and

Singapore actively sought out Japanese animation and television programs, even if they had to resort to pirated copies. Stories of Ikkyū, conveyed through the animated series, are part of "shared memories" across Asia for those who grew up watching them.[28] The *Code Words of the Great Teachers* is also a transnational endeavor, incorporating monks from different countries to situate Chinese Buddhism at the center of a pan-Asian religion. This story about Ikkyū sits at the nexus of two different cultural flows, that of Buddhism and that of contemporary popular culture. Parents or children may already be acquainted with Ikkyū stories, which the Dharma Drum series uses to convey a broader message about Buddhism.

There is a shared repertoire of stories about Ikkyū's childhood, and the narratives chosen for the Dharma Drum picturebook show Ikkyū outsmarting adults. In "A Witty Novice Monk," Zheng Lier includes two standard stories from Ikkyū's childhood.[29] Zheng opens with an account of the court politics in Japan at the time of Ikkyū's birth, which explains the concerns for his safety that led to him being placed at a monastery at only six years of age. Doing so removed the suspicion that he was being groomed for rule.[30] As Zheng tells it, although there were many other young novices, Ikkyū had trouble making friends at first, but eventually won over his peers with his quick thinking.

Visually, Ikkyū first appears in a special relation to the Buddha, affirming his subsequent behavior as Buddhist. The opening illustration of Ikkyū in the monastery shows him standing on the palm of a Buddha statue so that he can dust under its chin; a tear has formed at the corner of the Buddha's eye, and he looks like he is trying to withstand being tickled. This concisely conveys how Ikkyū will subvert the expectations of the monastery. The illustration also suggests a family relationship between the young Ikkyū (just six years old) and the Buddha (in the form of a sensate statue) through the way that Ikkyū treats the Buddha with familial affection rather than reverence.

The centerpiece of "A Witty Novice Monk" is the story of how Ikkyū and his pals gorged themselves on a sweet treat and avoided the repercussions. The young monk discovers that every day the master, after morning lessons, goes to the kitchen and has a spoonful of something sticky from a jar. Ikkyū asks the master what he is eating, and is told that it is "medicine" (*yao* 藥) for adults, but "poison" (*duyao* 毒藥) for children. The next day, Ikkyū returns to the kitchen to look for the jar, and finds it on a high shelf, whereupon he accidentally knocks it to the floor. The contents begin to leak out the lid, and Ikkyū gives them a taste—it is "malt sugar, which kids love to eat." Ikkyū calls over all the other novices, and they eat the entire jarful. Then some novices worry aloud that the master will be angry when he discovers what they have done. Ikkyū's solution is to smash the jar. When the master returns Ikkyū says that he broke it accidentally and that he ate the poison as a punishment, hoping to die. The master, knowing that he has been found out and outsmarted, can do nothing more than tell Ikkyū to clean it up.

Ikkyū takes what power is available to him, as a child and monastic subordinate. His naughtiness is mitigated by some key details in the narrative, such as the fact that he does not try the syrup until some of it leaks out accidentally. His behavior also seems justified by the fact that the master is deceptive from the start. The elder monk hides the syrup from the young novices, and he lies about what it is. Asserting that the malt syrup is medicine for adults and poison for children signals the gap he sees between children and adults, with only adults being able to understand what that difference means. He holds a position of knowledge and power, and assumes that he will go unchallenged; he also has the authority to punish if his instructions are not heeded. From what seems to be a position of weakness, Ikkyū figures out how to get what he wants (a sugary snack) and to force the master into an unwinnable situation—to discipline the children, he'd have to admit his lie. Ikkyū is both more clever and more moral than his elder.

Significantly, Ikkyū's actions are in service of his peer group, other children. He invites them to share the syrup, and then he alone takes the blame to spare others from the master's anger. It is the older novices who worry about the master's reaction, having been better acculturated into monastic life. In the illustrations, however, it is difficult to distinguish Ikkyū from all the other children, as they are dressed alike and have near identical facial features. The kids act together, with Ikkyū as their voice. Children are a group with needs and characteristics that distinguish them from adults, and they may benefit from acting collectively. Treating the novices as a group defined by their status as children heightens the contrast with adults as a category.

The illustrations reinforce and comment on the narrative in other ways. The master is gaunt, missing teeth, and is visually unappealing (there's no doubt who the villain is). Ikkyū is depicted more like a toddler than a six-year-old, giving him an oversize, round head, and what look like baby booties.[31] Ikkyū and other novices sit in the splay-legged fashion of preschoolers. A two-page spread (with no words) appears at the core of the story and shows the group of novices delightfully messy (Plate 9). There is a lot to look at in this lively illustration, from the different ways that the children are sticky to the cat and snail who are also mired in the syrup. But we should take note of the Buddha peeking around the upturned jar: with a half smile and a waving hand, he conveys amused approval. He is the other adult-type figure, so to speak, in the story, and his allegiance is with the children. We can read here a subversion of adult claims to religious authority, and the affirmation of childlike behavior as acceptably Buddhist. The master and the Buddha are opposing types of adults—the former seeing children as different, and the latter treating them as kin.

Ikkyū exemplifies the child-mind (*tongxin* 童心): creative and quick-thinking, he sees through the rules and moral posturing of adults. Although the abbot does not appreciate Ikkyū's free-spiritedness, the child- or childlike-mind has been valorized as providing an alternative to adult ways of thinking. In the early twentieth century, the illustrator Feng Zikai was one of the intellectuals who saw childhood as an idealized age, one of innocence that was a source of "endless creative potential and moral honesty."[32] For Feng, the childlike mind was something that adults could strive to recover, taking children as their models. In "A Witty Novice Monk," the second, shorter story told about Ikkyū shows an adult more receptive to the child-mind. The young monk was invited to visit a famous general, who had heard of Ikkyū's intelligence and wit. As recounted by Zheng Lier here, the general points to a screen depicting a tiger, claiming that the tiger emerged from the screen each day to cause trouble. He asks if the young monk can think of a way to tie him up. After carefully examining the screen, young Ikkȳu asks for a rope, forms a lasso with one end of it, and squats downs in front of the painted tiger. He then asks who is going to chase the tiger out so he can catch it. The general claps his hands, delighted to have found the young monk to be as "agile" (*jizhi*) as claimed. Unlike the disapproving abbot, the general is pleased with Ikkyū's quick-thinking and intelligence.

Ikkyu's child-mind has a Buddhist function and is something he retains in adulthood. We might note here that their conversation has the structure of a Chan encounter, with young Ikkyū playing along, but throwing the question of the tiger's reality back to the adult audience. He does not protest that the tiger cannot leap from the painted screen, but neither does he try to reach through or behind the screen to catch it. His response instead asks for his adult interlocutor to confirm or deny the tiger's reality. We see encounters between Chan masters and students structured in the same way, in which the goal is not to fall into affirming one side of a dualistic assertion. Here, Ikkyū's child-mind is akin to the awakened mind, and as such does not need to be restricted to childhood. Ikkyū's story concludes by noting that he was "not constrained by form or custom, using his quick-wittedness or unconventional behavior according to circumstances" to teach Buddhism.[33] Ikkyū's childlike mind becomes a vehicle for Buddhist teachings.

His childlike mind also suggests how people of different ages might inhabit different perspectives. What does it mean to have a child's mind as an adult? Children are often expected to develop "adult minds," in that they learn to conform to adult expectations and social roles. Retaining a child's mind requires unlearning—or relearning—through active effort. In the telling of Ikkyū's story, having a child's mind means acting without the usual cognitive or social constraints. Young Ikkyū is not the only one who exhibits this: the general's delight is possible because he can set aside his own expectations long enough to appreciate the young monk's response. He is a different kind of adult.

Rāhula and Ikkyū represent two different outcomes for naughty children. One is shaped *by* an adult, and one is shaped *against* an adult. Rāhula's story, despite having a child as its main character, centers the adult perspective, and Rāhula is brought in line with his father's expectations. Ikkyū's story, in contrast, presents a child's-eye view: if a mischievous young monk can use his cleverness for good in everyday situations within the monastery, then many impish children have such potential. For a picturebook with dual audiences, this message may resonate as much for adults as it does for children.

A Modern Exemplar

Shengyan's own story, told for children, incorporates these two perspectives—that of the child, and that of the adult looking at a child. If Ikkyū models Buddhist teachings through the child's mind, Shengyan shows how Buddhist messages can be discovered in childhood memories. Shengyan's story also suggests how modern monks might serve as exemplars for children, even if those children will not grow up to be monks. Stories about monks who lived during the early decades of the twentieth century or in more recent times do different work than historical biographies: they can show that living as a committed Buddhist is not part of the past or outside contemporary society, but fully part of it. When such stories are about living monks, they also serve to connect communities by providing portraits of leaders that may build their charisma or make them more accessible to followers. The stories told about the monk (or nun) themselves can make them more approachable, and the format can also work toward this end.

Told through popular media, the biography of Xingyun—whom we have seen as a commentator to the *Heart Sutra* in chapter 2—illustrates his work within society while making a monk who might be treated as a distant "great man" seem approachable to a range of audiences. Jack Meng-tat Chia notes that the illustrator of the comic-book version of Xingyun's life, Zheng Wen 鄭問 (b. 1958), spent a long time in preparation, making sure that he understood the arc of Xingyun's life. Its telling in comic form hews closely to the biography written by Fu Zhiying 符芝瑛. Both biographies emphasize Xingyun's activities in the world, from his smaller acts of compassion in his early years to the establishment of Fo Guang Shan and its international network. Zheng's illustrations use different perspectives and depictions of motion to add drama to the story. Chia observes that in this format Xingyun's life reads something like a Buddhist "rags to riches" story, as it shows how "traits valued in Buddhism—compassion, generosity, diligence, and determination—enabled a poor, modest monk to emerge as a worldling bodhisattva, who is able to bring the Dharma to every part of the world."[34] In a preface to the comic version of his life, Xingyun writes that he hopes this will be appealing to teenagers, as they are already familiar with the medium. In this case, illustrated texts are not intended for young readers but rather offer traditional topics in innovative, modern formats. We see this, too, in the animated film about the life of Yinshun produced by Great Love Television (Da ai dianshi 大愛電視), part of Tzu Chi's media efforts.[35] That the intended audience is adults is signaled by the opening to the film, in which Yinshun and his teacher Fazun 法尊 (1902–1980) discuss Buddhist philosophy in a secluded monastery. The Hayao Miyazaki–style animation is novel, but the content is not intended for children. Stefania Travagnin observes that this film depicts Yinshun as a Buddhist hero, and then connects him to Zhengyan. The animated film is used to argue for a dharma lineage, continuing in a new format a traditional function of monastic biographies.[36] The animated version of Yinshun's life differs from Xingyun's biography in that Xingyun had input in a way that Yinshun did not, pointing to a key difference between biographies of living monks and those who are historical figures.

Returning to Shengyan, his childhood is presented differently in texts aimed at children and adults. Both reflect the potential of self-narration of life stories. We know many details of Shengyan's childhood because he talks about it and has information that no biographer could have. For this reason, autobiographical texts generally provide more space for childhood. Miriam Levering, in her work on childhood in monastic biographies, points out that the autobiography of Hanshan Deqing 憨山德清 (1546–1623) is a "counter-example" to biographies with scant information about a monk's childhood. In his self-narration, Deqing talks about how family events prompted his early spiritual questioning. He also relates how his mother pretended not to care for him, to ease his transition to boarding away at school. Levering speculates as to how Deqing's childhood would have been handled by a traditional biographer, concluding that some episodes would have been omitted and others reshaped so that Deqing was "depicted . . . as intellectually and spiritually precocious in the Buddhist mold." Deqing himself emphasized "his relationship with his mother, on her role in shaping his choices, and on his own uncertainty about his monastic vocation"—showing the "not always ideal steps in one's formation that take place in childhood."[37] Without the need to show the child as destined for monastic life, autobiography can depict childhood with greater complexity.

In texts for adults, Shengyan's eminence does not begin with nature or nurture, but through serendipity. In his memoir *The Education of Master Shengyan* (*Shengyan fashi xuesi licheng* 聖嚴法師學思歷程), he begins with events that precede his own earliest memory. He describes the flooding of the Yangzi River that forced his family to move in the year of his birth and offers what little family history he knows. Shengyan talks about the poverty of his family and his village, and how lack of nutrition probably contributed to his childhood illnesses. He relates his early, intermittent education and how the religion he encountered was a mix of traditions. He entered the monastery at thirteen not out of a special belief in Buddhism but by happenstance: A neighbor, taking shelter from a storm in their home, remembered that she had recently visited a small temple that sought a little monk (*xiao heshang* 小和尚). As Shengyan relates it, his mother jokingly asked if he wanted to go be a little monk, and with no understanding of what a monk even was, he agreed.[38] *The Road Back* (*Guicheng* 歸程) covers similar ground, but adds a few anecdotes—when he was caught skipping school by his mother, how he mistreated one of his friends when she went blind, the bullying he received from classmates.[39] In both these autobiographies, Shengyan's youth makes up a small portion of the overall narrative, providing a backdrop to his studies and development as a Buddhist monk. The picture he paints of his childhood is generally bleak, reflecting the extreme poverty of the 1920s and 1930s, and the stress it placed on families. From his description of the multifarious religious activities of his village and the casual way that he first entered the monastery, Shengyan conveys that he had no special affinity for Buddhism as a very young child.

Master Shengyan's Naughty Youth (*Shengyan Fashi de wanpi tongnian*) uses stories about his youth to highlight his lack of precociousness and how meaning can be read into mundane childhood happenings. Aimed at children, the narrative focuses primarily on his early years, told from the first person. As we saw in his preface to *Code Words of the Great Teachers*, Shengyan recalls reading stories about monks as a child. He is thus well aware of the effects such stories have on children. *Master Shengyan's Naughty Youth* deliberately highlights his modest background and slow development. The first half of *Master Shengyan's Naughty Youth* concerns his years before entering the monastery, and much of his time in the monastery is as a young novice. Told in brief anecdotes, the book tracks his growth both in age and toward Buddhism.

His family's material impoverishment defines his childhood, as we learn in the first pages. The opening sentence establishes an opposition to the idealized way that childhood is often presented: "For my family, the New Year wasn't a celebratory affair." These words appear on red background, a red envelope that fills the foreground of the illustration (Plate 10). A gold coin tumbles out before a wide-eyed child. Behind him, two other people smile broadly and in the background door couplets are being prepared. The happy images of the New Year are ones that young children would recognize easily from their own experience, and from other picturebook treatments of this most important holiday. As in many children's books the illustration tells a different story than the text, here offering a contrast. The illustrations capture the celebratory spirit of the holiday, while the text reflects on its absence. Shengyan describes the days leading up to New Year's as ones of anxiety, as people came to collect their debts. The family had no money for new clothes for all six children, and as the youngest, Shengyan got hand-me-downs from his older siblings. His mother told them these clothes counted as "new" because they were newly washed and newly mended, and that it was most important that the clothes kept them warm and looked clean.[40] This message stayed with him, and he writes that he has consequently never been much concerned with clothes.

The illustrations introduce mending and repair as a significant theme. Here readers see five shirts on a drying rod with a young boy looking on from the foreground. There are patches on all the shirts, and looking carefully, the clothing is outlined with real stitches that have then been photographed. Illustrators do not always explain their process, but in this case a preface by Juzi 菊子 explains the variety of techniques used in illustrating *Master Shengyan's Naughty Youth.* (Juzi is also the illustrator for the story of Rāhula and has a recognizable style of drawing smiles.) Along with the stitching, multiple layers of different kinds of paper and collage create paintings with depth and texture. At least some stitching appears in all the illustrations, as Juzi identified mending or repair as a key theme in the narrative. It reappears explicitly in a later anecdote, in which Shengyan is desperate for a uniform to wear to school, so he doesn't stand out from the other children. Knowing the family cannot afford to buy one, he asks his mother to sew one. She says she cannot sew a uniform; the illustration shows her again mending clothes.[41] In these scenes of early childhood, lines of stitching signify mending and are connected with maternal care, but over the course of the book they transform into the lines of composition books and bookbindings. Juzi unifies these two aspects of Shengyan's development through illustration. Juzi also ties stitching to Shengyan's later mission: "Shengyan's great love mends the holes in the world, without ever stopping. Therefore, I insisted on using hand sewing so as to express true warmth and love in the Master's stories."[42] The acts of care performed by Shengyan's mother resonate through his later life, and, through the lines of stitching, into the picturebook as well.

When Shengyan concludes that his early years taught him to be content with simple clothes, he does not assign this religious meaning—although it would seem to connect to the simplicity of monastic robes—but Buddhist values do emerge in the second story he tells. This concerns a bunch of bananas brought home by his brother, and in this case being the youngest meant that Shengyan got a whole banana of his own. Bananas were exotic at the time, and few had ever tasted them. Shengyan decides to share his bounty with his schoolmates, and they each get one bite of banana. Shengyan delights in the happiness of his friends, and later extends this attitude of generosity to sharing the Buddhist teachings.[43] Shengyan, in these first stories, emphasizes the material impoverishment that shaped his worldview. Recalling these memories, Shengyan usually adds a line or two indicating what he learned from the experience.

Although these first two stories cast Shengyan in a sympathetic light, his childhood character is more complex and more realistic. Many of the stories that Shengyan includes center on naughty or mischievous behavior: he skipped school, he stole fruit from trees, and caught river crabs with his brother.[44] Each of these stories ends with a life lesson or other moral, and many of them also describe his parents' reactions. His mother is deeply disappointed when he skips school and beats him; his father tells him not to blame others for goading him on when it was his own stupidity that led him to climb a tree. Shengyan also recounts humorous anecdotes about his childhood. He felt embarrassed by his small head and small ears and was teased about them. Once when he was out in the fields with his brother, he was surprised by a water buffalo, fell off a bridge, and needed to be rescued. The family comes across as tight-knit, but not idealized; aside from shifting norms about corporal punishment, Shengyan's parents seem much like other parents. The setting likewise is not idealized: although he seems to recall a simple life in the countryside with fondness, his family's poverty makes it hard to romanticize it. The realistic (nonhagiographical) representation of his early years shows both Shengyan as a child and his parents as average, and this has important effects on the message of the book as a whole.

Shengyan's early time in the temple is where he learns to read life as imbued with Buddhist meaning; this is not what he expected, if he expected anything. He leaves home to become a novice at a young age (not specified here, nor a reason given), and he does not enter the monastery well prepared for what he will experience. He imagines that he will be fanning an old monk while he meditates and strolling around the mountain as if it was the precinct of the immortals. His explanation for such unrealistic notions shows the influence of early twentieth-century popular culture: "Because I saw performances like these in plays, therefore when I thought of my life as a monk, I thought it should be this way."[45] What he finds instead is a substitute family, centered on the older monk, who provides life lessons as he guides Shengyan through daily life in the monastery. (These lessons often come with a side of admonishment, as we saw in the opening paragraph of this chapter.) For example, the elderly monk sets young Shengyan the task of finding three identical bamboo twigs, which proves frustrating. Resigning himself to his punishment, Shengyan returns without having completed the task, only to be told that no two things are completely alike but there are similarities in difference, and differences in similarity.[46] Practical lessons about the importance of conserving water are extended to the karmic reward (*fubao* 福報) of being born as a human.[47] These moments of instruction are also a meta-lesson on how to move through the world: from everyday encounters, Shengyan draws a broader moral, either in the moment or in his reflections. Emulating Shengyan means learning from daily experience, even when that experience is one's own mistakes or failure. A precocious, perfect childhood would not afford such opportunities.

Nostalgia facilitates this meaning making. Adult readers of *Master Shengyan's Naughty Youth* might be struck by the depictions of rural life in the anecdotes and illustrations, from a wooden diabolo to oxen plowing rice paddies. More so than books about childhoods of the distant past, this account of Shengyan's life evokes nostalgia, if not for the younger years of the adult readers, for a lost or imagined time and place. Unlike his self-narratives for adults that specify his birthplace, the picturebook is stripped of such locators. The story could be in any countryside, making it available for overwriting with other memories or associations. Nostalgia has been a significant cultural phenomenon in East Asia, although often criticized for its shallowness.[48] Here, however, Shengyan draws lessons from his childhood by engaging with the emotions associated with past events. Psychologists have suggested that nostalgia, in that it prompts emotional review of the past, has positive effects for identity-formation.[49] In Shengyan's case, it is a Buddhist identity that shapes his personal narrative; the threads in the illustrations make material the connections between different parts of his life. As with Xingyun's commentaries on the *Heart Sutra,* which demonstrated how the scripture could be used to interpret everyday experiences, Shengyan's review of his childhood for Buddhist meaning can serve as a model for the picturebook's two sets of readers—backward-directed for adults and forward-looking for children.

There are two key narrative strands in *Master Shengyan's Naughty Youth:* one focused on education and academic achievement, and one centered on the implications of parental devotion. Shengyan's limited education meant then when he did begin formal Buddhist education—after his years as a novice—he was quite far behind. With the help of his fellow students, he manages to find his intellectual footing, and the book concludes with Shengyan editing the monastery journal and establishing his own way of teaching the dharma. The other narrative strand concerns Shengyan's parents, primarily his mother, and their sacrifices for the family when Shengyan was a young child. Recognizing what his mother had given up, Shengyan made a vow at an early age that he would earn enough money to give to his mother so that she would not have to worry about being poor. He was unable to keep his vow and do so within her lifetime, and so turned to helping others as a way of fulfilling his commitment and commemorating his parents. Vow-making is central to modern Buddhism, as we have already seen in retellings of Xuanzang's biography. Shengyan writes that he believes that making vows and redeeming vows is life's purpose. The illustration accompanying these words shows Shengyan—depicted so as to emphasize his cuteness—above a river of people. Cuteness prompts feelings of empathy and care, so the reader is meant to have an emotional response both to Shengyan and to all the other figures depicted as cute.[50] Shengyan's notion of vows would create a chain of good works, and these deeds would be facilitated by sympathetic identification with the other. Here, vow-making is affinity work that creates resonating connections. The last page suggests what effects might result: Shengyan's smile is echoed not only in the image of him on the bulletin board, but in the smile of the Buddha above. These echoing smiles across the final pages also remind us of the emotional attunement that happens between parents and children while reading.

The narratives address a dual audience of parents and children; the paratexts suggest what parenting lessons might be drawn from Shengyan's naughtiness. Reading this story as one might read one of the stories in *The Code of Great Teachers,* we can identify values that children should absorb: studiousness, family unity, compassion for society. The focus on positive traits could overshadow the idea of naughtiness (*wanpi* 頑皮) in the title and in the tales Shengyan recounts. Yet the prefaces emphasize naughtiness as key: the one written by the editorial section of Dharma Drum Culture (Fagu wenhua) is titled "From naughty little boy to little śrāmeṇera" 從小頑童到小沙彌. This preface highlights several ways in which Shengyan underwent a "metamorphosis" (*tuibian* 蛻變). Transformation requires a prior condition to have meaning, so it is important for the narrative that Shengyan begin as a normal, mischievous young boy. The transformations over the course of childhood form a narrative appealing to children and adults. The prefaces are meant for adult readers, typically parents, to guide them in understanding the meaning of the book. Naughtiness, and its potential transformation, has a different meaning when viewed through the lenses of children and of parents. Both might identify with a child who misbehaves, remembering from different temporal distances times in which they themselves got into trouble. For parents, however, they can also identify with Shengyan's parents, and may see their own children in this naughty little boy. The first preface, identified as a "recommendation," argues that there is a necessary connection between his naughtiness and his later success:

> If Master Shengyan hadn't had a naughty character, then he probably wouldn't have his present success. Naughty children are headaches for adults, but naughtiness is just a type of vitality in children. One could say that naughtiness is a kind of creativity. Adults don't like it when children are naughty because they hope that children will accept an adult value system and go along with adult wishes in their studies and activities. But once children completely accept adult thinking, then their lively creative vitality will diminish. If an individual is without the heart of a child, it's very difficult to face real trials and temptations, and to maintain one's ideals.[51]

These comments suggest that the book is to be read with dual perspective on the part of adults—as they remember their own childhood through the escapades of Shengyan, they also see the childhood of their children. Shengyan's naughtiness allows parents the opportunity to reframe the conduct of their own children. Behavior that may cause parents worry becomes an asset, and perhaps even a sign of future success. Presenting naughtiness as part of the child-mind and therefore as acceptable or advantageous inverts the expectations around childhood in traditional Buddhist biographies. Shengyan also moves between adult and child perspectives, offering his memories of what it felt like to be a child (embarrassed by his small head, being reprimanded by the teacher, being scared by a water buffalo) followed by his understanding of what these experiences taught him. The autobiographical mode offers an interior view of childhood that is missing from stories about Rāhula, Ikkyū, and other child monks. That Shengyan became a monk is central, but so is his metamorphosis (*tuibian*) through learning from everyday life.

Naughty Children Are Little Bodhisattvas Too

In picturebooks about young monks, children are both the audience for and the protagonists of the story. Mischief and naughtiness are defined by adults, and not all such behavior is in need of correction. Portrayals of young monks as imperfect and interested in fun make them like other children and highlight their difference from adults. Mischief and fun capitalize on the possibilities of childhood; experimentation and mistakes matter less when there is still time to change course. In Beauvais's formulation, children have the stronger currency and their unrealized time can be an advantage over adults.

The stories of Rāhula, Ikkyū, and Shengyan engage how the perspectives of children and adults differ. Presented as picturebooks, they assume an audience of both adults and children. Rāhula offers a straightforward story of misbehavior and correction. Ikkyū, in contrast, shows that adults may not always be right, and that childish fun—even messiness—can happen within Buddhist spaces. Shengyan reflects on the importance of childhood memories for adults, and how the lessons of childhood can pattern a process of lifelong learning. More than the other two stories, *Master Shengyan's Naughty Youth* shows the fluidity between childhood and adulthood. Perry Nodelman has argued that the reader of a children's book "is expected to experience a double awareness" of both childlike and not-childlike perspectives.[52] In many works, these perspectives are implied—readers assign child and adult perspectives to characters—but Shengyan makes them explicit. Shengyan switches between points of view, sympathetic both to the child he was and to his own parents, who had to deal with him as a challenging child. Shengyan also considers his youthful exploits from the vantage point of what he knows as an adult. Drawing lessons from childhood experiences, he points to how his own life forms a coherent narrative. By inhabiting his childhood self through memory, Shengyan reveals the different temporal perspectives of child and adult.

Shengyan's account of his own childhood, illustrated in *Master Shengyan's Naughty Youth,* offers a modern perspective on what makes a monk. Biographies of Xuanzang, as we have seen, follow traditional treatments of monastic biographies in providing only limited, and positive, information about life before tonsure. *Master Shengyan's Naughty Youth* inverts this, showing him as a troublemaker with typical childhood challenges. We can see continuations with the autobiographical tradition represented by Deqing, but Shengyan's youthful misdeeds also serve contemporary purposes. As with the "code words" series, the paratexts frame the story of Shengyan's childhood for parents, and present as positive what might be seen as negative. This also emphasizes a developmental view of children: they are not born with set characteristics but are shaped by their environment, including how their parents respond to them. Shengyan uses religious autobiography to make arguments about modern childhood and parenting, and how childhood, in all its dimensions, relates in a positive way to adulthood.

These stories also depict practicing Buddhism as something children can do *as children.* Adult models suggest how children might grow into Buddhism, as an adventurous spirit might be directed to pilgrimage, like Xuanzang. Rāhula, Ikkyū, and Shengyan are Buddhist already, but also children—their naughtiness distinguishes them from miniature adults. A Buddhist child has their own way of perceiving the world and acting within it.

5

Befriending Bodhisattvas

THERE'S A BUDDHA WHO CAN BE REACHED BY TELEPHONE, and another buddha who saves animals from fates as circus performers. We read about a bodhisattva who has undersea escapades (despite a long-standing association with a mountain in China), and one who guides a young prince on an Indiana Jones–type adventure. Along with the bodhisattva discussed in the introduction who helped a little boy deal with environmental pollution, these are new visions of suprahuman figures. This series of picturebooks juxtaposes transcendent and timeless beings with very contemporary situations and stories.

What do bodhisattvas and buddhas do, and how do they interact with us? These questions are often answered through stories, whether miracle tales that describe the bodhisattva's intervention in this world through their powerful effects, or through more extended narratives, such as the *Precious Scroll of Incense Mountain* (*Xiangshan baojuan* 香山寶卷), that elaborate a bodhisattva's appearance in the human realm. Literature for children cannot assume the same level of familiarity with these figures as works intended primarily for adults; it must introduce and explain buddhas and bodhisattvas. In doing so, this literature also argues for the type of relationship that the child-reader might have with the bodhisattva or buddha. This chapter will use a series of books published by Dharma Drum to demonstrate how these picturebooks transform bodhisattvas from figures of salvific intervention and distant exemplars of compassion into everyday companions and immediate models for children.

The picturebooks in *My Buddhas and Bodhisattvas* (*Wode fo pusa* 我的佛菩薩) show children with a direct relationship with buddhas and bodhisattvas, unmediated by religious clergy or parents. Rather, bodhisattvas are offered as transitional figures between parental care and independence. The model for this relationship is one of friendship, and the approachability of the bodhisattva is constructed through a visual idiom of cuteness, which renders Buddhist figures like children: unthreatening and in need of care. In these books, buddhas and bodhisattvas offer children companionship without expectation of the child's goodness, instead inviting them into prosocial collaborations. Through the child's independent relationship with the bodhisattva or buddha, these books depict a developmental model of Buddhist practice in which readers learn how to act in concert with such suprahuman exemplars. The books further encourage interactions with bodhisattvas and buddhas in tactile ways, through the inclusion of games and stickers. This is an introduction to the material culture of Buddhism, but it also prepares young readers to see the actions of Guanyin, Puxian 普賢 (Samantabhadra), and other bodhisattvas in the world around them. Becoming friends with a bodhisattva builds Buddhist agency.

Mothers and Mediators

Bodhisattvas and buddhas are usually portrayed as saviors and models of Buddhist virtues, rather than as friends or companions. An earlier picturebook, *Everyone's Mama* (*Dajia de mama*), answers questions about what bodhisattvas and buddhas do and how they interact with us in ways that keep these figures distant and mediated through adults. Written and illustrated by the nun Guofan 果梵 (b. 1949), and published in 1988 by a forerunner to Dharma Drum, *Everyone's Mama* introduces children to the bodhisattva Guanyin. The first pages of the book set the stage for *why* a child might want to know about this bodhisattva: sometime in the unspecified past an earthquake frightens a little girl at play. She rushes to her mother for comfort, who tells her that whenever she is afraid she can call on (*nian* 念) the bodhisattva Guanyin for protection (Plate 11). This prompts the little girl to ask about Guanyin and why calling her name helps. Through their dialogue, the mother explains who Guanyin is, her home on Mount Putuo (Putuo shan 普陀山), and her special capacity to hear people's entreaties—which the mother likens to radio transmissions. The examples of Guanyin's powers to save (from burning houses, typhoons, wild animals, and bad people) and powers of transformation (into rulers and so forth) are drawn from the *Lotus Sutra* chapter on Guanyin, although this is not flagged. Amazed by Guanyin's powers, the little girl says that she wants to worship Guanyin and become a bodhisattva herself. The mother lists several behaviors that are bodhisattva-like: helping the poor, not catching butterflies and dragonflies, helping animals in distress, and releasing animals (*fangsheng* 放生). The story concludes with the little girl declaring that Guanyin is everyone's mama and going with her dogs to worship the bodhisattva. The young girl's encounter with the bodhisattvas is through her mother, who acts as a mediating figure, and leads to devotional acts to Guanyin.

Guofan's nostalgic illustration style takes an ambivalent position: child-friendly, it also reinforces a narrative that keeps Guanyin somewhat distant. She works through traditional brush painting, simplifying the forms and streamlining details, and enlarging the heads of the figures she paints. Their facial expressions are conveyed through the simple lines of smiles, closed eyes, and eyebrows. She also adds fields of color to add brightness to the illustrations, and the overall effect is something like calligraphic cartoons. Throughout Guanyin is illustrated in her white-robed form, and her traditional iconography of willow branch and pure water is also explained in the text. Although Guanyin is depicted with a friendly and approachable mien, she is not actually in the world in which the story takes place. When she is shown rescuing people from calamity—the passages drawn from the "Universal Gate" chapter—clouds underneath her feet indicate her divine status and distance.

The little girl, and by extension the young reader, learn about Guanyin's salvific powers through her iconography without developing a personal relationship with the bodhisattva. The practice of calling on Guanyin is explained, but more emphasis is given to the child's relationship with animals. Setting aside one's butterfly net, helping a sparrow caught in the rain, and releasing fish back into a stream are all actions that children might easily undertake and enjoy. The little girl's embrace of her dogs at the end of the story mirrors her mother's hug at the beginning; caring for animals is training both for human relationships and for bodhisattva-like behavior. The illustrations of animal care late in the book echo similar ink drawings by Feng Zikai, connecting it to early twentieth-century efforts to illustrate Buddhism for popular audiences.[1] Imitating the bodhisattva is how the little girl can begin to act in a Buddhist way.

The story is preceded by two prefaces on the "origins" (*yuanqi* 緣起) of the book. In the first, aimed primarily at adults, Guofan relates her own mother's invocation of Guanyin, and how, following her mother's early death, she came to understand that following the teachings of Guanyin (*Guanyin famen* 觀音法門) had to be integrated into one's life through care of others. This realization prompted to her to want to make an artistic, modern version of the "Universal Gate" chapter (Pumen pin 普門品) of the *Lotus Sutra;* she settled on a childlike style to convey her sincerity. This preface concludes by offering the merit from the making of the book to all those who are inclined toward Buddhism. This account of her personal background with Guanyin and her creative process is accompanied by a second preface, directed at children (*gei xiao pengyou* 給小朋友). Here, Guofan relates a conversation she had with a four-year-old child she knows. The conversation started when

Guofan led the child—who had been crying nonstop—into the Buddha Hall. There they knelt before a statue of white-robed Guanyin, and Guofan whispered to him:

> "Look! The bodhisattva is watching you, saying, 'Yuqing isn't well-behaved!'"
>
> He inclined his little face, covered with tears, and stared with wide eyes. His face red with shame, he asked, "Teacher, is the bodhisattva really looking at me? Does the bodhisattva know I've been crying?"
>
> "Yes, that's right." Then I said, "The bodhisattva likes well-behaved children!"
>
> Still staring with wide eyes and facing the statue of Guanyin, he asked, "If I'm a good kid, the bodhisattva will like me? And mama will like me?"[2]

It is this encounter that provided the specific inspiration for Guofan to write a children's book. However, the bodhisattva that she presented to Yuqing is very different from the motherly savior figure in the body of the book itself. This bodhisattva surveils children and has preferences for well-behaved ones. Yuqing may have related to Guanyin as a mother—as implied by the title—but as a mother who wants good (*guai* 乖) children. The bodhisattva was not there to help the little boy, but rather to monitor him. Such a presentation does not encourage the child to see the bodhisattva as friendly. What moved the little boy in the preface is unlike what motivates the little girl in the story to emulate Guanyin. We can read the story of the fictional girl as an intervention: if children learn early who Guanyin is, they will want to take her compassion as a model for their own lives, as Guofan herself did at a much later age.

Guanyin is figured as a mother in both the anecdote in the preface and in the story itself. *Mama* is used in the title, rather than "mother" (*muqin* 母親); the latter is a noun describing a role, while "mama" is a term of address used by children.[3] Even more than "mother," "mama" puts the person using it in the position of child. And indeed, there is a shift from biological mother to bodhisattva mother: in the preface Yuqing was led away from his mother (to provide her some relief from his crying jag) and to the statue of Guanyin. There he was prompted to see the bodhisattva as akin to his mother, observing his behavior and having a positive or negative reaction to it. By the last line of the dialogue quoted above, Yuqing had made the connection between maternal approval and that of the bodhisattva. In the story itself, the little girl runs to her mother (whom she naturally calls "mama") when frightened by the earthquake and is then taught to call on the bodhisattva. Although not explicit, the bodhisattva is suggested as a replacement for the mother: instead of calling for her mother, the little girl can instead call on Guanyin when she needs help. For both Yuqing and the little girl in the story, Guanyin evokes certain feelings and so forming a connection to the bodhisattva has an affective dimension. Further, over the course of the story, Guanyin is offered as a model for behavior. A series of equations are made: Guanyin is everyone's mama, the little girl is her dog's mama, anyone with a compassionate heart is Guanyin. Little girls are expected to be like their mothers, but Guanyin becomes the figure the little girl seeks to emulate. Indeed, because the bodhisattva is "everyone's mama," the little girl and her mother end up in the same relationship to Guanyin: they are both her "children." What one needs to do to call on the bodhisattva is simple, the basic act of invoking a name that children do naturally. There is, as presented here, no special ritual involved: one calls (*nian* 念) Guanyin's name and worships (*bai* 拜) her.

As one of the earliest Buddhist picturebooks in Taiwan, *Everyone's Mama* is a bridge between an older tradition in which the bodhisattva is a distant figure and one in which Guanyin comes into this world in the present. Throughout the story, the bodhisattva is referred to with the third-person pronoun for gods and spirits (*ta* 祂). She is depicted as a model for emulation but also an object of worship, and, through the introduction, as a figure who rewards good behavior. Yet there is the suggestion that Guanyin might appear in this world: What would it mean for children if she did so? What other ways might a child relate to a bodhisattva?

Cute Friends

Published two decades after *Everyone's Mama,* the Dharma Drum series *My Buddhas and Bodhisattvas* includes stories about Guanyin and three other bodhisattvas (Dizang 地藏, Wenshu 文殊 or Mañjuśrī, and Puxian) as well as four buddhas (Siddhartha, Amitābha 阿彌陀佛, Mile 彌勒 or Maitreya, and Medicine-Master Buddha 藥師佛). Apart from Siddhartha, all the stories focus on the capacity of bodhisattvas and buddhas to rescue living beings, but also on children's ability to form direct relationships with these suprahuman beings. That buddhas and bodhisattvas could be friends is established by making them cute, through their use of first-person address, and through the types of roles the narratives give to young protagonists.

In *Medicine-Master Buddha's Birthday Present* (*Yaoshi fo de shengri liwu* 藥師佛的生日禮物), the buddha is adorable and charming, and quickly forms a clear bond to the primary human character, a young girl called Little Cao. The opening pages emphasize Medicine-Master Buddha as fun, an attribute not typically associated with bodhisattvas. The story opens on top of a birthday cake, where the buddha's helpers Moonlight Bodhisattva and Sunlight Bodhisattva are making figures out of whipped cream to the delight of Little Cao.[4] Medicine-Master Buddha did not have to be summoned by special means; he has simply appeared, knowing that Little Cao's mother and father must work overtime at the hospital and so cannot celebrate their daughter's birthday with her. By the second page, the buddha and the little girl have established a friendly intimacy and sit together at a table; hanging behind them is a picture of Little Cao with her family (Plate 12). The goal of the story is to bring these two groups together, and the penultimate spread shows the parents sitting with Little Cao and Medicine-Master Buddha at a large round banquet table. Having Medicine-Master Buddha at the family table underscores their closeness, as well as the potential of home as a place to encounter suprahuman figures.

In the course of the narrative Little Cao learns about Medicine-Master Buddha, his companions, and the twelve generals that protect him, as well as how the medicine he uses is made. They visit the hospital where Little Cao's parents work, and there distribute medicine, which transforms the hospital into an amusement park, freeing the parents from their overtime obligations. In his reader's guide, Ding Min 丁敏, a professor of Chinese literature, concisely expresses how these two goals of the narrative relate: "How can one close the gap between the 'Great King of Doctors,' (*da yi wang* 大醫王) and young children, and make them feel closer to Medicine-Master Buddha, while also causing them not to fear doctors—who are Medicine-Master Buddha's helpers on earth—so much?"[5] In other words, how can Medicine-Master Buddha be made into a friendly figure?

Medicine-Master Buddha's accessibility is not just conveyed through where he is (the family home), what he does (play with whipped cream), and how this makes the little girl feel (happy and loved), but also through how he looks. While retaining the iconographical features that distinguish Medicine-Master Buddha from other figures, he has been made cute. His cuteness removes the distance between him and the little girl by depicting them in similar ways; this in turn facilitates their friendship. Medicine-Master Buddha's head is oversize, about a third of his body in total, and is almost completely round. This roundness is echoed by his hair curls. Although we cannot see his feet, his hands are disproportionately small. Medicine-Master Buddha is always smiling broadly, the corners of his mouth almost reaching the rosy circles on his cheeks. His nose is tiny, and his eyes are perfectly round circles when open, upside-down u's when closed. His pendulous ears are rendered as smooth and elongated. Medicine-Master Buddha, his attendants, and the little girl are illustrated as cute. (With their more oblong heads, the parents are perhaps a bit less cute.) As with the smiles in *Master Shengyan's Naughty Youth,* the visual similarity between Medicine-Master Buddha and Little Cao (seen clearly in Plate 12) can be connected to the bodily attunement that characterizes close relationships, such as between parent and child. The illustrators of the other books in the series have distinct styles, but their depictions of buddhas and bodhisattvas are all cute: they have oversize heads, large eyes, and rounded forms. To show a small child in this way is expected. To make buddhas and bodhisattvas cute is new, and changes how these figures are perceived.

Cuteness is defined by infantilization in the positive sense, employing a constellation of features found in human infants, but also in very young animals—such as kittens with big round eyes and puppies with giant ears and paws that are awkwardly large. In some cases, the limbs of a person, animal, or object are shortened or attenuated, contributing to a sense that cuteness is connected to weakness or physical incapacitation. These features have somatic and emotional effects. Depicting non-babies with the features of babies elicits affection for them, and the desire to care for them. This care may take the form of touching, which is evoked by softness, fuzziness, and smallness; as Sianne Ngai observes, "smallness and blobbishness suggest greater malleability and thus a greater capacity for being handled."[6] Although products for children are often marked by cuteness—and children attracted to their charms—many adults find cuteness appealing too.[7]

The global aesthetic of cute shares a number of visual features, but cuteness is also shaped by specific cultural environments. Ngai's work examines cute within the context of the Anglo-American-European avant-garde movement; Disney cute, for example, was connected to a nostalgia for rural life and nature.[8] In the Taiwanese context, the visual idiom of cute is part of an East Asian sphere of popular culture, where the *kawaii* 可愛い aesthetic of cuteness emerged out of 1970s Japanese consumer culture and mass media—both as a response to it, and facilitated by it.[9] Cuteness in Japan was an alternative to traditional arts,[10] and it formed a key part of trans–East Asian popular culture because of its distance from traditional ethnic or national culture.

In Taiwan cuteness is part of pan-Asian popular culture but also has its own meanings. Japanese products, such as the Sanrio family characters and Doraemon, are often well-received in Taiwan because of "cultural proximity," but they exist alongside other Asian media imports, many in Mandarin.[11] As in Japan, Taiwanese cute culture can be a form of resistance, and a means to recast gender roles.[12] Tzu-I Chuang has argued that femininity and weakness were initially key elements of cute, beginning with Hello Kitty–themed promotions at McDonald's in the late 1990s. As cute came to be manipulated by young women who saw a form of power in claiming cuteness, its specific gender associations began to drop away by the early 2000s. With cuteness no longer the primary domain of young women, it could be deployed in different ways, such as by political figures.[13]

Appropriating cuteness in the service of Buddhism draws the religion into conversation with popular culture, but also creates a space for playing with relations of power.

Cute-ifying human figures and anthropomorphized animals is common in picturebooks of all sorts, even before cuteness was ascendent in Asian popular culture. Monks, too, have been depicted as friendly and adorable in books and other media.[14] However, cuteness has particular significance when illustrating buddhas and bodhisattvas, figures that have typically been represented in ways that signal their difference and apartness from human beings. Instead of creating suprahuman figures that are the object of offerings, beyond the reach of human hands, making buddhas and bodhisattvas cute invites touch, even if only imagined. Dharma Drum is not unique in treating buddhas and bodhisattvas this way: in the two-volume *Four Great Bodhisattvas* published by Fo Guang Shan in 2017, illustrator Xie Meizhen 謝玫真 also depicts Puxian, Dizang, Guanyin, and Wenshu as cute. These cute bodhisattvas contrast with the monks covered in the paired two-volume set on the eight great founders from the same year, who are depicted with relatively realistic proportions.[15] This different treatment has to do with the relationship between buddhas and bodhisattvas and the human realm. Unlike monks, who are human and therefore part of everyday life, there is a distance separating buddhas and bodhisattvas from humans, and cuteness becomes a way of bridging that distance.[16] When they are cute, buddhas and bodhisattvas become objects of affection, not awe, and invite connection over reverence.

Iconography

In *My Buddhas and Bodhisattvas,* cuteness facilitates the identification and memorization of iconographical elements by simplifying the forms and ornamentation of the buddhas and bodhisattvas. Along with his wide smile, Medicine-Master Buddha wears a monastic robe, holds a blue bowl in one hand and grasps the stem of the purple-leaf plum (which has medicinal uses) in the other.[17] The cute-ified Amitābha has a head roughly as large as his body, pendulous ears—exemplifying the touchable blobbishness Ngai identifies as a quality of cute—that stretch from his hairline to his chin, a big smile, and rosy cheeks. His curled hairstyle (*luofa* 螺髮) and uṣṇīṣa (two of the thirty-two major marks of a buddha) are decorated with swirls of varying sizes. Although his eyes are not particularly large, he is often depicted as winking, and his facial expressions are animated. To distinguish him from other buddhas, Amitābha is also shown on a lotus, connecting him to his Pure Land even when he is elsewhere. Maitreya, the buddha of the future, likewise is shown with bodily proportions that signal cute, and is also often winking. As the future buddha, Maitreya is still a bodhisattva and is depicted with princely trappings associated with pre-buddhas. He has a crown, flowing hair, two jeweled necklaces, and two golden armbands that serve to signal his status. The bodhisattva Dizang is often represented as a monk with a staff (for opening the gates of hell, although that is not part of his story in this series), and this is how he is presented here, with an infant-like bald head and the usual large ears.

In *Bodhisattva Guanyin, Change, Change, Change!* (*Guanyin pusa bian, bian, bian!* 觀音菩薩變變變) establishing the iconography of the bodhisattva Guanyin is as important as the plot itself, and forms part of an iterative Buddhist education. This picturebook goes further than *Everyone's Mama* in attention to iconography, reinforcing it through matching and other visual games (discussed below). Guanyin is depicted draped in flowing white robes; beneath her white headdress there is a crown with the image of Amitābha. This representation of Guanyin first became popular in the Song dynasty and remained one of the most prevalent ways of depicting the bodhisattva in late imperial China.[18] On the cover of the book is another manifestation of Guanyin, here in her "thousand-armed" (*qianshou* 千手) form. This depiction also appears once inside the book, with the explanation that she has different "treasures" (*baowu* 寶物) to aid people with different needs. The thousand-armed iconography is conveyed through a multitude (roughly three dozen) of arms holding different objects; the illustrator, Cai Yalan 蔡雅蘭, connects the two representations by using the same face. Guanyin's many other manifestations are referred to only once, on a page in which children are asked to match Guanyin's shadow to her transformation, which turns out to be "Fish-Basket Guanyin." Easily identified because of the large fish she sits atop, no explanation is given of the significance or history of this form of Guanyin.[19] At the back of the book, there are notes for parents about the contents of each illustration, but they simply describe the image and provide little help for those not already familiar with this form of the bodhisattva. Fish-Basket Guanyin references a story ill-matched for the preschool audience of the book: A beautiful woman carrying a basket of fish appears in a village one day and makes herself sexually available to any interested man. However, once they have relations with her, the men lose their desire forever, having been compassionately cured of this affliction by the bodhisattva in disguise. She dies young, is buried by the roadside, and a short time later a monk appears and recovers her skeleton, the bones of which are linked by a golden chain. This postmortem miracle is common to stories of Guanyin's appearances. Rather than offer a summary of the narrative, the notes for parents simply emphasize the transformation itself as a manifestation of "inconceivable power of her compassionate vow."[20] As the full story is not included here, this unexpected material can only serve to prime young readers for future encounters with Guanyin's various manifestations. Here those manifestations are both cute-ified and simplified to their essential elements. By creating familiarity with the bodhisattva's iconography, the book participates in an iterative process that assumes readers will loop back to Fish-Basket Guanyin at a later stage in their Buddhist education.

The books in *My Buddhas and Bodhisattvas* use four different illustrators, but there is a similarity in the style they employ, reflecting the aims of this series: vivid colors and cute characters are stimulating and appealing, and invite interaction. The palette of colors is bright, and for the most part the images are made up of solid shapes with minimal shading. These choices in style are meant to contrast with traditional ways of depicting Buddhist deities: Zheng Mingjin 鄭明進, the illustrator who wrote the guide at the end of the story of Maitreya, praises Jun Yi 君宜 for her splendid (*jingcai* 精彩) illustrations of people and animals.[21] The guide for the book on Guanyin was written by Xu Suxia 徐素霞, an artist and illustrator of children's books herself, who observes that the illustrations "have especially avoided the relatively solemn mode of depiction in traditional Buddhist images, and have chosen a more lively design style."[22] Cuteness is part of an innovative artistic approach that is still recognizably Buddhist. The visual dimension of these picturebooks is the most immediate way that the buddhas and bodhisattvas are made approachable—yet learning their iconography is also an important part of what the illustrations must convey.

Voice

Voice further frames the reader's relation to these figures: All eight buddhas and bodhisattvas speak directly to the children in the series *My Buddhas and Bodhisattvas*. The use of first-person voice is a way of imagining friendship and connection between the bodhisattva and the reader. In *Bodhisattva Guanyin, Change, Change, Change!* we find Guanyin using first-person address from the very beginning. There are two starting points to the book, a preface titled "Introducing the Leading Role," and the first page of the story proper. The dense text and layout (with just two small illustrations) of the two-page preface might lead many readers to skip over it as paratextual material. It begins with "Hi kids! I am Guanyin!" The bodhisattva calls children *xiao pengyou* 小朋友, which literally means "little friends," a common address to children used by many adults, especially teachers. This opening address from a buddha or bodhisattva echoes what children would hear from friendly adults on a daily basis.

The use of the first person is a technique that contributes to "character identification."[23] Frequent readers of children's books are likely to have encountered the first person in other stories and be familiar with the perspective shift it elicits. In *Bodhisattva Guanyin, Change, Change, Change!,* like the other books in this series, the primary characters are young children with whom the young reader is expected to identify. The reader does not see through the lens of Guanyin's "I"; rather, the first person encourages children to see themselves as the object of her address. Yet if parents are reading the book aloud, they will take on Guanyin's first-person voice: Given that this bodhisattva represents compassion, this offers a connection between parental types of care and those of the bodhisattva, a link already seen in *Everyone's Mama.* Creating these associations are part of affinity work that seeds Buddhist futurity within the family.

The illustrations take a different perspective: we see the buddhas and bodhisattvas smile, move, and act, which also means that we are not seeing the events of the narrative from their first-person perspective. Perry Nodelman, scholar of English-language children's literature, points out that this is quite common in picturebooks, with most illustrations showing the speaker rather than what the speaker sees. First-person visual perspectives in other media, such as in film, are also rare.[24] The words of the story thus come from "the person we're looking at" as they do in real life, or in staged performances.[25] We are accustomed to the disjuncture between narrative and visual points of view, but this can have different functions. If the words and the pictures convey different things—a mismatch between the narrator's understanding of the situation, and how it would appear to a third person—the effect can be ironic or humorous. This is not the case here, as Guanyin always has a correct grasp of the situations before her. Rather, this use of the "I" is closer to books in which authors use "first-person narrators to bring an aura of conviction to their fantastic stories."[26] The alignment between narrative and visual viewpoints works to create confidence in the bodhisattva as a trustworthy figure.

The Child's Role

What the child characters are asked to do—and indeed that they play active roles—further establishes that their relationships with the buddhas and bodhisattvas are defined by friendly intimacy. The use of voice calls the reader to play the role of helper. In *Bodhisattva Guanyin, Change, Change, Change!* the last line of the preface and the first line of the story both address the reader in the second person, as someone who might be recruited to assist others as Guanyin does, thereby recognizing children's capacity for moral action. The preface concludes, "I hope you can be like me, and become a good helper to everyone!" The next page repeats this sentiment: "After you read my story, will you want to be my little helper, so that we can help people together?"[27] The question format prompts an answer, presumably affirmative, from the reader. Guanyin adds that there is a test to become her assistant, which takes the form of the puzzles embedded in the book. Through the use of "I" (*wo* 我), and "you" (*ni* 你) Guanyin begins a conversation with the child-reader, and establishes that the child is expected to *do* something.

The minimal plot of *Bodhisattva Guanyin, Change, Change, Change!* focuses on rescuing a child who has been kidnapped by monsters. The rescue of the child is never in doubt, but the figure of the monster allows the book to establish what monsters like and what they fear, and through this device works to establish proper forms of behavior for children. Children are told that "monstrous methods" (*yaofa* 妖法) cause them to "crave sleep, crave eating, crave playing, love crying, love being angry, love performing, love picking on the weak."[28] The bad tendencies or behaviors are separated from the children themselves, and Guanyin's "you" includes children who might engage in them. The behaviors prompted by these "monstrous methods" can and should be changed: they distract children from attending to others, and, in the context of the story, from rescuing their friend. The monster is lonely, and so having friends—who can support good conduct—is important. Indeed, with their friends, children practice identifying positive behavior through a game that occupies the last pages of the book (discussed below).[29] Friendship is the model for the child-reader's relationship with the bodhisattva and also for their interactions with peers.

Children mirror the bodhisattva in their ability to change. The preface talks about Guanyin's capacity to change (*bian* 變) into all different kinds of helpers, listing several of the forms that appear in the "Universal Gate" chapter of the *Lotus Sutra* along with her thousand-armed manifestation. The bodhisattva's different manifestations in the world are one way to understand the word "change" in the title. The story offers other interpretations of "change": Special types of words bring about change, by eliciting the aid of the bodhisattva and by scaring the monster. Further, children themselves are objects of transformation, through learning what will make them good assistants to the bodhisattva. This, in turn, allows children to be Buddhist agents, and to bring about change in their world. Although the narrative elements are different, these are themes that were also present in *Master Shengyan's Naughty Youth* (chapter 4), with its emphasis on his metamorphosis that in turn had much wider effects.

Medicine-Master Buddha's Birthday Present also presents the child's friendship with a buddha as an important step toward emulating that figure. Medicine-Master Buddha introduces himself in the preface by describing the light-filled splendor of his Pure Land to the east. He explains that he is able to dwell in this wondrous place because of the twelve vows that he took; these are not given in full, but Medicine-Master Buddha's brief explanation emphasizes their connection to making sure that people do not suffer illness.[30] (As we have already seen, vows are an important way to commit to transformative acts.) The preface concludes with the Buddha recruiting children to be "little Medicine-Masters" themselves, a role made possible by their friendship.

For most of the story, Little Cao and Medicine-Master Buddha are on a mission together; as the focalizer, the young girl shows that children can regard Medicine-Master Buddha as a friend. Facial expressions work to show the connection between the two characters: Both the buddha and the little girl are almost always depicted smiling broadly. Often their eyes—white circles with black dots for pupils—show that their gazes, and thus their smiles, are directed at each other. The buddha is pictured as winking multiple times, and in the illustration of the family at the table, Little Cao winks back at him. Winks work because the winker can assume that the other party knows what is intended by the gesture; the wink affirms special knowledge between two people. These winks emphasize the friendly intimacy that has been established between the buddha and the child. Bodily postures and gesture further reinforce this. Little Cao shows the Buddha a photo she has taken, stretching out her arm, and kicking her feet in excitement. The Buddha seems to place his hand on Little Cao's back to guide her through a maze, and again when he shows her the process of making medicine.[31] In the latter image, she gives him a thumbs-up, and smiles broadly. From the moment he appears with a cake, Medicine-Master Buddha is presented as a friendly, approachable figure. It is through their friendship that the little girl learns about making medicine and comes to imitate this Buddha in extending healing to others. In the hospital, she holds a blue bowl just like Medicine-Master Buddha, visual confirmation of their parallel roles.

Games and Other Scriptive Things

Games are central to the design of *Bodhisattva Guanyin, Change, Change, Change!* and *Medicine-Master Buddha's Birthday Present,* and teach children how to act in Buddhist ways. Games reinforce recognition of the buddhas and bodhisattvas, promote prosocial behavior, and introduce Buddhist material culture, doing so in a way that is more participatory than the narratives. At the end of the story about Guanyin, parents are given an explanation of the use of games in a reader's guide (*daodu* 導讀).[32] Here, Xu Suxia writes that the game format is an "active method" (*huopo de fangshi* 活潑的方式) for leading children to understand more about the bodhisattva and her visual representation. The reader's guide at several points emphasizes vision (*shijue* 視覺) or the eye-catching (*xingmu* 醒目) nature of the illustrations. The game dimension of the book, beyond simply offering children something to do as they are being read to, also opens up to deeper learning. Recalling that the narrative focuses on defeating a monster, Xu writes that it is a personification (or monsterification) of our own internal cravings and desires, created to make this theme more obvious. Xu writes that parents can use the game related to the monster's trickery to explore this more sophisticated concept. The game asks children to be little Guanyins and functions to highlight the connection between cause and effect: if they behave positively, then they will advance, while negative attitudes will bring them to a stop. Xu notes that having children intuit this correlation through the game is a better method of instruction than nagging them (*suisui nian* 碎碎念).[33] Play is better than overt didacticism and fosters a more companionable parent-child relationship.

The game potential of Buddhist cause and effect was recognized by Ming dynasty monk Ouyi Zhixu 蕅益智旭 (1599–1655), who wrote instructions for a game called *Selection of Buddhas* (*Xuanfo tu* 選佛圖) that was modeled on a game in which players competed to advance through government bureaucracy. In Ouyi Zhixu's version of *Selection of Buddhas,* players start at a very low level and aim to advance through higher religious attainments to achieve Buddhahood. Movement on the board is dictated by rolling dice; Beverley Foulks McGuire says that this represents the "uncertainty of karma." She writes that "each square provides an occasion to concentrate on good or virtuous stages of religious development," and that in this way it may function like a confession ritual, bringing self-awareness of a player's real faults.[34] Although children and parents are unlikely to be familiar with this earlier Buddhist game (and the paratexts do not mention it), they may well have encountered *Chutes and Ladders,* a modern game based on an Indian one; the original *Snakes and Ladders* incorporated the idea of moral progress, akin to *Selection of Buddhas*.[35]

These games are examples of what Robin Bernstein has called "scriptive things." According to Bernstein, things are distinguished from objects by performance: "things script meaningful bodily movements and these citational movements think the otherwise unthinkable."[36] Scriptive things require or "hail" bodily response, developing in those who use them "performance competence." Bernstein sees performance competence as parallel to Jonathan Culler's "literary competence" and describes the competent performer as one who "understands how a book or other thing scripts broad behaviors within her or his historical moment—regardless of whether or how the performer follows that script." For Bernstein, the act of turning a page is a simple example of performance competence, but books also explain to children how to relate to objects and people in their world, ideas that they may then reproduce in their play.[37] Douglas Guerra notes that board games are "scriptive things par excellence" that create "indirect opportunities . . . for habitual orientation and reorientation."[38] Some games may require that the players arrange their bodies in particular ways (such as four players around a board), and talk in specified ways about the action of the game. Games require that players attend to a predetermined set of information (property rents in *Monopoly,* for example, or attributes of birds in *Wingspan*). A game is a bounded exercise in attention building. The attention it teaches then may be brought out of the game, and into everyday interactions.

Through their use of games and other interactive features, the books in this series present ways to develop in children a specifically Buddhist "habitual orientation" toward the world, as well as Buddhist performance competence. In *Medicine-Master Buddha's Birthday Present* the story centers on the distribution of medicine so that the sick can be cured, and Little Cao reunited with her family. Several games explain the process of creating traditional medicine, the most elaborate of these depicting the various stages of taking a fruit or berry and creating pills from it. Little Cao and by extension the reader start at the top of the right-hand page and are instructed to chart a path through different activities shown within leaf-shaped bubbles. Little Cao is not alone is this endeavor: Medicine-Master Buddha waits for her at the end, as he does in all the pathway-type games. To follow the correct path, players must avoid those bubbles not associated with the process of making medicine. These could have been filled with anything—out-of-order activities such as picking berries, or unrelated processes such as fixing a car—but the "wrong" bubbles show Little Cao engaged in everyday play: swimming, singing karaoke, watching television, playing with blocks. The text admonishes young players that they cannot "goof off and take a break with Little Cao." Making medicine benefits others, at least in this story, and it is counterposed to selfish fun. Without explicitly saying so, the message of this game is that working on behalf of others means setting aside some or all idle pleasures. A narrative could make this point as well, but the game creates an active choice.

The final game in *Medicine-Master Buddha's Birthday Present* also centers around choices made by a young reader: they are to select the correct path between an ailing planet earth and one that is shiny and happy, advancing through stars that show Little Cao behaving in eco-friendly ways or not. The correct path takes Little Cao through gardening, turning off a faucet, cleaning her neighborhood, bicycling, and recycling. The alternatives are eating lots of snacks, leaving a faucet running, driving in a car, shopping to excess, and not picking up after her dog. Her facial expressions reinforce the correct reaction to behavior: as she gobbles snacks, finds herself with too many shopping bags to carry, and ignores dog poop, her eyes grow wide with alarm at the situation she is in. As with the rest of the book, Little Cao is pictured alone for all activities, except for when she is in a car—and then the driver disappears in the fold of the book, hardly visible at all. Almost all these activities a child would likely be doing with an adult, but depicting Little Cao alone emphasizes the personal choice children have in their everyday lives. Although the goal is to join Medicine-Master Buddha as a helper, it is her own actions (and that of the reader, choosing on her behalf) that allow her to complete the path correctly. The visual dimension of this game lacks specifically Buddhist content; the text explains that doing these good deeds will "make the sick earth transform into a beautiful, healthy world just like Medicine-Master's Pure Land." This eco-consciousness is part of modern Pure Land thought: Yinshun, in his writings on different Pure Lands, saw the eastern realm of Medicine-Master Buddha as the most appropriate model for how to transform the human realm. Yinshun even went so far as to liken Medicine-Master Buddha's vows to Sun Yatsen's principles of the people. Such theories are well beyond *Medicine-Master Buddha's Birthday Present,* but the book is seeding a connection both between the earth and Medicine-Master's Pure Land, and between personal activities and global transformation.[39]

The game that appears at the conclusion of *Bodhisattva Guanyin, Change, Change, Change!* parallels *Selection of Buddhas* in tying advancement to certain kinds of behavior and knowledge (Plate 13). Unlike the older game, it is impossible to go backward; a player can only lose a turn, which is the result of landing on one of two squares depicting bad behavior (not being helpful, fighting over toys). Most squares represent an opportunity to carry out helpful or beneficial acts, and this balance of good and bad possibilities conveys a positive assessment of children's potential on the part of the game designer. Helping one's parents, singing songs, and sharing toys lead to advancement, as does calling Guanyin's name and imaginatively helping the bodhisattva save others. The game couples good behavior with Buddhist acts, intertwining them to convey the idea that a Buddhist child—a little bodhisattva—is one who engages in prosocial acts at home and with friends.

In addition to this game, *Bodhisattva Guanyin, Change, Change, Change!* also scripts habits of seeing and reading by structuring interactions with illustrations in the book. On several pages, children are asked to point to the illustrations that match Guanyin's iconography, and this elicits a cataloging of a bodhisattva's or buddha's features so as to identify them. They are told to trace the mantra that runs from the little boy to the bodhisattva, a kind of proto-writing practice, and are asked to identify the character for "empty" (*kong* 空) in the reproduced text of the *Heart Sutra,* a pre-reading practice that identifies the key term of the text. Another page asks children to follow a series of 108 white dots: the reason given in the story is to save the children caught in the waves, but the dots resemble rosary beads in appearance and number, suggesting how similar objects might be manipulated in the real world. A rosary is analogous to a line of dots, and children will know to follow the beads. These activities prepare the child as a Buddhist ritual actor to take first steps toward performance competence. By frequency, the most important capability fostered by the book is identification of the bodhisattva Guanyin through her iconography and in various forms. Following the book's instructions, children practice looking to certain features of the bodhisattva, and through these attributes know both that it is Guanyin as well as what powers she holds. Likewise, they are taught to attend in a different way to special kinds of texts, and that words have potency. These are beginning skills that will be developed in later encounters with Buddhist material culture.

Each of the books in this series includes two pages of stickers in the back, with text telling children to place them wherever they like. Stickers are coveted items for many children and provide a special type of sensory pleasure. In many of the books, the stickers include various other characters featured in the narrative alongside the primary bodhisattva (only the Maitreya book does not include a sticker of the focal buddha or bodhisattva). For Medicine-Master Buddha—whose sticker includes Little Cao—he is accompanied by seven of his guardian generals. The book on Siddhartha includes only stickers of the Buddha; this is true too for Guanyin. Without any instructions about where to place the stickers, children have freedom to make their own selections; this contrasts with the controlled nature of the games within the book, with their specific pathways and solutions. Stickers are "scriptive things" of a different sort, suggesting that children could transform their environment by decorating it. This is how stickers function for adults as well, and stickers of mantras or "namo Amituofo" can be found decorating laptops and taxicab interiors, among other places. Children have the opportunity to play *with* these figures, moving them from book to surface, and perhaps moving them one or more times after that. The narratives show children interacting with buddhas and bodhisattvas, and the stickers offer a limited way for child-readers to do the same. Like paintings or statues of buddhas and bodhisattvas, stickers also bring the buddhas and bodhisattvas into domestic spaces. However, they do so in ways that leave open how and where the images will be placed, potentially without appropriate attention to how Buddhist icons should be treated. By incorporating buddhas and bodhisattvas into spaces that belong to children, the stickers encourage familiarity and interaction but also present interpretative possibilities in the way the books themselves do not.

Beyond scripting children as future ritual actors, the interactive features in *Bodhisattva Guanyin, Change, Change, Change!* and *Medicine-Master Buddha's Birthday Present* encourage children to think of themselves as moral actors, reinforcing the roles given to children by the narrative. By becoming Medicine-Master Buddha's helpers or little Guanyins, children are endowed with powers and prompted to act in the world. It is noteworthy that there are no adults depicted in the story about Guanyin, even though they are referenced in the text. The children rescue their friends with the aid of the bodhisattva, not adults. Bad behavior and good behavior are shown solely among children.

Transitional Objects

Parents and other adults are frequently absent in the other books in the series as well. In *Bodhisattva Dizang's Magical Treasury* (*Dizang pusa de shenji baozang* 地藏菩薩的神奇寶藏), the main child character is a little boy who is the prince of a fictional kingdom. In *Amitābha Buddha's Big Adventure* (*Amituofo da maoxian* 阿彌陀佛大冒險), the narrative is put in motion by a little girl calling on Amitābha for help. Likewise, in *Puxian Bodhisattva's Great Battle against the Trash Monster* (*Puxian pusa da zhan laji guaishou* 普賢菩薩大戰垃圾怪獸) a little boy turns to the bodhisattva for help with a monster and a challenging living environment.[40] Adults are depicted in scenes representing problems—the noisy neighbors, a street scene with people wearing face masks as a way to deal with pollution from cars and scooters—but not in those illustrations showing the little boy learning good behavior.

Bodhisattvas and buddhas, in this series, take the place of responsible, caring adults who guide children in their moral and social development. They are transitional figures on a child's path to independent agency. A clue to their function as parent-substitutes comes through the stuffed animal that accompanies Little Cao in *Medicine-Master Buddha's Birthday Present*. The little yellow dog with floppy brown ears goes with her everywhere: he's shown in a wagon, on her lap, next to her on a chair, being carried in a little bag, and most often nestled in her arms. All the primary illustrations of Little Cao include the dog as well: he is not just a toy, but a constant companion to the little girl. The stuffed dog is a "transitional object," the term coined by the child psychologist D. W. Winnicott to describe the objects to which very young children often become attached. Children often take transitional objects everywhere they go and do not want them to be altered in any way, such as through washing. The importance of transitional objects persists from infancy into early childhood, and children tend to need them more often at times of separation, at bedtime, or when in emotional distress. They can be cuddled, something that is also elicited by cuteness, and further must have "warmth," "texture," or "something that seems to show it has vitality or reality of its own."[41] Winnicott explains that the transitional object stands in for the first relationship the infant has (the mother, or more specifically the mother's breast), but unlike the parent, the transitional object is under the complete control of the child. Transitional objects provide a reliable alternative to a parent who may not always be available as a source of comfort to the infant.[42] No attention is drawn to the little stuffed dog in *Medicine-Master Buddha's Birthday Present,* but his appearance conforms to when transitional objects are most important: with her parents working on her birthday, the little girl is never separated from another object that provides comfort.

For most children, as they acquire language and have wider experience in the world, the transitional object loses its importance; it is not forgotten or discarded but instead is "relegated to limbo."[43] Yet some teenagers and young adults continue to rely on transitional objects to provide feelings of safety and security.[44] In her study of dolls and puppets modeled after the gods—collector's items that elicit strong emotional attachment—Teri Silvio has suggested that a "younger generation of Taiwanese are reconceptualizing gods as Winnicottian transitional objects."[45] In the *My Buddhas and Bodhisattvas* series, bodhisattvas or buddhas are offered as alternatives to transitional objects, providing reliable companionship to children when parents are absent. The symbolic source of comfort is transferred from an external object to an imagined other.

My Buddhas and Bodhisattvas opens the possibility that suprahuman beings do not need physical form to offer the same kind of attachment as transitional objects. The series is aimed at a developmental phase of childhood that is especially suitable for transferring attachments from a physical object to an imagined other.[46] Not all Buddhist books for children give target ages, but this series identifies its audience as four- to six-year-olds. This is an age at which the use of transitional objects is often coming to an end, as children develop more robust social relationships. The absence of parents in the narratives suggests that children may often need to look outside the family for comfort and help.[47] Buddhas and bodhisattvas thus are alternatives both to parents and other adults, but also to transitional objects. Further, the target age of this series also corresponds to the emergence in children of a theory of mind—the understanding that they have mental states (including thoughts, emotions, perceptions) and that others have *different* mental states.[48] This usually happens around four years old, and is important for the growth of empathy, fairness, and compassion—which requires imagining other people's perspectives—but also for the emergence of ideas about God and other suprahuman beings.

Imagining Other Minds

For children to understand such beings, they need to be able to attribute a different kind of mind to them—one that knows *more* than their own mind or the minds of other people. Studies have shown that young children in monotheistic cultures understand that God has different perceptual abilities, and that God makes things like mountains, but not machines.[49] Although children develop a notion of God as different at quite a young age, it is not clear from studies whether they model God on humans, gradually coming to believe that God is a human with special properties, or whether they begin by seeing God as a completely different sort of being.[50] Whatever the model, they are not reasoning from their own experience, and must rely on testimony from others, most often parents.[51] Learning about other minds requires the mastery of a certain kind of language, namely that which allows for the representation of mental states (know, think, feel, remember). Stories are an important way that these representational skills are developed: listening to and understanding a story demands "the use of language as an *internal* personal representation, one derived from the external presentation" and it "requires the child to represent in mind a reality that is at odds with the known and present reality."[52] In other words, children do not have direct experience with bodhisattvas as living beings, but stories in which bodhisattvas address them in the first person provide a way to mentally represent them as speaking subjects. Reading stories about nonhuman agents, such as God or a buddha, support the child's development of language around different kinds of mental states. Because parents are often reading books with children around five years old—the point at which theory of mind emerges—children are also receiving information from the testimony of their parents as to what should be believed, and how confidently it should be believed. This is not only the domain of literature for children. T. M. Luhrmann writes:

> Faith traditions also train their followers to experience their gods directly, in effect training them to have more immediate sensory evidence of the invisible other. But before they get there, followers must know their god through the stories about him or her. They must be able to imagine their god as person-like, and they can do that because of the way the god has been described in their sacred books, in their gatherings, and by other followers.[53]

The books in the *My Buddhas and Bodhisattvas* series offer shared descriptions of what buddhas and bodhisattvas are like.

Research about how children develop belief in other minds and in supernatural beings such as God has taken place primarily in the United States and other Western countries; we might reasonably wonder how well such accounts work for non-Christian communities, such as Buddhists in Taiwan. One cross-cultural study examined religious and scientific belief among adults in the United States and China and found that there were "striking cross-national similarities in the role of religiosity and consensus in the evaluation of unobservable scientific and religious entities." Adults in both places saw religion and science as clearly defined domains, and that their belief in religious entities was influenced by their own religiosity—that is, whether they were part of a religious community.[54] Although this particular study did not look at children, what mattered for adult religious belief was their community. It seems likely that the presence or absence of religious community, beginning with the family, has a similar influence on children's development of belief in other minds.

When buddhas and bodhisattvas speak in the first person there is no doubt, at least in the narrative, about the accuracy of their representations about what they know, and what they experience. In *Bodhisattva Guanyin, Change, Change, Change!,* what the bodhisattva knows relates to the monster, who is the only other nonhuman in the story: it likes some things and hates other things.[55] However, Guanyin does *not* know what is in children's minds, or when they would need her assistance; the story opens with her saying that she "hears" (*ting* 聽) a little boy calling her for help. This is true in *Puxian Bodhisattva's Great Battle against the Trash Monster* as well, when the little boy asks the bodhisattva for relief from noisy neighbors. Likewise, Amitābha, in *Amitābha Buddha's Big Adventure,* receives a phone call that alerts him to the needs of others. In *Medicine-Master Buddha's Birthday Present,* how the buddha ends up at Little Cao's birthday is unclear, as the story starts after his arrival. That he does *not* know the thoughts and desires of the little girl is suggested when the buddha asks Little Cao what her three birthday wishes are. Buddhas and bodhisattvas are not omniscient with regard to the contents of human minds; they do not see into children's minds and anticipate their needs. Rather, they need to be summoned through communication—telephone, speaking, a repeated phrase like a mantra—that is not all that different from how children might summon their parents, although certain kinds of language have special associations with buddhas and bodhisattvas. The limitation of the bodhisattva's knowledge gives children an active role in their relation to them. Buddhas and bodhisattvas exceed parents and other humans in that their perception of those who need them works at longer distances. They also have specialized knowledge of nonhumans, as well as abilities that far surpass humans. The books in the *My Buddhas and Bodhisattvas* series depict buddhas and bodhisattvas using their special abilities to help children. They play a comforting role in children's lives, as an alternative or supplement to their own parents. But children are not simply passive recipients of this care.

Competent Children

My Buddhas and Bodhisattvas communicates how adults think about children's abilities as religious actors, and how those abilities might be developed.[56] Presenting buddhas and bodhisattvas as companions or parent-alternatives who will come when called reflects a focus on children's agency that, in the terms of Richard Flynn, attends to "children's competence and capability as social actors."[57] Buddhas and bodhisattvas befriend children to help them develop agency, especially in stories grounded in this-world challenges. In *Puxian Bodhisattva's Great Battle against the Trash Monster,* for example, the bodhisattva coaches the young protagonist in resolving social conflict and developing personal responsibility. Through the bodhisattva's guidance, the little boy learns to act in the world in a way that he has agency within it. This is perhaps even more true in the *Medicine-Master Buddha's Birthday Present:* with her parents working on her birthday, the little girl is in a situation that reflects her own lack of control and inability to have her desires met. Although some of what they do is fantastic—creating magical medicine that they then distribute—the presence of the buddha gives her agency, and her shared wink with the buddha at the end suggests the way she has developed independence from her parents. In these stories, the voices of bodhisattvas and buddhas teach children how to approach interpersonal relationships (e.g., sharing) and how they might act to improve their world (e.g., cleaning up trash). Games provide practice for taking these actions. Growing into one's role as a social actor is intertwined with assuming agency within a Buddhist world. *My Buddhas and Bodhisattvas* anticipates these future roles, and creates affinities to facilitate their realization.

Becoming Bodhisattvas

The visual representation of the bodhisattvas is part of telling stories about who they are and what they do: cuteness is a way of integrating bodhisattvas within a world of cuddly animals and imaginative play while also retaining iconography that bridges different sets of readers. Visual and material forms of the bodhisattva shape reception for different audiences. A comparison with women's devotional practices in late imperial China is instructive. By the Ming and Qing dynasties, Guanyin had taken on feminine attributes—many of which were part of the illustrations in *Bodhisattva Guanyin, Change, Change, Change!*—and these encouraged new forms of women's devotion. As Yuhang Li has shown, women saw ornamentation through objects that referenced the bodhisattva's iconography as a way of "becoming Guanyin."[58] Women also embroidered images of Guanyin using their own hair, a practice that echoed other bodily sacrifices but also transformed part of them into the image of the bodhisattva. Portraits of figures as bodhisattvas (such as the portrait of Emperor Qianlong 乾隆 as the bodhisattva Wenshu) suggested that some human beings can *be*—or at least *act as*—bodhisattvas. The wearing of jewelry, embroidery and other handcrafts, and portraiture were not specifically religious practices, but if carried out in special ways allowed lay Buddhists to instantiate their bond with the bodhisattva in material form.

These picturebooks use the idiom of contemporary children's culture to likewise imagine new relationships with bodhisattvas and buddhas; cuteness makes these figures available for imitation and identification by children. Thinking back to *Everyone's Mama,* the picturebook discussed at the beginning of this chapter, it conveys the idea that children could call on a bodhisattva, and that they can act in relation to the bodhisattva—worshipping on their own—but also in imitation of her, through gestures of kindness. The *My Buddhas and Bodhisattvas* series, written two decades later, intensifies and expands these efforts; they are more clearly scriptive things, trying to evoke specific types of interaction from children. The cuteness of Guanyin in Guofan's book is amplified in the later works, by moving from the traditional brush painting style to vividly colorful illustrations more in line with anime and cartoons. Cute-ifying buddhas and bodhisattvas does more than bring them into alignment with other materials for children; it fundamentally changes the nature of these suprahuman figures. Cute things are meant to be touched and cuddled, so a cute bodhisattva conveys not only approachability but inverts the expected relation, opening the possibility that the bodhisattva could need care as well. In these stories, children are asked to help the buddhas and bodhisattvas with various tasks, and their willingness to do so may be influenced by the care impulse elicited by cuteness. Children are also taught how to interact with a bodhisattva or buddha: the use of first-person address and the frequent use of questions creates a dialogue between the reader or listener and the bodhisattva. Internalized, such questions can come to serve as means to interpret other encounters through a bodhisattva lens ("what would Guanyin do?"). These dialogues suggest that children can have friendly, informal relationships with bodhisattvas.

The picturebooks examined in this chapter direct children's interaction with the material object of the book itself, through the extensive use of games. These games require children to touch the book to a far greater degree than the average storybook, which might only call for pointing or page turning. Children are asked to point in these books too, as they identify iconography and discern differences. They are also prompted to trace pathways. This prepares children for later material encounters with Buddhism, as touching the 108 dots will later be replaced with beads on a rosary. Encouraging children to find the right route in some games moves from literal to metaphorical pathways, in which they are asked to evaluate good and bad behavior. These simple activities cultivate a Buddhist sensibility about daily life, in which prosocial behavior is linked to more explicitly religious acts. Building on the picturebooks discussed in chapters 2 and 3—which showed how the lessons from Buddhist scriptures and biographies might be applied in modern life—*My Buddhas and Bodhisattvas* writes new stories about bodhisattvas that bring them into contemporary childhoods. These narratives provide imaginative models for thinking *about* bodhisattvas and thinking *like* them.

These stories are framed as introductions and point toward the iterative nature of Buddhist education. The emphasis on iconography assumes that young readers will be encountering these buddhas and bodhisattvas again and will need to recognize them. That practicing Buddhism is developmental extends to parents as well. On a simple level, the books acknowledge a dual audience by providing guides for adult readers with more advanced information and perspectives. Parents are also an audience for the stories themselves, and if they read out loud, they will take on the voice of the bodhisattva, saying: "I am Guanyin!" The language that the bodhisattva or buddha uses to talk to children thus becomes language that parents themselves use: a mother becomes Guanyin by reading aloud to her children and this is part of her own Buddhist education. Largely absent in the narratives themselves, the role of parents in religious instruction is implied rather than depicted. In the next chapter, we will turn to how the space of the family is represented as an important site in which one learns to be Buddhist.

PLATE 1. Illustration of water and waves from the *Heart Sutra* © 2009 by Grimm Press Ltd. Text copyright © Master Hsing Yun. Illustrations copyright © Giuliano Ferri

PLATE 2. Mr. Winter from "I Only Want to Build the Third Floor," illustrated by Wu Xiaofang. Copyright Foguang Culture Co., Ltd.

PLATE 3. Illustration of the greedy dog on a bridge. *The Heart Sutra* © 2009 by Grimm Press Ltd. Text copyright © Master Hsing Yun. Illustrations copyright © Giuliano Ferri

PLATE 4. Final spread repeating vignettes from multiple stories. *The Heart Sutra* © 2009 by Grimm Press Ltd. Text copyright © Master Hsing Yun. Illustrations copyright © Giuliano Ferri

PLATE 5. Young Xuanzang beneath a pine tree. *Hsuan Zang* © 1998 by Grimm Press Ltd. Illustrations copyright © Robert Ingpen

PLATE 6. Xuanzang facing a pirate. Copyright Foguang Culture Co., Ltd. Source: *An Illustrated Book of the Founders of the Eight Schools* (*Bazong zushi tuwenshu* 八宗祖師圖文書, 2017), page 17, drawn by Xia Yilan.

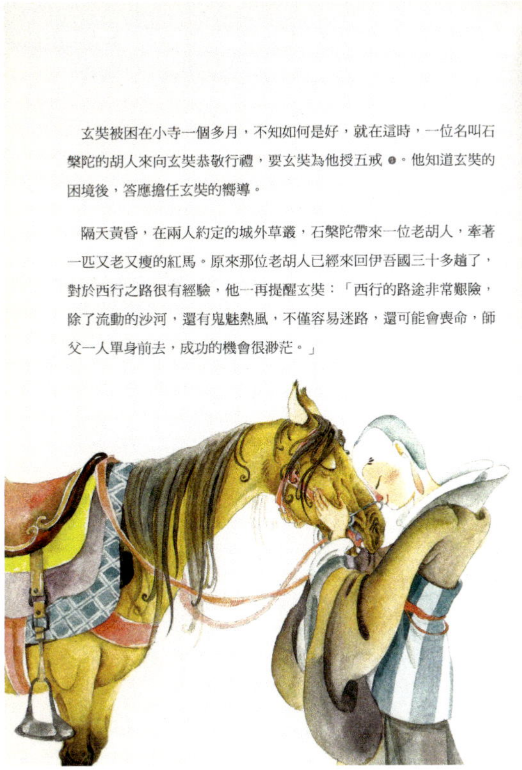

PLATE 7. Xuanzang with his horse, from "The Adamant and Unyielding Explorer," in *Code Words of the Great Teachers* A. Copyright Dharma Drum Mountain Cultural and Educational Foundation.

PLATE 8. Rāhula, from "Whose Kid Is So Naughty!," in *Code Words of the Great Teachers* H. Copyright Dharma Drum Mountain Cultural and Educational Foundation.

PLATE 9. Ikkyū and his friends in "A Witty Novice Monk," in *Code Words of the Great Masters* A. Copyright Dharma Drum Mountain Cultural and Educational Foundation.

PLATE 10. Opening spread from *Master Shengyan's Naughty Youth*. Note that the character *fu* 福 is stitched. Copyright Dharma Drum Mountain Cultural and Educational Foundation.

PLATE 11. From *Everyone's Mama* (*Dajia de mama* 大家的媽媽). Copyright Dharma Drum Mountain Cultural and Educational Foundation.

PLATE 12. Little Cao celebrating her birthday in *Medicine-Master Buddha's Birthday Present*. Copyright Dharma Drum Mountain Cultural and Educational Foundation.

PLATE 13. Game at the end of *Bodhisattva Guanyin, Change, Change, Change!* Copyright Dharma Drum Mountain Cultural and Educational Foundation.

PLATE 14. Illustration of the jade ornament in *The Parking Dragon*. Copyright Gaya Mountain Foundation 財團法人伽耶山基金會.

PLATE 15. Deceased friends and family members in *Whose Dream Is Longest?* Copyright Gaya Mountain Foundation 財團法人伽耶山基金會.

PLATE 16. Mother and daughter making offerings together, in *Firefly Makes a Vow,* by Fang Suzhen 方素珍.

PLATE 17. Talking coal and tree from "The Ancestor of Trees," in *Interesting Plants.* Provided by Tzu Chi Humanitarian Foundation.

PLATE 18. Dust mite poop factory from *Dust Mite Dingding's Diary of Moving House*. Provided by Buddhist Tzu Chi Medical Foundation.

PLATE 19. Wanted poster for COVID-19, from *The New Coronavirus Declassified!* Provided by Tzu Chi Humanitarian Foundation.

PLATE 20. Board book in the shape of a little girl, *I Love Fruits and Vegetables, I Love the Earth.* Provided by Tzu Chi Publishing Company 慈濟人文出版社.

PART III

Worlds

6

How to Be a Buddhist Family

DRIVING HOME ONE DAY, a little boy asks his father whether there are aliens (*waixing ren* 外星人) in the celestial realm presided over by Medicine-Master Buddha (Yaoshi fo), a query that captures the curiosity and puzzlement of young children trying to understand religious worlds. Children don't know what the parameters of Buddhism are, and their questions have different motivations than those of adult believers, who may not ever think to bring extraterrestrials into the same sphere as Buddhist deities. Beyond the content of the little boy's question, the context in which it is asked is also significant: the little boy and his father are going about their daily activities, and the question comes at the end of a wide-ranging conversation about family history, of which Buddhism is only one part. This story, *The Parking Dragon* (*Tingche long* 停車龍), illustrates what Buddhist families might look like in the early twenty-first century. Published by Incense Light (Xiangguang),[1] an influential educational organization, *The Parking Dragon* places Buddhist education within the everyday life of families.

Domestic spaces are frequent settings in picturebooks, and as places for Buddhism they associate the religion with families in positive ways while also commenting on modern family life. These settings carry a warm emotional valence: Mavis Reimer writes that "a nurturing and safe family home is a primary setting of many texts of children's literature, with kitchens and bedrooms within that dwelling often used metonymically to convey the core emotional qualities ideally associated with home." Further, "the family home as a primary setting" demonstrates that one significant project of children's literature is to "facilitate the development of the sense of self in young readers."[2] Who is at home and who is part of a family are important and frequent topics in picturebooks, and there is an extensive literature on the significance of representation in children's literature.

Picturebooks that show families with same-sex parents, with family members of multiple ethnicities, or including people with disabilities not only reflect and affirm real families but also promote their wider acceptance. The families that appear in children's literature reflect changing social norms, and in the case of the Buddhist picturebooks, how religious life fits within those norms. Although what a home looks like—from its architectural features to the configurations of family members—may differ across cultures, the positive associations of this setting transfer to those subjects depicted within their spaces.

In the Incense Light picturebooks, we see the development of three related ideas: First, the home and other domestic spaces are natural places for religious education, and this education can be integrated into the routines of everyday life. Thinking back to the previous chapter, this is a feature of modern Buddhist picturebooks more broadly. The bodhisattva Puxian and Medicine-Master Buddha visit the homes of children, showing these domestic spaces as sites where Buddhism happens too. Second, this religious education happens through an ongoing and iterative family conversation about Buddhist beliefs and rituals that reflects a natural approach to parenting. Because adults and children are part of the same conversation, these picturebooks affirm the child's perspective. Departing significantly from older top-down models of religious education of children, this conversational style aligns with contemporary models of parenting that seek to nurture children's innate interests and strengths. Third, this family Buddhism is gendered: along with other domestic tasks such as cooking and child care, in the pages of picturebooks mothers are more frequently shown as talking to their children about Buddhism, creating the conditions for later connections and development. Through close readings of three picturebooks, this chapter explores how narrative and illustrations represent families as sites for beginning Buddhist formation.

Families in Buddhist Literature

Although aliens and parking woes may mark *The Parking Dragon* as belonging squarely to the late twentieth or early twenty-first century, the integration of Buddhism with family life is a concern with a much longer history. In Buddhist stories about families, many present filial relationships within a Buddhist framework. Scriptures such as *The Scripture of the Vast Kindness of Parents That Is Difficult to Repay* (*Fumu enzhong nanbao jing* 父母恩重難報經)—dating to the Tang dynasty—argue for the heavy ritual obligations children have to their parents. This apocryphal scripture is one of a number of medieval texts on the theme of the burden of parenting and the necessity of filial piety. The text explains the mother's contribution in each month of pregnancy, and sets out a series of extreme sacrifices by children, all of which are said to be insufficient to repay even a tiny fraction of what they owe their parents. In the scripture's conclusion, the Buddha reveals that copying this very sutra and carrying out other Buddhist deeds (confession, charity, supporting the three jewels) is the only way to repay one's parents.[3]

Other premodern Buddhist texts foreground the tensions around family differences in religious commitment. The stories of Mulian and Princess Miaoshan 妙善, along with many tales in the precious scroll tradition (*baojuan*), have family relationships at their center.[4] Mulian and Miaoshan are good Buddhists with families who are not. Mulian's mother behaves in unethical ways, most often described as eating meat and refusing to donate to monks, and this lands her in the depths of hell after death. Mulian's devotion to her and his assiduous practice allow him to locate her there, and then to appeal to the Buddha for help in rescuing her from her dire postmortem fate. Miaoshan is likewise the most pious person in her family, wishing to become a nun rather than be married off. Her father objects in the most violent way possible, burning the nunnery to the ground. In exile, Miaoshan continues her cultivation, and comes to her father's aid when he falls ill. At the end, she is revealed to be an incarnation of the bodhisattva Guanyin; awed, the whole family converts. Both these Buddhist families focus on adult children, and their relationships with their parents. Because they have religious commitments while their parents do not, these Buddhist children seem to be born, not made; texts about them do not directly explore how parents might inculcate Buddhist values in young children.

The idea of a modern Buddhist family—of nuclear family life organized primarily around Buddhist beliefs and practices—emerged out of the era of political and cultural reforms in the early twentieth century. Mothers in particular were responsible for the education of children within the home, including religious instruction. For this, they might have relied on the works of Chen Hailiang, discussed in chapter 1, for guidance. Changes in family life over the course of the twentieth century have continued to reshape what Buddhism means within the context of home. Modern mothers continue to play a larger role than fathers in the lives of their children, but their own social roles have shifted. They are more likely to be working outside the home, and their children are often busy with extracurricular activities. The sources they draw on for images of Buddhist families include parenting advice but also picturebooks that tell stories about family life. In the case of Incense Light, adult education classes also indirectly serve to shape religious education within the home.

The Incense Light Approach to Buddhist Education

The educational efforts of Incense Light (Xiangguang) reflect the needs of modern families. Incense Light began with a local temple: What would become the Xiangguang Temple began as a place to house a statue of Guanyin believed to have miraculous powers. The locus of devotion to this statue was a rural village outside Jiayi 嘉義, centrally located in the western part of the island. Following the rebuilding of the temple (the main hall of which had been destroyed by an earthquake in 1943) in the early 1970s, supporters made a request to BAROC for an ordained monk or nun to serve as leader. This was seen as a way to ensure the survival of the temple, but also would provide an opening to build up a monastic order of nuns.[5] Xinzhi 心志 (b. 1939), the nun recommended by BAROC, received the precepts from Tianyi 天乙 (1924–1980), one of the most important nuns in the postwar period: born in Gaoxiong, her native fluency in Taiwanese allowed her to be a go-between for monks who had fled China at the end of the civil war. Tianyi wanted nuns to play a significant role in Taiwanese Buddhism and sought to ensure that they were well-educated. Both Xinzhi and Wuyin 悟因 (b. 1940), the nun who succeeded her at Xiangguang Temple, studied at a Buddhist seminary in Taibei, and became friends there. Wuyin and Xinzhi have very different personalities, with Xinzhi described as being the more nurturing of the two. As Xiangguang Temple grew, however, Xinzhi came to believe that Wuyin would be more suited to lead its expansion, especially since many of the nuns were college-educated. Wuyin was the driving force behind Incense Light's development and in many ways functions as the founder.[6]

Education became a major focus of Xiangguang Temple, and the nuns looked to models from abroad to inform their approach. They invited a Christian organization, the Institute of Cultural Affairs (ICA), to offer short courses at the temple so that they could study their educational methods. As Yü Chün-fang explains, the ICA pedagogy was intended to "create free exchanges between teachers and students and make the classroom atmosphere more lively and dynamic."[7] Like many other Buddhist organizations, Incense Light expanded rapidly in the 1980s and 1990s, following the lifting of martial law and easing of other restrictions and facilitated by economic development. Incense Light nuns built on the skills and practice of the early years of the organization to develop educational programs aimed at lay Buddhists. The adult classes became both their core mission and the primary means of economic support.[8] According to Yü, these courses are fundamentally different than traditional Buddhist education because they integrate students as active learners. Buddhist publications such as books and journals are consumed passively, and large dharma lectures—a common format—likewise represent one-way communication. Incense Light's adult classes are either kept small or include small group discussions, so that students have the opportunity to make presentations and ask questions. The teachers find ways to actively engage students, such as an exercise in which eating an apple serves as a way to learn about mindfulness and impermanence.[9] The framework for adult education is modeled in large part on public middle schools, from the length of the semesters, to the three levels of coursework (elementary, intermediate, and advanced), to the use of student leaders and assistants. Field trips, performances, and competitions serve to create communal bonds among the students while also providing reinforcement of in-class lessons. The textbooks that form the core instructional materials cover both "mainstream and Mahāyāna Buddhist tenets" and "use nontraditional language to present Buddhist teachings."[10]

The lessons learned in the classroom setting and in supplementary activities are meant to be applied in everyday life. This goal is reinforced through personal essays on assigned topics, many of which are not specifically Buddhist but require reflection through a Buddhist lens.[11] Knowledge from the Incense Light classes is also applied through public service, such as teaching in youth detention centers and offering counseling in public middle schools.[12] Incense Light also has classes for college-age and younger students. The latter are offered through a program called Buddha Garden (Buda yuan 佈達園), established in 2000, and reorganized in 2008. The program was intended in part to provide child care during adult classes: "In order to meet the needs of modern families and to support students in the adult education classes, so that even more people could study Buddhism with focus, we set up the Buddha Garden so that parents and children could each enjoy their part, and also to come a step closer to putting into effect the ideal of the integration of Buddhism into the life of the household."[13] For children, the goals of the classes are to provide an introduction to the basic concepts of Buddhism, develop a good attitude and corresponding behavior, and to establish good moral character. Elaborated, there are three objectives:

1. To give children a pleasant way to study Buddhism, and to cultivate quality interaction between parents and children.
2. To use Buddhism to help children learn to awaken themselves and awaken others,[14] to establish a good attitude and behavior, and the capacity for self-expression.
3. To incorporate Buddhism into children's lives and ethics, and by means of Buddhism promote the healthy development of body and mind.[15]

The classes are mixed age, including students from age four to age eleven. To meet the challenge of teaching different levels, each class has both lead and assistant instructors. The courses incorporate storytelling, games, performances, and arts and crafts, such as puppets of important monks and dioramas of Buddha-lands. The embodied pedagogy and diverse classroom activities are similar to the approach taken in adult classrooms. The Buddha Garden children's classes are scheduled for two nights a week, for sessions that last just under two hours. This program is supplemented by summer camps.

Incense Light is characterized by its commitment to and innovation in lay education. Their educational efforts focused first on adults and expanded to include children as young as four years old. With introduction of the Buddha Garden, Incense Light has been able to provide both parents and children the opportunity to study Buddhism in ways that can be integrated into family life. Although the educational program is not gendered, there are far more women than men among adult participants; the practical effect of women's greater interest in these classes is that mothers are more likely to be involved with the religious education of their children. The Incense Light approach to picturebooks is as innovative as their classroom practices: in the series we will examine, major Buddhist concepts are integrated with new stories and creative illustration.

Creating Spaces for Conversation

Let us return now to *The Parking Dragon,* the story about the father and the son with which I began the chapter. It is one of six books in a series published by Incense Light with the title "Wise Images of the Six Consciousnesses" (Liu shi zhi hui 六識智繪), published between 2011 and 2014.[16] The six consciousnesses are produced out of the experience of the sense organs when they come in contact with sense objects, and the Buddhist schema adds ideation (*yi* 意) to sight, hearing, smell, taste, and touch to yield six consciousnesses corresponding to the six senses. Although the narratives themselves are not Buddhist, there are Buddhist elements in each one, woven into the story to illustrate that clergy, temples, deities, and ideas of the afterlife are natural parts of children's lives. The sensory world that these books describe is fundamentally Buddhist. And with their focus on family spaces, these picturebooks show home as a specific sensory realm that can be made Buddhist.

The head nun of Incense Light Temple, Wuyin, expands on the role of the senses in Buddhism in her introduction, which appears at the beginning of each volume in the series. After imagining a dialogue between the sense organs, Wuyin writes:

> The six senses are a key part of Buddhist theories of cultivation. Vexation and delusion are produced by the contact of sense-organs, sense-objects, and sense-consciousness, but we cannot

> because of this cover our eyes, pinch our noses, close tight our mouths. Instead, we must try our best to benefit ourselves and others through the way we think about, react to, and carry out seeing, hearing, smelling, tasting, and touching. We could even say that we must go through the senses to study and practice the Buddha-dharma: the six sense-organs are important, as they are places where we can study and cultivate. Thus these picturebooks that take the six senses as their topic have come into being.

The six senses are the source of suffering, but being hampered by this, Wuyin argues, is not productive. She recommends reorienting the view of the senses from sites of suffering and attachment to place of Buddhist study and practice. The aesthetics of the books—both in terms of their stories and in their illustrations—are an example of this positive, Buddhist use of the senses.

The senses provide the organizational framework for the series, but all but one of the stories center on family interactions rather than Buddhist explications of sensory experience. This may be because, as Hong Wenqiong has noted, the terminology about the six consciousnesses is well above the cognitive level of young children.[17] *The Parking Dragon* (*Ting che long*) is the book associated with the nose (*bi*), but the story centers on the conversation father and son have while driving home together. Smells play a small role in that conversation: the little boy likes his father's smell, and likes the smell of the cello, too. The father affectionately calls the little boy "stinky" (*chou* 臭).[18] Smells are closely connected to memory and emotion, and sensory scene-setting early in the story suggests how they work to create family bonds. As the story opens, the boy is enjoying a spring rain when his father swoops in to tuck the child under his umbrella. They get in the car, and we see the little boy hugging his father from behind; the first two illustrations are of father and son embracing, establishing their intimacy. The next several pages look in on the pair from the perspective of the windshield, the rounded illustrations of the car's interior placing the focus on their conversation, which turns more serious when the boy asks if cars can die.

Death is the central topic of this story, as we learn that the young boy's mother has passed away. Her absence forms the background for everyday observations about the rain slowing, the people in the car next to them (funny looking), and pretending they are swans. This last idea segues into an anecdote about the father and mother as children: they grew up as neighbors and had picnics with pretend food made out of what they could find around them. The little boy clearly enjoys hearing about family history and asks the father to tell the story of the "parking dragon," a stone ornament that the parents bought at the jade market when the mother was pregnant. They thought the dragon was cute, and with four little feet and big eyes, they imagined it looked like the developing fetus of their child. It brought them good luck in finding parking spots, and the mother herself wove the knot used to hang it. "What is mommy doing now? Can she see us?" the child breaks in. The father replies, "When mommy got sick, she liked best to recite the *Medicine-Master Sutra,* and she hoped to go to Medicine-Master Buddha's jeweled realm in the east, where it is said no one will get ill."[19] This is the point at which the little boy asks about aliens; the father replies that he supposes so, without dwelling on the question, and suggests that the boy's mother misses them and is watching them even at that moment.

The illustrations transform the family car into a welcoming domestic space. They are bright but dreamy, with the car traveling through the streets of their town but also imaginatively on the strings of the jade ornament and the extended fingers of the mother's hand. The illustration of the father putting on the child's seat belt links the father's curved arms with the belt, and the child's closed eyes and happy smile convey the sense that he is being hugged. Thinking about setting, here it functions to enhance and expand the story.[20] The car represents the family unit and is a space of safety. The car is similar to a Volkswagen Beetle, with a rounded roof. Cozy, it seems just big enough for father and son. Often homes, especially kitchens, are the domains of mothers, and in this story the homelike space has been transferred to the automobile. Home need not even be a location but could be a symbolic object—such as the jade dragon ornament—or a set of practices. As David Morley has observed, home may be "a mobile, symbolic habitat, a performative way of life and of doing things in which one makes one's home while in movement."[21] The time and space of the daily commute becomes a place to perform home and family, which here includes Buddhism.

The car also references the even more intimate space of the womb—the site where families are produced. Illustrations that appear to be looking through the windshield reinforce the car's roundness, making the car into a womb-like space. Too, the jade dragon ornament is round, and relates to wombs both through its origin story and through representations of the little boy as a fetus or infant at its center, and of the mother in the same position, held by two green hands. Taking the car as a symbol of the family, it is what allows them to move safely through the everyday world, but also through memory and imagination. The road the car travels on transforms into a sea lane among turtles, and then the road becomes a river that takes them into the parents' childhood. The road changes again, becoming a ribbon of gold that connects and encircles the dragon, then the outstretched hands of the mother, before finally resolving into the street that leads to the family's apartment complex. Bound together as a unit, father and son navigate a simple trip home but also more complex emotions.

The Parking Dragon works as much to teach parents how to interact with their children as it does to tell a story to entertain or instruct children. The story opens with the physical and emotional affection between father and son—beyond their first embraces, the father spends some time scratching his son's back, at the boy's request, joking that he is like a mangy dog. Although the father doesn't answer all the boy's questions—for example, the question about whether cars can die—they are treated seriously. The child feels comfortable asking them, and thinking imaginatively, and the presentation of such questions as dialogue normalizes them as part of family interactions. That is, both parent- and child-readers would learn from the example of such questions that they are appropriate. While the matter of a car's afterlife may seem unimportant, it is part of the young boy's attempt to work out what his mother's death means. When he asks where his mother is now, and whether Medicine-Master Buddha's world has aliens, the father does not dismiss the questions. Parent-readers can easily imagine that such questions have been repeated on many drives home, or in other contexts. By showing how this father navigates his child's queries, this book provides a model for parent-child conversations.

Background Buddhism

The Buddhist content of the story is handled lightly, and centers on the mother's devotion to the *Medicine-Master Sutra*. Medicine-Master Buddha, as we saw in the previous chapter, is closely associated with health and wellness, and here the primary sutra associated with this buddha is important as a means of preparing for one's next life. The mother is said to read or recite (*nian* 念 could mean either) the *Medicine-Master Sutra,* which almost certainly refers to Xuanzang's translation, the full title of which is the *Scripture on the Merits of the Original Vow of the Medicine-Master Gemlike Radiance Tathāgatha* (*Yaoshi liuliguang rulai benyuan gongde jing* 藥師琉璃光如來本願功德經). The Buddha describes the vows made by Medicine-Master Buddha when he was a bodhisattva, the first of which was that he would achieve awakening. A number of the vows concern sentient beings that are suffering in various ways: those who have been born with physical and mental limitations, who are born in female form, who have been ensnared by the legal system, those who have been forced into misdeeds by privation. For this story, the seventh vow is the most relevant: "If there are sentient beings who are beset by many illnesses, with no means of relief or recovery, without doctors or medicine, and without family, poor and suffering greatly, my name need only to enter their ears, and their illness will be removed, their body and mind at peace, their family and daily needs all present in abundance, and they will be able to achieve unexcelled awakening."[22] The sutra also explains that the Medicine-Master Buddha presides over a Pure Land equal in beauty and wonder to that of the western Pure Land of Amitābha. The *Medicine-Master Sutra* was a popular text in the twentieth century, with lectures on it by Taixu and Yinshun, who saw the scripture as integral to Humanistic Buddhism. Medicine-Master Buddha's vows focus on the transformation of this world, meaning that his Pure Land in the east could serve as a model for the "Pure Land in the Human Realm."[23] The scripture continues to be popular, and especially lends itself to Buddhist approaches to medicine and palliative care.[24] In *The Parking Dragon,* the mother's illness is not explained, but it is not surprising to see her turning to this sutra.

Another Buddhist idea is presented obliquely through the illustrations. On the largest illustration of the jade parking dragon, there is a mandala-like design added to the center, with a fetus or infant of the little boy surrounded by symbols connected to the conversation they are having about their family. Concentric circles depict elements of his city, with rain prominently falling on the buildings in the outermost ring (Plate 14). Here the circular jade dragon is inscribed with four characters: "one form, one flavor" (*yixiang yiwei* 一相一味). This is a phrase from the fifth chapter of the *Lotus Sutra,* "The Parable of the Medicinal Herbs" (Yaocao yupin 藥草喻品). The Buddha lists several of the varied types of plants growing in different environments, and says that when it rains, the water reaches each plant equally, giving them what they need to flourish. The Buddha then explains that his teaching is like the rain, reaching everyone, and of "one form, one flavor," even though the particulars of the teaching may vary to meet the needs of individuals.[25] This is another way of expressing one of the central messages of the *Lotus Sutra:* that there is a single teaching, or vehicle, of the Buddha, and that the three vehicles are expedient teachings for people of differing capacities.[26] That the story of the little boy's trip home with his father takes place during a rainstorm—with rain falling equally on all the cars in the city—takes on new significance, given the allusion to this parable.

The Buddhist content of *The Parking Dragon* assumes different levels of understanding. Not all readers, whether child or adult, will notice the words on the parking dragon, and make the connection with the *Lotus Sutra.* For those that do, it is a reminder of the adaptability of the Buddhist teachings, and here it may be important to recall that the original passage distinguishes between the roots and stalks, stems and leaves of plants of small, medium, and large size. The little boy in the story may wish to imagine that Medicine-Master Buddha's realm has extraterrestrials in it, and such a belief does not impede his understanding of the realm where his mother might be reborn. Likewise, the child-reader may not understand the six consciousnesses that underpin this series but will still gain something from the story.

"One form, one flavor" is a way of thinking about the different levels of readings available in children's literature.

The Parking Dragon offers one example of what being a Buddhist family might mean: father and son talk about difficult topics in the course of their everyday lives, and Buddhism is part of how they understand life's challenges. Other books in this series also show Buddhist families who are dealing with health or other kinds of difficulties. *Flying Shoes of One Hundred Fabrics* (*Huifei de baibu xie* 會飛的百布鞋) is focused on the touch, or the body (*shen* 身), through the story of a little girl who is unable to walk or speak. She longs for a pair of flying shoes that will carry her to all the places she cannot go. She asks for small pieces of cloth that others have blessed—a particularly special piece was given by a nun, whose practices of making full prostrations and reciting the names of the buddhas infuse the fabric.[27] Her grandmother hand-sews these scraps into shoes as a present for her tenth birthday. The book about the tongue (*she* 舌) and taste, *Flowering Branches and the Fullness of Spring* (*Huazhi qunman* 華枝春滿) is about twin sisters with mental disabilities who sell rice balls (*fantuan* 飯糰) at a cart in a park, following them through a day. They are likened to the bodhisattva Guanyin by one of their customers. Buddhism, in various ways, forms the background to these families' lives.

Teaching through Talking

Whose Dream Is Longest? (*Shei de meng chang* 誰的夢長?) makes Buddhist instruction more explicit. This story focused on *yi*, thought and ideation, and, much like *The Parking Dragon,* a family conversation makes up the narrative. It opens with a young girl asking, "Mommy, why do people have to eat?" As the mom cooks dinner—vegetarian fried rice—she talks with her two daughters about dreams and what animals they'd like to be. Their older brother comes in just as they are about to eat, and they continue talking about dreams, with the little girl wondering whether animals dream. This leads to the mother talking about a dream that she had while on a seven-day retreat dedicated to Guanyin (*Guanyin qi shi* 觀音七時). Guanyin played a major role in the dream, opening the mother's iron heart to release a troop of monkeys, after which the bodhisattva pulled an enormous snake out, followed by an alligator and a horse. The older sister interrupts to talk about her dream, but the younger sister circles back to her mother's dream, asking her what it meant. This gives the mother an opportunity to recount how she asked a Buddhist master about it, and he explained that it meant her mind was like a monkey and her thoughts like a horse (*xinyuan yima* 心猿意馬). The monk also congratulated her, as the dream reflected how she was able to dispassionately remove the poison of anger and arrogance from her mind.

Following the mother's description of her dream, the elder sister then launches into an account of her own. Her dream was about having hot-pot—depicted extra-large in the center of the illustration—with their grandparents, and a girl she was friends with in primary school. Her older brother chimes in that these are all people who have passed away (*guren* 古人). The mother immediately invokes Amitābha's name and says that they should perform rituals on their behalf at the next opportunity. The illustration shows a monk or nun meditating with a rosary on a lotus leaf, surrounded by other blooming lotuses, as the deceased walk away from the reader. Their backs are turned, although the school friend has turned around to say goodbye (Plate 15). On the next page, and concluding the story, the brother breaks in to complain about how long everyone's dreams are, and to say that he is going out to have the rabbit's teeth trimmed.

There are several Buddhist practices in this story, beginning with the retreat the mother attended. Contemporary Buddhist retreats are often structured as seven days in length, and can also be devoted to Chan, or Pure Land practice. Charles Jones, writing about the latter, explains that retreats can also be shorter in length, and no matter how many days they occupy, the flow of each day is roughly the same. It begins with the morning liturgy, breakfast, periods of recitation and meditation broken up by the noon meal and perhaps an instructional talk, and a final service to dedicate merit. Even one day of such practice is intense, and longer periods more so. Jones relates that he had a brief vision that was interpreted by both laity and clergy as the Pure Land; such visions were explicitly part of the goals of the retreat he participated in.[28] The mother's dream was not of something described by Buddhist scriptures, but likewise seems to be clearly the result of an intensification of practice. The dream in the context of a recitation retreat reflects the long-standing importance of dreams for the evaluation and interpretation of spiritual progress. The recounting of this dream covers four two-page spreads, representing a significant portion of the book, and it is the longest dream discussed. The mother and the bodhisattva Guanyin appear in three of the four illustrations: In the first, the mother is wearing the simple lay uniform used for retreats, and she is seated cross-legged in a meditation posture, eyes closed. Guanyin, depicted here in her white-robed form, sits slightly behind her, reaching in front to open the mother's heart. They are surrounded by a troop of comical monkeys. The next illustrations show Guanyin in a more active role, removing the snake and the alligator from the mother's chest. Lotus blossoms and clouds indicate the otherworldly nature of the bodhisattva. As with all the illustrations in *Whose Dream Is Longest?*, human figures are depicted with large heads and tiny necks; they look a bit like balloons tethered to thin bodies with long limbs. Eyes are large and wide set, with other facial features much smaller. With muted colors, the effect is less cute and childlike than some children's books. Along with older children as characters and more complex discussion of Buddhist practices, the quirky illustrations suggest an imagined audience that is older than that of *The Parking Dragon*.

The mother serves as the family authority on Buddhism through her links to Buddhist institutions. In *Whose Dream Is Longest?* we see her performing affinity work: creating for her children connections to Buddhist persons and practices. Her children have been asking questions throughout the mother's account of her dream. The mother, like Buddhist practitioners before her, turns to someone more experienced to interpret it. The monk whom she consults analogizes the animals to states of mind. The "monkey mind" is one that clambers from one thing to the next. The expression appears frequently in Chinese Buddhist texts, as far back as the early fifth century; it most popularly appeared in *The Journey to the West*, in which the metaphor took the form of the character Monkey.[29] "Thoughts like a horse" conveys the way the mind rushes from one thing to the next, and is used both on its own, and in combination with "monkey mind." Based on the monk's interpretation, he associates the snake and alligator with anger and arrogance; both animals are considered base and dangerous, and the snake is often associated with the physical form. The monk who interpreted the mother's dream is known to the whole family, and the elder sister asks if it was the "cockroach monk." This is not, it turns out, an insult, but rather a sobriquet the monk has taken because he "goes where people do not want to go, eats what people do not want to eat, and wears what people do not want to wear."[30] The accompanying illustration shows him in a rocky landscape wearing patched clothing, reinforcing his renunciation.

The mother's dream represented individual Buddhist practice, while the final dream recounted by the older sister offers a glimpse of the social and ritual dimension of Buddhism. The sister has dreamt of a number of deceased people, prompting the mother to say that at the next dharma assembly (*fahui* 法會) they should make sure the deceased receive the "precepts of the underworld" (*youming jie* 幽冥戒). "Dharma assembly" is a general term for ritual services; precepts for the dead are a part of the Water Land Assembly (*shuilu hui* 水陸會) and also rites associated with Dizang. The children haven't heard of this, and the mother explains that she learned about this ritual from the monk. In the same way that the monk interpreted her dream, she acts as the authority in explaining her child's dream. Describing the ritual, she characterizes the conferral of the precepts as a "gift" (*liwu* 禮物) and as a "warm blessing" (*wennuan de zhufu* 溫暖的祝福), putting the ritual in terms more understandable for children. Knowing both how to interpret the dream and what to do in response, the mother is the Buddhist expert in her own home. Her role vis-à-vis her family parallels the monk's (both the specific monk mentioned here, and in the abstract) role in relation to laity as a whole. *Whose Dream Is Longest?* reflects hierarchies of knowledge and expertise, and depicts the mother drawing on her authority in non-dogmatic ways.

The Buddhist elements here, and in *The Parking Dragon,* show religion as integrated into everyday family life. The mother participates in rituals that require commitment and dedication and has an ongoing relationship with a monk; this allows her to be the conduit of Buddhist knowledge for her children. Discussing her dream, and how it has been explained by the monk, offers an opportunity to introduce concepts of mental distraction. Her Buddhist knowledge allows her to interpret her daughter's dream, taking the meal with the deceased as a signal that they still have demands on the family that can be addressed through ritual action. All of the dialogue is happening during the family dinner hour: there are pets and toys in the illustrations, and the older brother talks with a mouthful of chocolate. As with *The Parking Dragon,* family conversations are central to home life. The mother is patient and engaged with her children: she doesn't dismiss the little girl's comments that she doesn't want to eat, and that she wishes she were a cat. Based on the content of their conversations, this is also clearly *Buddhist* parenting. The narrative, such that it is, is not focused on Buddhism, but Buddhism comes up quite a bit. Buddhist topics are discussed, and then the conversation moves on. Buddhism is just part of something families talk about and use to make meaning in their lives. *Whose Dream Is Longest?* represents a particular kind of Buddhist family, and a modern model of parenting.

Setting aside their Buddhist content, the conversations that are at the center of each of these narratives represent one paradigm of contemporary child-rearing. A comparison is instructive: *Whose Dream is Longest?* is a striking contrast to how an ideal Buddhist family is represented in an early example of Buddhist storybooks in Taiwan. Ci'en Publishing's *A Trip to the Western World of Extreme Happiness* (*You xifang jile shijie* 遊西方極樂世界, 1978) imagines that the children of Taiwan have an opportunity to compete for seats on a rocket to the Pure Land, which they will visit as tourists. The selection criteria are belief in Buddhism, proper behavior toward parents and teachers, and good health and character. Four of the children selected are neighbors, and their parents are described as "sincere Buddhists" who have imparted the "positive influence of the Buddhist teachings" to their children. When they receive the good news, the youngest immediately puts her hands together and thanks Amitābha and Guanyin. As a family they offer incense to the Buddha and bow before him. They also sing Buddhist hymns, something the children prove very adept at over the course of the story. We learn that one of their grandmothers recites scriptures every day, and that one mother makes a vow to be reborn in the Pure Land after evening services each day. As author Lin Shimin depicts it, the ideal Buddhist family—one that produces children worthy of visiting the Pure Land—has a statue of the Buddha, and perhaps an image of Guanyin. The family engages in daily Buddhist practice of recitation, hymns, and offerings.[31] Through exposure to the Buddhist devotion of their parents, children absorb both attitudes of piety and specific behaviors. They are a Buddhist family because they do Buddhist things together, an approach that aligns with Chen Hailiang's earlier recommendations for Buddhist families. It is also a top-down model of religious education, in which parents have information that is transmitted to and then performed by children.

Not only is family hierarchy clear here, but there is greater distance between the children and figures like buddhas and bodhisattvas. In contrast to the engagement with bodhisattvas we saw in the previous chapter—where children were invited to touch images and play with stickers—the bodhisattva in *A Trip to the Western World of Extreme Happiness* first appears as a statue to be reverenced. Even when the children interact with bodhisattvas and Amitābha later in the story, it is depicted as an exceptional encounter with somewhat distant authority figures; the average child could not expect to speak with a bodhisattva in their everyday world. As with Guofan's description of Guanyin as preferring only good children in the preface to *Everyone's Mama,* the children here get to encounter bodhisattvas solely because they exceed their peers in being good Buddhists (a naughty child could hardly have won this contest). In contrast, *My Buddhas and Bodhisattvas* and the Incense Light picturebooks have shifted the framework of Buddhist family education from didactic to developmental.

Approaches to teaching children about Buddhism are influenced by modern parenting styles. When *A Trip to the Western World of Extreme Happiness* was published, there were no skyscrapers in Taiwan, and other details in the book suggest a setting that has only recently begun to modernize. Ideas about parenting have changed alongside family life.[32] Many parents do not want to re-create their own childhood experiences, instead aspiring to ideals of "natural growth" that allow children to develop in their own directions and at their own pace. But parents may also be constrained by the reality of multiple demands on their time. Absent parents were represented in the story centered on the Medicine-Master Buddha in the last chapter, with both mother and father so dedicated to their work as doctors that they could not find time for their daughter. The fictional families of *The Parking Dragon* and *Whose Dream Is Longest?* fall closer to the "natural growth" approach. The little boy in *The Parking Dragon* is perhaps too young to have academic expectations placed on him, but his time with his father seems unhurried, with space for joking around and cuddles. The ages of the children in *Whose Dream Is Longest?* are never given, but the brother is old enough to do things on his own: when we are introduced to him, he has just come back from recreational mountain climbing. The family eats together, and they talk through the meal. Both fictional families seem to be cultivating skills of social communication and creativity, as the children wonder about cars dying and why people need to eat. It is perhaps not surprising to see family time represented idealistically—rather than showing kids immersed in screens during dinner—but conversations are a way for parents to attend to their children. Through these conversations, the mother not only cultivates a sense of family but connects her children to a Buddhist worldview.

These dinnertime discussions recall the importance of interactive classrooms in Incense Light's adult education. But the importance of conversation and attention between parent and child extends beyond Incense Light; other parenting advice written from a Buddhist perspective similarly stresses these kinds of interactions. Dharma Drum added a reader's guide (*daodu*) by Xu Suxia, a painter and children's art educator, when they published a translation of the *Peaceful Piggy* series on mindfulness.[33] Xu's postface for *Moody Cow Meditates* (translated into Chinese as *Baotiao niu de xinqing guanzi* 暴跳牛的心情罐子) focuses on how parents might aid their children in learning how to imagine difficult emotions. Xu writes that children are most concerned with being understood, which can only happen by talking to them. Xu instructs adults not to rush the process of calming children, and once children are calm, parents can talk to them about the situation, perhaps followed by meditation. A conversation should acknowledge the child's feelings of anger, and convey that parents are not focused on punishment or placing blame. Xu concludes by reiterating that it is important for adults to see the child's perspective, and from there lead the child to try to understand how others think.[34] In other words, learning anger management is facilitated through parent-child conversations, and good parenting means paying attention to what children say.

Conversations with their children benefit parents as well: In "Face Problems, Then Set them Aside" (Miandui wenti, fangxia ta 面對問題，放下它), the author Xiao Ya 曉亞 gains perspective from a conversation with her son. She is involved in a minor car accident, but can't let go of it, playing the scene over and over again in her mind. Her son doesn't understand why she is preoccupied and tells her just to pay the other driver—there's nothing more to think about after that. Xiao Ya observes that he is able to live entirely in the moment. She connects this to a frequent saying of Dharma Drum's founder Shengyan: "Face it, accept it, handle it, and set it aside" (面對它，接受它，處理它，放下它).[35] She then revisits the different parts of the car accident and its aftermath to show how Shengyan's words could have helped her handle it better, all prompted by a brief conversation with her child. Talking to one's children represents an approach to parenting that meshes well with forms of modern Buddhism that emphasize its relevance in the world. Put another way, parenting and Buddhist practice are symbiotic (for Buddhists), with views on one influencing the other. The families imagined in the Six Consciousness represent a distinct approach to parent-child interactions that resonates with real-world parenting advice.

The picture of parenting that emerges from Xiao Ya's anecdotes reflects the intensification of child-rearing over the last two decades—an intensification that makes it clear how parenting itself can be a religious enterprise. That a parent and child reading a book like *The Parking Dragon* can be religious practice is clear; parenting in this way is part of what is termed "lived religion." Robert Orsi calls attention to the active world-making functions of lived religion, describing it as an "intersubjective" process that happens through engagement with others, including children. Orsi writes, "Lived religion cannot be separated from other practices of everyday life, from the ways that humans do other necessary and important things, or from other cultural structures and discourses."[36] The home and family then become rich sites for lived religion, as parents and children collaborate on creating realms of meaning.

Writing about American families, Kathryn Lofton goes further to argue that parenting itself is a religion. Tracing changing attitudes about children and child-rearing from the early years of America, Lofton shows how parenting discourse became more scientific and specialized. By the end of the twentieth century people were also leaving churches in greater numbers and needed new outlets for their devotion. Linking these developments, the resulting intensification of parenting meant that mothers and fathers sought the most developmentally appropriate stroller, the best way to prepare nutritious meals for their children, and invested countless hours in education and enrichment. Lofton concludes,

> Students of religion investigate how human beings solve problems in communities and how communities create concepts of the human. In its twentieth- and twenty-first-century incarnation, parenting has become such a site of problem solving and imagination. . . . If religious orthodoxy is understood as a submission of individuals to a comprehensive theological system, parental orthodoxy could be conceived as a submission of individuals to the work of parenting as the determinant of its practitioner's lives.[37]

In its goals and in the way that it serves as an organizing commitment, parenting, the way that upper-middle-class Americans do it, is a religion. Given a shared global parenting culture, much of this religiosity might also be identified in other places, with appropriate regional variations.

Lofton's insight resonates with Chinese traditions of family education and parenting. Ji Zhe argues that *jiao* 教 is a meta-concept, "signifying the sum of discourses and practices about the transmission of moral values for which religion, education, and politics were basic and concrete forms."[38] For example, *jiao* appears in the modern compounds *zongjiao* 宗教, *jiaoyang* 教養 (bring up, educate) and *jiaoyu* 教育 (educate), showing how *jiao* is a part of multiple discourses including that of parenting. Ji notes that in the early twentieth century the "fusion of religion and education"—a part of which took place in the family home—was separated and rearticulated in the process of forming secular public spaces such as schools.[39] Although the state tried to intervene in family life, and although child-rearing was subject to ideological pressures, parenting remained in the private sphere. We might then revise Lofton's assertion from the Taiwanese perspective, and say that parenting is *jiao*. Within the modern home, *jiao* continues to bring together religion and education in reimagined ways.

In the late twentieth and early twenty-first century, mothers continue to play a dominant role in family *jiao*. Even as modern women have taken on new roles outside the family, their roles within the family have expanded as greater resources are devoted to children. It is no surprise that mothers play a leading role in children's books that represent early education, but Lofton's insight allows us to see that the converse is also true: educating and caring for their children is a central part of how mothers define themselves. Showing how Buddhism contributes to parenting allows religious identity and parenting identities to complement and support each other. A parent reading a picturebook like those discussed in this chapter is an essentially religious act both from the perspective of parenting, and of Buddhist education. If a parent in Taiwan reads their child a book about a bodhisattva, we would unproblematically categorize this as religious. But parents in Taiwan also submit themselves to the "work of parenting" and to the work parenting does on them. Parenting means creating new rituals, and it can often mean developing a new sense of ethical engagement, as mothers and fathers build relationships with their children. Both parenting and Buddhism education are directed at future goals, ends that are best facilitated through connections in the present.

Buddhism Is for Mothers

The depiction of families in the *Six Consciousness* series also highlights how Buddhist stories are gendered, and how Buddhist activities are likewise gendered. Looking at Buddhist children's literature more broadly, Buddhist history is depicted as predominantly male, while the Buddhist present is female. This is apparent in historical surveys of Buddhism. Regardless of publisher, collections of biographies of eminent figures in Chinese Buddhism, whether they are intended for adults or children, overwhelmingly emphasize monks. This reflects the biases of source texts, but also a selection process that sees historical exemplars as primarily adult men. Likewise, the home has not always been figured as a primarily female religious space. It is the place where fathers instruct sons, as in Xuanzang's father reading the *Classic of Filial Piety* (chapter 3), and where sons learn to make offerings to the patrilineal ancestors. In the face of a patriarchy that had religious dimensions, women's roles and practices could seem secondary. Yet childhood is often centered around the mother: women have always had the primary responsibility of caring for and educating children, and women are likely thus the first Buddhist teachers a child encounters. Consequently, books that depict Buddhist childhoods are more likely to feature adult women characters. Even an exception reveals how this dynamic works: *The Parking Dragon* features a father talking to his son, but the mother is deceased, which has placed the full responsibility of parenting on the father. But *within* the narrative, it is the mother who is Buddhist. She recited the *Medicine-Master Sutra* and aspired to rebirth in that Buddha's realm.

Gendered roles are very clear in *Whose Dream Is Longest?* The story begins with the mother in the kitchen cooking, talking to her youngest daughter. The father is absent for the entirety of the narrative and is never mentioned. Although we cannot know that he is not deceased, when the older daughter relates her dream of eating with relatives who have passed away, he is not included. It is more likely that he is simply working long hours or working abroad. This is a common pattern in Taiwanese families, in which mothers are more likely to supervise extracurricular activities and afterschool time. Fathers, in turn, work longer hours and travel more.[40] In the absence of the father, there are three male characters in the story: the older brother, the monk, and a veterinarian who appears in one of the final illustrations, as they take their rabbit's teeth to be trimmed.[41] The latter figure represents professional expertise outside the home, which is also how we might characterize the monk. As I have discussed, the mother turns to him for explanations of her dreams and other sorts of Buddhist training. The older brother suggests how men are less well anchored in the domestic sphere: he comes back from hiking and is the one who instigates going out to the veterinarian. The mother is the center of the home, both for family care—cooking, and conversation with her children—and for Buddhism, as she also teaches her children through her own experience.

Other books in this series also foreground female members of the family. *Flowering Branches and the Fullness of Spring* shows twin sisters preparing and selling rice balls, and although both their father and mother are mentioned in the narrative as transmitting their cooking methods, neither are depicted. In *Flying Shoes of One Hundred Fabrics,* the young girl's primary caregiver is her grandmother. The pair is depicted together four times, while the illustrations show the girl with her mother and with her father once each. The full family appears on the final pages, to celebrate the girl's birthday. The girl and her grandmother are shown in everyday tasks, such as sewing and drawing, while her activities with her parents are special trips, out of the ordinary. The family shown in this story is a reminder of the importance of grandparents, and in particular grandmothers, as part of the support system for modern families. In these picturebooks, children are represented as spending most of their time with mothers and grandmothers, who then play a primary role in moral and religious education.

The Boat of the Great Vow (*Dayuan chuan* 大願船) shows family-centered Buddhism transmitted through three generations of women—grandmother, mother, and daughter. The setting is unusual, taking place on a boat rather than in a home or neighborhood, as in the other stories in this series. Because the boat trip is for a Buddhist purpose, there are lots of ritual elements in the environment: the little girl goes to sleep listening to the monks chant the evening service, watches them do walking meditation, and admires the altar set up for the dharma assembly (*fahui*).[42] The girl's most important teacher is her grandmother, who is serving as the cook for the trip. She is illiterate but was taught the *Diamond Sutra* by a monk. She recites a different verse as she prepares each meal. For breakfast, it is: "There is no view of self, view of others, view of sentient being, or view of life span."[43] At lunchtime, she recites "Give rise to the mind without dwelling anywhere," and at dinner, "All conditioned dharmas are like a dream, an illusion, a bubble or a shadow; like dew and like lightning, you should contemplate them in this way."[44] The little girl absorbs these even though they are beyond her understanding: "Although she did not understand the meaning of these phrases, she learned them by heart."[45] The source of the scripture is ultimately the monk who taught it to the grandmother, but she transmits it to her granddaughter by integrating it into her daily life. It is also the grandmother who tells her about the function of the dharma assembly, which is to help the sentient beings who are lost in the ocean. During their conversation, the girl's mother chimes in that the offering will release the recipients from their wandering.[46] For this family, practicing Buddhism is something that the female members do together.

The prominent role of mothers and other women is not a special feature of Incense Light picturebooks, but rather illustrates a pattern in contemporary Buddhism. In other stories we have looked at, mothers are central to childhood education, and when that childhood education includes Buddhism, it means that women are primarily responsible for its transmission. Thinking back to the anecdote that we saw in chapter 2 about the boy stepping on the rotten eggplant—part of Xingyun's explication of the *Heart Sutra*—the mother provided the child with reassurance and guidance. In Shengyan's account of his youth, which we saw in chapter 4, his mother is the heart of the family both emotionally and economically, as she repairs clothes and makes sure the family gets by—and it is her dedication that he vows to repay. In a book published by a commercial press, *Firefly Makes a Vow* (*Yinghuochong qu xuyuan* 螢火蟲去許願, 2007) a mother and daughter offer incense to a small statue of Guanyin tucked in the hollow of a tree (Plate 16). The two of them are entreating the bodhisattva for the health of a son, but it also seems an opportunity for the mother to impart ritual knowledge: this is why we would visit Guanyin; here she is, on a forested mountain trail; this is what we do.[47] As with *The Boat of the Great Vow*, this story shows a glimpse of Buddhist knowledge passed on from mother to daughter.

Not only is family Buddhism more likely to be the domain of women, the conversational style—modeled in the Incense Light picturebooks—is also gendered as female in contemporary Buddhism more broadly. For example, we see this reflected in the experiences of the *bōmori* interviewed by Jessica Starling. Temple wives are expected to maintain a constant presence, not only for the formality of welcoming any visitors but because they are especially skilled at interacting with the laity. One husband observes, "it is much easier to talk to a woman than a man, and that is important to our parishioners." His wife explained that she offers tea, and then listens to "whatever they want to talk about" rather than try to discuss Buddhist teachings with them.[48] Another *bōmori* was praised for her ability to provide a conversational outlet for a student who was being bullied, and for creating a safe space within the community. Starling notes that this encounter had no specifically Buddhist content, but that "if the encounter between the laity and the temple is handled correctly, a lasting connection may be made."[49] The picturebook mothers, like Starling's *bōmori*, are good at fostering the conditions for conversation. Because they do so in domestic spaces (rather than temples), it is the Buddhist content of their conversations that creates connections.

Buddhist Affinities

In domestic spaces depicted in the *Six Consciousness* series parents, primarily mothers, create connections between their family and Buddhist institutions and practices, what I have termed "affinity work." Mother and grandmothers in these picturebooks make meals, teach life skills, hold conversations with their children, and introduce, often in oblique ways, Buddhist ideas and practices. We recognize these activities as the labor of homemaking and child-rearing. But they do more than this: through affinity work, mothers create and maintain connections to Buddhist networks. The family in *The Boat of the Great Vow* is close enough to the group of monks performing the ritual offering at sea to be invited along on the boat; the grandmother also had a connection to the monk who instructed her in the *Diamond Sutra*. In *Whose Dream Is Longest?* the mother attends retreats and has an ongoing relationship with a monk, who interprets her dreams. Although we might characterize these as personal, individual relationships, the mother and grandmother use these connections to help facilitate religious education within the family. Mothers cultivate ties that bring their children into Buddhist networks and produce family *yuanfen*. This affinity work appears natural, not as a special effort.

Affinity work also connects to the iterative nature of Buddhist education we have seen elsewhere. The parents depicted in these stories do not assume that Buddhism must be delivered in discrete packages of doctrine or scripture, or even in ways that flag them as lessons in Buddhism. Rather, parents talk about Buddhism in everyday ways that invite return to the topics. The different ages of the children in *The Parking Dragon, Whose Dream Is Longest?*, and *The Boat of the Great Vow* allow us to imagine what this iterative education might look like: the little boy who is curious about where his mother went after death could grow into the middle daughter in *Whose Dream Is Longest?*, whose dream about deceased family and friends prompts a plan for ritual offerings. The children in these stories develop connections to Buddhism through years of casual conversations like those depicted, circling back to the same topics in new ways.

The *Six Consciousness* series envisions a Buddhist childhood given form through family interactions. Buddhism is integrated into family routines, and home life is not apportioned into religious time and other time; they flow together. Scriptures, for example, are recited during daily tasks or referenced through everyday objects (we are reminded of Rāhula's footwashing bowl discussed in chapter 4). Children are shown as having their own questions, dreams, and ideas, and while these may be different from those of their parents, they are part of the same conversation, literally. Understanding children as independent thinkers and full-fledged family members informs parenting choices. Treating the child's perspective as valid and important contrasts with top-down parental instruction, and so, through picturebooks and supplementary materials, parents are taught the value of listening carefully and responding to their children. This, in turn, is meant to shape their own habits of thought and interpersonal interactions. The Incense Light picturebooks imagine children and adults not as different kinds of Buddhists, but as religious actors co-constituted through family life.

7

Making Science Buddhist

CONSIDER THREE VIGNETTES, from three different books:

> While a smaller tree and a lizard look on, a talking tree of considerable age scolds a piece of coal for calling him "kid": "I'm already one hundred and eight years old, and everyone calls me 'Grandpa Tree.' Now a little guy like you comes along and calls me 'kid'—does this mean I should call you 'Grandpa'?" The cheerful piece of coal only provokes the tree more by asserting they are all part of one family, and then goes on to explain how coal comes to be.

> We read: "Although our lifetimes are very short, no more than two or three months, we can produce over two thousand poops." This text, and the first-person description of how this poop causes allergies, accompanies an illustration of a dozen dust mites working a factory assembly line of emoji-style poop. Many of the mites are clearly delighted with their work, but there's an inspector present in case any of them fall short.

> In a board book, a group of chickens and their chicks gather in an agitated huddle, some of them with beaks open to cheep angrily. Other chickens are more downcast, depicted with a tear at the corner of their eyes which they wipe at with hand-like wings. Two of the chicks have fallen down, and have their eyes closed, as if sick or even dead. An arm reaches in and has grabbed one unlucky chicken by the neck. The text on the left-hand page reads: "In order to make animals grow up more quickly, people put unhealthy things in their food, even to the point that if one animal

> gets an infectious disease, they will all be killed together whether healthy or sick."[1]

These three books all develop empathy for nonhuman entities through anthropomorphism. The first two books use dialogue, cuteness, and positive emotions to elicit interest in scientific explanations of common phenomena. The third vignette, implying that chickens feel sadness as humans do, is more stridently didactic, part of a book promoting vegetarianism to young children. These three books are part of a body of children's literature that integrates scientific inquiry with being Buddhist, even when that religious identity is not made overt. The Tzu Chi picturebooks discussed in this chapter show that scientific knowledge transforms how children act in the world, a message that becomes more pressing and more Buddhist the closer it is to the child's own body. Picturebooks about the natural world, often distant from the child's lived experience (rhinos and coal mining) are presented with scientific neutrality, even as they use strategies such as cute-ification and dialogue to allow the reader to develop affective relationships with nonhuman beings. When the topics involve the child's own body—hygiene, disease, and diet—they also attend to what the child-reader can do. This is clearest in the case of vegetarianism, where children are represented as autonomous young Buddhists making their own choices about practice, which are reinforced by fictional friends and shared in family settings. If you understand science, these books argue, you will act in Tzu Chi ways.

The Science of Humanistic Buddhism

Buddhist thinkers of the early twentieth century endeavoured to tie their tradition to scientific reasoning as part of their efforts at modernization and reform. As Eric Hammerstrom argues, the 1920s were a key decade for these developments: Buddhist interest in science gained currency at the same time that anti-superstition movements were underway.[2] Buddhist intellectuals argued modern science confirmed Buddhist cosmology and epistemology, and that modern science could be explained through terms drawn from Buddhist thought. Western biomedicine was another site for Buddhism's engagement with science, with Buddhist authors arguing both that developments in medical science supported views expressed in scripture and that Buddhist teachings could supplement medical interventions by addressing spiritual needs.[3] If scientific thinking was part of modern life, it was an approach that Buddhism could take as well. The ideology of scientific progress dominated the twentieth century, changing how Chinese Buddhist thinkers related to scientific endeavors. Although there is still interest in how Buddhist concepts might align with science, now more emphasis is placed on how Buddhist ethics might temper or guide the use of science, especially in activities relating to medicine and environmentalism.

In modern Taiwan, Buddhist Compassion Relief Tzu Chi Foundation has been at the forefront of Buddhist medical and environmental efforts.[4] Tzu Chi was founded in 1966 by the nun Zhengyan.[5] Born in Taiwan during the period of Japanese colonial rule, Zhengyan is connected to the early twentieth-century reform movement through her teacher Yinshun, who studied with Taixu. Yinshun wrote widely on matters of Buddhist doctrine and is often associated with the phrase *renjian fojiao,* although he did not focus on Buddhism as a movement for bettering society.[6] Zhengyan's social engagement, rather than deriving from her teacher, was influenced in large part by Christian missionaries, whom she observed caring for Taiwan's marginalized populations.[7] Indeed, unequal access to health care was part of what prompted Zhengyan to establish Tzu Chi as a young nun. Initially the organization relied on small donations and the sale of handicrafts. Women volunteers formed the core of the early Tzu Chi organization. In addition to a concern with providing health services, Tzu Chi's major endeavors include disaster relief (both within Taiwan and globally), and environmentalism. With a long history of good relations with the government, Tzu Chi offers social services that supplement those offered by the state and in the process negotiates the roles religious organizations play in modern Taiwan.[8]

Institutional growth is possible because individuals find compelling the Tzu Chi approach to integrating Buddhism into modern life. C. Julia Huang has argued that Tzu Chi's medical mission—core to their overall mission—reflects a "double process of secularization of Buddhism and sacralization of medical science."[9] A hospital in Hualien was Tzu Chi's first major construction project and there are now six additional hospitals across Taiwan, along with a medical college and a bone marrow bank. As Tzu Chi established hospitals and health clinics, they showed "how medical care rationalizes Buddhist charity with modern and scientific institutions."[10] Donations are not funneled into monasteries and temples but into institutional forms that have legitimacy outside the sphere of religion. The lobby of the Tzu Chi hospital in Hualien is dominated by a large mural of the Buddha treating a sick monk. This illustrates Huang's second point, that Tzu Chi has transformed medical care "into a Buddhist sacramental practice." Volunteer work is understood through a Buddhist lens, especially in the "exclusive" volunteer retreats that take place at the hospital and the Abode of Still Thoughts (where Zhengyan lives, and the religious heart of Tzu Chi).[11] Likewise, organ donation and cadaver donation are given Buddhist meaning by tying them to *jātaka* stories and the perfection of giving (*dānapāramitā*) that is a core part of the Buddhist path.[12] Tzu Chi exemplifies a culture-centered approach to medicine that is growing in importance within the health-care field, offering a holistic vision of community care in contrast to one that focuses on the individual.[13] Not only does Tzu Chi provide new, Buddhist, models for approaching medical practice, its hospitals and medical college are the sites of the production of new scientific knowledge.[14] Tzu Chi demonstrates how science, in the form of biomedicine, can be almost seamlessly merged with modern Buddhism.

The secularization/sacralization process allows for a flexible use of Buddhist terms and symbols, without undercutting the Buddhist motivation at the base of Tzu Chi activities. Tzu Chi is registered as an NGO, and in some contexts their philanthropy appears as secular and transnational.[15] For example, the hospital in Hualien extends its Buddhist identity well beyond the mosaic in the lobby, referring to white-clad nurses in ways that evoke the bodhisattva Guanyin and calling the vests worn by volunteers "little *kāṣāya*," (*jiasha* 袈裟), a term for monastic robes.[16] In contrast a Tzu Chi medical clinic in Southern California might submerge much of this explicitly Buddhist identity, even as it is part of the same compassionate mission. Yet Buddhist motivations are operative even if they do not appear on the surface. This applies to other Tzu Chi efforts, including, as we shall see, in children's books—these need not be identifiably Buddhist to be fully Tzu Chi.

Tzu Chi's environmental efforts can also be understood through Huang's twofold process of secularization and sacralization. The organization's environmental mission originates in Zhengyan's personal experience: on her way to deliver a lecture in Taizhong in 1990, she saw litter and trash on the streets, and at the end of her lecture, she encouraged people to help do something about the situation. Recycling was the first environmental endeavor Tzu Chi undertook, and it was in response to a real-world problem. In parallel to their medical mission, this is a way of repackaging Buddhist austerity within a modern, scientific discourse. The sites for environmental action can then be sacralized, as through the use of the term *daochang* 道場—a place for rituals or religious practice—for recycling centers. Recycling is not an isolated act but part of a process of self-discipline and a means to cultivate a reorientation to the modern world and its emphasis on consumption.[17] Although Tzu Chi started with a focus on environmental protection, which can have an immediate, local effect, they subsequently introduced climate change and related terms into their publications, further incorporating scientific discourse into their environmental practice.[18] For Tzu Chi, pollution and the climate crisis may reflect spiritual problems, but they also require scientific approaches to reach a solution. Thus science must be taught alongside Buddhist dharma. Although their medical mission and environmentalism are thoroughly Buddhist in concept, there are good reasons to aim for an audience that may not be motivated primarily by religious ideas. In a pluralistic society, environmental protection and health care are goods that transcend particularistic moral commitments; marking them as religious might be an impediment rather than a benefit. Consequently Tzu Chi's medical and scientific children's books often make little or no mention of Buddhism—with important exceptions.

More broadly, Humanistic Buddhism's commitment to social improvement entails engagement with scientific and technological discourse. Although this chapter focuses on children's books produced by Tzu Chi, and although Tzu Chi is particularly invested in medical care, many other Buddhist organizations have also taken up environmental causes. Dharma Drum, for example, includes "natural environmentalism" (*ziran huanbao* 自然環保) as one of four environmentalisms; the other three are spiritual environmentalism (*xinling huanbao* 心靈環保), ritual environmentalism (*liyi huanbao* 禮儀環保), and life environmentalism (*shenghuo huanbao* 生活環保). Spiritual environmentalism has priority, requiring the transformation of internal attitudes and perspectives. The four environmentalisms move from inner to outer, with natural environmentalism being the last in the series, and the only one that explicitly engages with nonhuman parts of the environment.[19] As another example of Taiwanese Buddhist environmental work, the nun Zhaohui 昭慧 (b. 1957) founded the Life Conservationist Society and has been deeply engaged with cross-cultural dialogue on the treatment of nonhuman animals.[20] Environmentalism is an important way in which Buddhist engagement with science has been transformed in contemporary times, channeling inquiry and knowledge into ethical practices on the level of the individual. Tzu Chi picturebooks take children as the audience for this type of Buddhist formation through scientific study and real-world action.

Why Coal Is Cute and Rhinos Talk

The introduction to this chapter included a brief section of the story "The Ancestor of Trees" (Shu de zuxian 樹的祖先) about a piece of coal that falls off a truck, leading it to explain to a nearby tree how it too was once a tree. The process to become coal takes such a long time that even though the coal seems newly dug from the earth, it is much older than the tree.[21] The little piece of coal is equipped with eyes, a small nose, and a mouth; the two trees with whom the coal converses are also furnished with eyes, noses, and mouths (Plate 17). The story only occupies a few pages, but this is enough to establish that each has an identifiable personality and speaking style. There's also a lizard who helps to move the conversation forward. The little piece of coal, despite being the eldest, is the character through which focalization occurs: as the smallest, the coal is the most childlike, and it has to explain itself to "adult" figures who seem to know better. As with the friendly buddhas and bodhisattvas discussed in chapter 5, depicting the lump of coal as cute makes it more appealing and thereby more likely that the reader can sympathize with its challenges. Although there is no real danger—the trees after all cannot move—the narrative tension hinges on how successfully the little piece of coal can communicate the reality of how trees and coal are related.

This communicative aspect is a competency the story wants to inculcate, It is emphasized in a text box titled "Intrapersonal Intelligence" (*neixing zhineng* 内省智能) with a prompt for discussion: "Have any of your siblings or friends ever been blamed for something they didn't do? Did you have to help explain their innocence? What did you do?"[22] This translates the coal's encounter with the big trees into the everyday skill set of young children. It is also part of the overall agenda of this series of books. "The Ancestor of Trees" appears in *Interesting Plants* (*Youqu de zhiwu* 有趣的植物), which offers six stories to explain how plants propagate and how they protect themselves. The book in turn is part of a series entitled "The Multiple Intelligences Collection" (Duoyuan zhineng baodian 多元智能寶典). The concepts of "intrapersonal intelligence" and "multiple intelligences" (often abbreviated MI) come from the work of developmental psychologist Howard Gardner, who has outlined eight different kinds of intelligence: linguistic, musical, logical-mathematical, spatial, bodily-kinesthetic, naturalist, interpersonal, and intrapersonal.[23] Gardner's ideas have been influential globally, with a significant impact on education in Taiwan; there are hundreds of books, workbooks, and toys with *duoyuan zhineng* 多元智能 (multiple intelligences) in their names or titles, all part of a parenting approach that seeks to best prepare children for academic success. "The Multiple Intelligences Collection" from Tzu Chi integrates these intelligences into each book by inserting themed pages on developing different intelligences. In *Interesting Plants,* a "naturalist" page has children sprout seeds in different conditions; a "logical/mathematical" page offers a math problem related to mangrove seed pods; for "interpersonal" intelligence, children are asked to think about sharing fortune and difficulty with their peers; to develop "linguistic" intelligence, readers are asked to identify poems describing trees; for "visual/spatial" intelligence, children pick the shortest path for a hedgehog to travel.[24] Only the personal intelligences (intra- and inter-) suggest an ethical outlook, and the examples in the book connect to the stories by analogy, rather than through the subject matter. That is, learning about plants does not explicitly lead to treating plants differently. Nor is learning about coal and how it is created connected to the environmental problems of coal extraction and use. Indeed, the idea that trees should "respect" (*qijing* 起敬) coal might even suggest the opposite.[25] Scientific knowledge is presented for its own merit, not with the intent of explicitly shaping behavior.

The appearance of scientific neutrality is an important characteristic of "The Multiple Intelligences Collection." *Little Secrets of Animals* (*Dongwu de xiao mimi* 動物的小秘密) opens with a story about a rhinoceros who is very itchy, a consequence of the parasitical insects that live on her skin.[26] A bird comes to her aid, taking up residence on her back and eating the insects. The rhinoceros calls the bird her private doctor (*siren yisheng* 私人醫生), and the bird also aids the rhinoceros by alerting her to the presence of a hunter, which the rhinoceros chases off. Contemplating the gun dropped by the hunter, the bird tells the rhinoceros that it contains tranquilizer darts that would allow the hunter to take her horn and sell it. Shocked, the rhinoceros acknowledges that her poor eyesight would be her downfall if not for the help of the bird. The narrative at this point is interrupted by a page in a different font titled "Supplemental Knowledge" (*zhishi dabutie* 知識大補帖), explaining that in Chinese medicine rhinoceros horn is efficacious for alleviating fever and counteracting poison, and this is the reason that rhinos have been hunted almost to the point of extinction. The phrasing used—"the clinical experience of Chinese medicine"—gives credence to its curative properties. This page also adds some details about which rhinos have two horns, and which only one. The medicinal value of rhinoceros horn is not questioned, nor is a course of action suggested to prevent the rhinoceros from going extinct. The narrative goes on to provide more information on the habits of rhinos: Seeing it wallowing in mud, a young sika deer comments to its mother that the rhinoceros is very dirty. The deer mother explains that the this is a way for rhinos to protect their skin and to ward off mosquitoes.

Talking animals serve to impart knowledge about the rhinoceros. In the course of these few pages the reader learns about the symbiotic relationship between the rhinoceros and the bird, why the rhinoceros is a threatened species, and the reason behind the rhino's unclean and unattractive appearance. The story does not tell readers what to believe or to think, but provides them with information to help understand how human practices are connected to the animal world. Likewise, no lessons are made explicit at the end of the story, as is often done with children's books.[27] However, there are clear takeaways: we see here animals working cooperatively, the threats posed to animals by human behavior, and the misunderstandings that can arise when one species judges another by its own standards. That the animals are given voices makes it easier for readers to grasp their perspectives. The rhinoceros and the bird chat together like friends, and the dialogue between the two deer mimics human parent-child interactions. The scientific knowledge is imparted in such a way as to also help the child-reader see the world from the animals' point of view. In her preface, author Zeng Weihui 曾維惠 makes clear the link she sees between understanding and protecting, writing, "To make children understand animals, to draw near to animals, and to protect animals is a very important and interesting task."[28] Conservation must be preceded by knowledge, conveyed in language appropriate to children. And acquisition of knowledge is facilitated by positive emotions: finding the animals adorable and relatable helps readers learn about them. Elsewhere Zeng connects intellectual development with emotional growth, writing "by widening children's intellect one is also able to promote attachment between parent and child, making the family more harmonious."[29] Stories about animals have positive social effects even when they do not explicitly address human behavior. As we will see, the emotional dimension of these stories will become more prominent as the topics move closer to the child-reader's body and self.

Looking at the world from the perspective of a talking animal or plant can encourage empathetic behavior in a general way. The coal in *Interesting Plants* serves to focalize the reader's attention, as does the rhinoceros in *Little Secrets of Animals*—like most of the other animals depicted, he has an oversize head, big eyes, and short limbs. The sika deer have big eyes and long eyelashes, and wear clothes. As with other examples of cuteness, this serves to make the animals and plants seem as if they need care. In one of the plant stories, there's even a character named "Ginseng doll" (*renshen wawa* 人參娃娃). These are the same strategies that any children's book would use to make plants and animals appealing; there is no suggestion that Buddhist ideas such as inherent Buddha nature or reincarnation have informed these depictions.

The effects of looking carefully at the world of animals may help to form environmental attitudes later in life, especially if children are not immersed in nature. A study in Australia found that when adults involved in environmental protection were asked to recall favorite childhood reading material, they were more likely to name fictional accounts of nature than scientific books. For the authors of the study, this suggested that fantasy and imagination were important in creating pro-environmental worldviews.[30] Sociologist Bengt Larsson points to how "eco-edutainment" fits into the pedagogical attitudes found in "advanced liberal democracies": children are expected to be autonomous and active, and to participate in "their own socialization" into responsible citizens and "ecological selves." This early learning is part of an expected lifelong education that "places individuals in a greater space of responsibility, morally and geographically" with regard to environmental problems.[31] For the readers of Tzu Chi's "The Multiple Intelligences Collection," cultivating ecological knowledge is presented as part of the multifaceted development first championed by Howard Gardner. Relating the stories to specific skill development prompts multiple connections, but imaginative engagement with the plant and animal characters does not lead directly to action in these narratives. Simply knowing about animals, plants, and their worlds would seem to be enough. Other Tzu Chi children's books deepen the perspective-taking seen here, however, and are more explicit about the actions children might take.

Books are not the only way in which Tzu Chi educates children about science and the environment, and introduces them to advocacy for social action. To take just one example, the television program titled "Calling Dr. Clever" (Hujiao miao boshi 呼叫妙博士) has an adult scientist guide the explorations of young students. An episode about barbecuing on the mid-autumn festival (*zhongqiu jie* 中秋節) exemplifies how the program integrates cultural knowledge, scientific learning, and environmental activism: Two girls first learn about the traditions of the mid-autumn festival, and then the negative effects of one of those traditions, barbecuing food. They learn about the air pollution caused by charcoal smoke, then visit a scientist who explains the chemicals produced when food is barbecued and their effect on the body. The girls make a video trying to change people's habits, emphasizing these points and the waste of using disposable items. There is nothing ostensibly Buddhist about this episode or the program generally, but the integration of knowledge and social action reflect the dominant Tzu Chi strategy for teaching environmentalism.[32]

Our Bodies, Our Buddhist Selves

Dust mites are much more intimately connected to humans than rhinos are, but much less charismatic. Humor works to bridge the gap. At the back of *Dust Mite Dingding's Diary of Moving House* (*Chenman dingding banjia ji* 塵蟎丁丁搬家記) and following the story, a page announces that it will offer a "great declassification of bugs" (*chongchong da jiemi* 蟲蟲大解密). The first file to be declassified is that of the dust mite, through a series of questions: What are dust mites? What kinds of dust mites are there? What kinds of environments do dust mites like? What are the special qualities of dust mites? How do dust mites cause allergies? Dr. Zhu, illustrated at the top of the page with an oversize head and a kindly smile, is the implied guide through these questions. On the second page, an illustration of a little boy airing a blanket in the sunshine accompanies a discussion of how to prevent dust mites in one's home. The bottom of the page includes four references, to a government guide, hospital website, an issue of *Scientific American* for Taiwan, and the website of the Taiwan Environmental Pest Management Association. The presentation of information assumes that getting rid of dust mites requires first understanding them as insects: how big they are (measured in microns, not very), how many types are found in the dust of Taiwanese household (sixteen), and what humidity they prefer (60–80%).[33]

The story itself might be described as gross-out fiction from a medical perspective. Gross-out fiction uses bodily functions (e.g., burps and farts) or other disgusting things in a humorous way. Gross-out fiction is often seen as successful in attracting children's attention in ways that more serious approaches may not. The gross-out aspect of dust mites comes to the fore in the early pages of the book. The second spread shows a magnified image of what dust mites do while we are sleeping and features a dust mite wearing a hat made of poop, handing more poop to another mite. The page following is the depiction of the poop factory noted above, where the illustrator seems to have delighted in cramming as much poop as possible into two pages (Plate 18). The medical perspective is present here as well: it is not just that dust mites are excellent at producing poop, but this poop leads to allergic reactions. The first pages show Dingding the dust mite winning a prize for causing the most allergies. The poop factory is overlaid with bubbles showing the effects of dust mite allergies: sneezing, runny rose, coughing, and rash.

The story is set in motion when Dingding returns home with his prize and finds his home uninhabitable because of a new dust mite cover. He finds his family—lined up in a style that evokes immigration lines—and they move to an uncle's house, occasioning more descriptions of the dust mite life cycle (eating habits, egg production). Cleaning prompts Dingding to move several more times, and he takes up residence in a stuffed animal, on a dog, and in a sofa. It concludes with Dingding narrowly avoiding being washed. The reader is encouraged to take the perspective of Dingding: it's through his eyes that we see the world, imagining his joy when he wins the prize, his panic when he cannot find his family, and his longing for his old home. Dust mites are pictured enjoying family meals, reminiscing over photographs, and celebrating births, just as humans do. But peril fills Dingding's world, as he has to avoid human cleaning efforts—this is the mirror image of the peril caused by the dust mites themselves, responsible for so much of human allergies. Seeing how many places the dust mites live, the reader may come away feeling that the world is contaminated, even if they might sympathize with the plight of Dingding's family.

Compassion for dust mites is a complicated thing. The treatment of dust mites here shows the challenges of bringing together scientific knowledge and medical thinking with Buddhist perspectives. As with the treatment of animals in the previous section, readers are encouraged—through the use of focalization—to take the perspective of the dust mite. In terms of allergies, however, dust mites are antagonistic to humans. Although the reader might sympathize with Dingding, the goal of the book would seem to be to get rid of dust mites. The concluding pages following the narrative talk about "preventing" (*yufang* 預防) dust mites, but based on the information offered about dust mite lives, washing bedding in hot water as recommended will *kill* dust mites. The narrative asserts that the mites simply "move house," and is careful not to show any being killed or to use words that imply that they are killed. Were this not a Buddhist book, "moving house," might even be taken as a euphemism for death. As we will see in the next section, Tzu Chi promotes vegetarianism within the context of caring for all living things. In Chinese Buddhist history, this care for all living things has often extended to insects, if not with the same attention as with larger animals: monks used mesh to sieve out insects before drinking, and vinaya texts instructed them on how to avoid irritating insects without causing them harm.[34] *Dust Mite Dingding's Diary of Moving House* continues this tradition by sidestepping the fate of dust mites in the narrative. This is the most Buddhist aspect of these books, and one that is likely to be overlooked by many readers.

Dust Mite Dingding's Diary of Moving House is part of the Tzu Chi series "Public Medicine for Children" (Yipu tongshu 醫普童書). In addition to dust mites, the series covers other insects such as rove beetles (which irritate the skin), biting midges, head lice, and tsutsugamushi mites, which cause scrub typhus. The series also includes books on more general health issues that children might encounter: colds, allergies, ear infections, dental caries, stomachaches, and accidents.[35] These books are part of an effort to provide better scientific and medical education for children, consonant with Tzu Chi's mission. In an internal report, a Tzu Chi representative explained that the series came about through the efforts of a doctor affiliated with the pediatrics unit at one of Tzu Chi's hospitals, with the aim of providing information with more "public credibility" (*gongxinli* 公信力) than what was available on the web or elsewhere. Through the series children were intended to gain general medical knowledge that they could put into effect through everyday efforts to protect their health and maintain good hygiene. These books connect knowledge with action. The Tzu Chi representative noted that this would have positive effects on the household and society: better health knowledge, put into practice, "would reduce the rate of illness and accidents, decreasing the financial burdens on the family, lessening the amount of effort parents put into care, and lowering society's hidden medical costs."[36] This same report—on an event at which parents and children were encouraged to read the books together—included attestations from both parents and children. One third grader said a book about Haemophilus influenzae, described as a green monster in a black forest, left the deepest impression, while also conveying the importance of good hygiene and seeing a doctor when ill rather than trying to treat yourself with medicine. His mother added that she bought the books to supplement her own experience.[37]

The public health role of these picturebooks can be seen in the rapid production of *The New Coronavirus Declassified!* (*Xin guanbingdu dajiemi*

新冠病毒大解密) in June 2020, just months after the coronavirus was declared a global pandemic. The books in the "Public Medicine for Children" series all contain a fair amount of information about the science behind the illness and for its treatment. *The New Coronavirus Declassified!,* however, is exceptional in this regard. The narrative begins with the most well-respected virologist of an imaginary country explaining the different kinds of scientists who are doing research on the new coronavirus and the precautions they must take in the lab. The virologist then explains the composition of a coronavirus (including that it is neither living nor nonliving),[38] how it differs from other viruses, and the history of infectious diseases (Plate 19). She says that the coronavirus known as COVID-19 likely jumped from bats to humans, elaborating that infections from bats were once not very likely because of infrequent contact, but because humans have destroyed the natural environment and encroached on the territory of bats—even eating them at times—the risk of infection has increased.[39] The virologists continues by explaining how it is transmitted, what happens once it is in the lungs, symptoms, treatments, and preventative measures. This brief summary cannot capture the scope and level of detail of *The New Coronavirus Declassified!,* which skillfully combines public health, the science of viruses, and the process of scientific research in such a way that even well-educated adults are likely to learn from it.[40]

The author's note at the story's conclusion highlights the social dimensions that are implied in the story. Liu Yijun 劉怡均 (Ingrid Liu) is the president of Tzu Chi University in Hualien, and a molecular neuroscientist. She was invited to write *The New Coronavirus Declassified!* by the Tzu Chi Culture and Communication Foundation 慈濟傳播人文志業基金會, signaling that the publishers felt that this was an important topic meriting a prominent author with exceptional scientific credentials. Although the objective of the book is to provide timely information on COVID-19, Liu takes the opportunity to counteract the stereotype that senior scientists are men by making the virologist a woman. The interrelationship of the humans and their environment is also important to Liu: "We wanted to make the viruses cute, because everything in the world is interdependent: if humans are able to respect the lives of other species, and cherish the environment, then the chances of hostile encounters with viruses and other sources of diseases will be diminished."[41] Here Liu reinforces a point made earlier with regard to human interactions with bats, which also connects two domains in which Tzu Chi is active—medicine and the environment. She also points to the importance of aesthetics (cuteness) in shaping affective responses that in turn have real societal effects.

Children's picturebooks are an important vehicle for scientific education. In her author's note, Liu relates a conversation she had with her friend, the prize-winning children's author Xing Jiahui 幸佳慧 (Arlene Hsing, 1973–2019). Xing teased Liu that scientific research is read by only a few hundred people, while picturebooks reach a much wider audience, and influence both the children who are the primary readers and the adults who share books with them. Xing encouraged her friend to translate her scientific knowledge into picturebook format. Liu took from this conversation the importance of reaching different age groups as a way of enlarging the influence of scientific research.[42] Liu's concern with multiple audiences for public health information has a parallel with creating Buddhist literature for children, as a means of reaching different audiences and expanding influence. For Tzu Chi, scientific literature for children is part of their religious mission, and it more often takes the form of characterizations of environmental interrelatedness than overtly Buddhist statements.

Donations amplify the social effects of this literature. Although books in the "Popular Medicine for Children" series are sold in bookstores, Tzu Chi has also provided copies free of charge to places where they felt they were needed. In 2018, a branch of the organization gave over three thousand books to twenty-three elementary schools in Taidong, with the aim of closing the urban-rural gap in medical knowledge.[43] Because they have no explicitly Buddhist content, the books in the "Popular Medicine for Children" series allow Tzu Chi to promote their mission in places that might be less welcoming to religious content. But even if children or their parents do not connect the books to Tzu Chi, promoting good health is a significant part of the organization's mission, as we have seen. Like "The Multiple Intelligences Collection," the contents of these books do not signal their Tzu-Chi-ness or even a Buddhist perspective. This is in some sense a natural conclusion to the interest in combining Buddhism and science—that the two would be so seamlessly merged that the religion need not call attention to itself.

Little Vegetarians

Vegetarianism is different, and for Tzu Chi eschewing meat is part of religious identity. Other reasons, such as health or a desire to consume a less resource-intensive diet, also support vegetarianism. The third book excerpted in the introduction to this chapter, *I Love Fruits and Vegetables, I Love the Earth* (*Wo ai shuguo, wo ai diqiu* 我愛蔬果，我愛地球), is a board book in the shape of a young girl standing with a basket of vegetables. From the cover she smiles at the prospective reader, accompanied by both wild (monkey, snail, crocodile) and domesticated animals (rabbit, chicken, cow) (Plate 20). The little girl is dressed in a white shirt and dark blue pants; the apron that she wears follows this color scheme, as do her socks and shoes and the ribbons in her hair. Blue and white are the colors of the Tzu Chi uniform, and it is as easily recognizable on this book cover as it is in the streets of Taibei. Most of the children in the book are depicted wearing clothes in a range of colors and styles, but this cover image and the image of three young volunteers (*xiao zhigong* 小志工) midway through the book mark out an identity as Tzu Chi member as a possibility for children.[44] Richard Madsen notes the significance of the term *zhigong* instead of the more common term for volunteer, *yigong* 義工: rather than emphasize the voluntary aspect *zhigong* conveys obligation and "an enlightened acceptance of one's duties toward others."[45] This uniform is a visual way to signal that one is a "Tzu Chi person" (*Ciji ren* 慈濟人), another expression that the organization uses to indicate their mission and identity.[46] Putting on the clothes of a Tzu Chi volunteer, the child enters into a web of social responsibility—which includes the nonhuman.

In this book, Tzu Chi identity is further defined as one that cares for all beings *and* the planet through vegetarianism; compassion is linked to environmentalism. The first page quotes Master Zhengyan: "We should maintain a mind of gratitude towards nature," and explains that because all living beings live together, people should take care of life and value natural resources. Vegetarianism is one way of cherishing the earth.[47] These opening pages redefine Buddhist eating practices as part of broader environmental thinking, a theme that continues throughout the book. *I Love Fruits and Vegetables, I Love the Earth* also uses metaphors of health to talk about the earth; a healthy human body is tied to a healthy planetary body. On the second pictorial spread, the earth is anthropomorphized, depicted as having a fever: a thermometer sticks out of its frowning mouth, sweat rolls down its face, and an ice pack rests atop its head. The text explains that the earth's temperature is rising because so much land has been converted to raising animals, reducing the number of plants that can remove carbon dioxide from the atmosphere. The following pages elaborate, adding that animal farts (*fang de pi* 放的屁) contain methane, which traps the heat of the sun.[48] This is accompanied by an illustration of a mother polar bear and her baby on an ice floe barely large enough for the two of them; the text uses polar bears, along with seals and sea birds as examples of animals that will be most threatened by climate warming. Having established the environmental effects of raising animals for consumption, *I Love Fruits and Vegetables* turns to the relationship between human and nonhuman animals, pointing out that we are only one of the many species that live on earth, that we are akin to animals, and should feel their suffering when they are caged. The passage quoted in the introduction to this chapter also speaks to the cruelty of raising animals, and on that same page the designers render one sentence in red ink: "Roughly a thousand animals are killed each second."[49]

After offering examples of animals that are vegetarian, *I Love Fruits and Vegetables* turns to children who have promoted vegetarianism. The book concludes with an explanation of how to eat healthily as a vegetarian and, in its last lines, ties vegetarianism back to the environment: "Beginning with eating vegetarian, we can work together for the well-being of the earth and live together happily with animals."[50] The illustration reflects this prospective happiness with a little girl dancing in a forest with a chicken, goat, pig, and rhinoceros, all anthropomorphized to varying degrees. This mode of depicting animals—cute and like humans—reinforces what Lina Verchery has termed "ontological continuity," the idea that all beings in the six paths of rebirth are not as different as their current forms would suggest.[51] When cows smile in the same way little girls do, it is easier to see why one should not eat the other. To think about this picturebook as part of affinity work, we see human connections being extended to other species. Because these entanglements are part of a Buddhist worldview, cultivating an understanding of them—through shared reading—is a part of building cross-species *yuanfen*.

I Love Fruits and Vegetables also uses scientific rhetoric to persuade children to take up vegetarianism. It does so through the use of terms such as carbon dioxide (*eryang huatan* 二氧化碳), methane (*jiawan* 甲烷), and infectious disease (*chuanran bing* 傳染病), which are more sophisticated vocabulary items than found in most board books. The use of terms such as "carbon dioxide" also assumes that the reader understands that the atmosphere is made up of gases that must be balanced in a particular way. This is not explained in the book itself, which only points out that plants absorb carbon dioxide without explaining why this would be desirable. Scientific rhetoric is also present in the use of statistics: that there are 8.7 million species on earth, that 100 million animals are slaughtered each year, that this amounts to 1,000 animals killed each second. Even the section on what to eat reflects a scientific approach, arguing that legumes contain the same kind of nutrition that meat does.[52] The use of scientific rhetoric suggests that this is an important way of looking at the world, one that exists alongside moral persuasion.

The scientific explanation of why one should practice vegetarianism adds to standard Buddhist arguments. Fundamentally, the reason that Buddhists do not eat meat is rooted in the injunction against killing. This rule has been interpreted in various ways as it relates to the consumption of meat: First, it was initially intended to apply only to monks and nuns and was understood to mean that animals could not be slaughtered for their benefit; meat received on begging rounds was acceptable. That Buddhist monastics are wholly vegetarian in China, and consequently in Taiwan, is a result both of new translations of scriptures and of lay practice; vegetarianism as a

Buddhist practice became firmly rooted in China during the medieval period. Even before vegetarianism was standard monastic practice, it had been taken up by lay Buddhists, building not only on Buddhist scriptures but on earlier traditions of fasts and diet restriction as well as ideals of compassion.[53] The most prominent lay Buddhist to practice vegetarianism was Emperor Wu of the Liang dynasty (Liang Wudi 梁武帝, r. 502–549), who not only abjured meat himself, but also held imperial debates on the matter of monastic vegetarianism and issued an edict banning Buddhist monastics from eating meat. The advocacy for vegetarianism begun during the early sixth century proved determinative for Buddhist practice going forward.[54] Vegetarianism found further support in the *Brahma-Net Sutra* (*Fanwang jing* 梵網經), which contains precepts to be conferred on lay Buddhists. In addition to the major precept that forbids killing, this scripture also includes a minor precept explicitly addressing the consumption of meat, arguing that it stunts compassion.[55] In short, from the medieval period onward, Buddhist monastics were expected to be vegetarian, and lay Buddhists very often were, at least for some periods of time. It became part of the way that Chinese Buddhists signaled their religious identity.[56] As for historical examples of *children* practicing vegetarianism, medieval monastic biographies treat the inability to consume meat or secret vegetarianism as a sign of preordained commitment to Buddhism.[57] In households with Buddhist practitioners, children would have been exposed to vegetarianism, and it would not be surprising to find them following suit.

By the early twentieth century, vegetarianism was promoted as a Buddhist practice appropriate for children. In Chen Hailiang's "A Child's Buddhist Reader" (Fohua ertong duben 佛華兒童讀本), mentioned in chapter 1, vegetarianism is introduced at the very first level of readings. The concluding portion of the text focuses on the treatment of animals: Children are told that all animals have mothers and fathers, all fear death just as people do, and should be protected. Humans have a special role, because they are king among the animals, and excessive killing reflects a bad king. The final verse of this text reads: "Do not kill animals to eat / Little friends, you must put this into practice!"[58] Not eating meat is presented as a core Buddhist practice alongside recitation of the Buddha's name and reading scriptures. The importance of keeping a vegetarian diet is reiterated in the subsequent six levels of instruction. Interspersed through this section are reprinted illustrations by Feng Zikai; most of these illustrate nonkilling, further emphasizing the importance of keeping vegetarian. Its presentation of vegetarianism as an essential Buddhist practice for children marks an important moment in constructing Buddhism specifically *for* children. We see this too in *A Journey to the Western World of Extreme Happiness* (discussed in chapter 6): One scene describes a magical banquet at which whatever the children order immediately appears on the table before them. They know to order soy-braised tofu, fried cashews, steamed lotus root, bitter melon and tofu skin, mushrooms with bean sprouts, and seaweed soup, along with many kinds of fruit—all of it vegetarian.[59]

This emphasis on vegetarianism in China and Taiwan contrasts with children's literature in Japan. Japanese Buddhism has a more ambivalent relationship with vegetarianism, interpreting the injunction against killing as applying to the act itself rather than meat produced from it. Barbara Ambros's study of the picturebook *Partaking of Life: The Day That Little Mii Becomes Meat* shows how the expression of sincere gratitude before a meal creates a "sacrificial logic" that permits the consumption of meat. Written by Uchida Michiko, a disciple of Jōdo Shin Buddhism, the story centers on Little Mii, a spent dairy cow deeply loved by a little girl. Due to the family's economic circumstances, Little Mii must be sold. After she is slaughtered, a small portion of Little Mii's meat is returned to the family; the young girl is made to eat it as an acknowledgment of the cow's sacrifice for the family. *Partaking of Life* is graphic in its description of how the cow is stunned before slaughter (while omitting the slaughter and its aftermath) to show both the sacrifice of the cow and the nobility of the slaughterhouse worker, who does work that makes possible the health and well-being of others.[60] Although a sophisticated treatment of the moral complexities of the meat industry, there's no question that a similar scene in Taiwanese Buddhist children's literature would be in the service of converting the reader to vegetarianism.

Although vegetarianism is common to all Buddhist groups in Taiwan, it is an important part of Tzu Chi organizational culture, both linked with eco-consciousness and expressed through the aesthetics of the group. In stores established by Tzu Chi under the name Jingsi 靜思 (Still Thoughts, taken from the name of the organization's hall in Hualien), cookbooks are among the publications offered for sale. The stores also carry reusable utensils and bowls (disposable chopsticks are especially discouraged), and a range of tastefully packaged vegetarian condiments, fast meals, and supplements. Larger bookstores often have a café attached, sharing the same aesthetic of natural materials and neutral colors, serving simple vegetarian food. Vegetarian cooking shows are broadcast on Tzu Chi's television channel. Although not unique to Tzu Chi, these commercial and media efforts demonstrate the degree to which vegetarianism has been woven into a positive sense of identity.[61]

Making the material form of the book in the shape of a young Tzu Chi volunteer points, in an almost literal way, to the formation of children by way of it. In addition to the Tzu Chi volunteer uniform, gestures also signal Buddhist identity: on the second page of the book a little boy greets a rabbit with his hands held palms together in front of his chest, a near-ubiquitous Buddhist salutation.[62] More significantly, testimony from children shows readers examples of their peers both being vegetarian and advocating for it. A five-year-old volunteer observes that plants can just regrow, while when animals die they are reborn; a nine-year-old is quoted as saying that animals are our friends, and that having them killed for the sake of a meal is inhumane. Some of the children are named: Little Xuan points out the illogic of eating fish to become smarter, because humans are clearly smarter than fish already, while Rourou is even careful not to step on ants while she is walking. The list of exemplary children concludes with praise for their "good hearts which cannot bear to harm animals" and a hope that "other little friends can join them in eating vegetarian!"[63] By taking the shape of a little girl, the book presents itself as one such friend, who will open the reader to other friendships. This is akin to the intimate relationships with bodhisattvas and buddhas we saw in chapter 5, but here other children replace suprahuman figures as exemplars. *I Love Fruits and Vegetables* pushes the idea that children can be autonomous religious actors even further: not only do children in the book act as Buddhists (by being vegetarian), but they can also persuade others to do so. Children can cultivate affinities with other children, leading to socio-religious action.

Tzu Chi identity is also emphasized through the use of quotations from Master Zhengyan, as we have seen above. Four times throughout the book, a brief phrase from Zhengyan is added at the bottom of a page in a different-colored ink. Both child- and adult readers might skip over these—they are not necessary to understanding the book's arguments—but they serve to reinforce the Buddhist nature of the pro-vegetarian arguments being made. This tells us something about how the science of environmental change relates to being Buddhist or a member of Tzu Chi (nothing identifies Tzu Chi or the views presented in the books as "Buddhist"). As I noted above, the book opens with a discussion of the impact of meat consumption on the climate, turning later to arguments based on the mass killing of animals and a sense of shared existence to further advocate for vegetarianism. Vegetarianism is in tension with the perceived health benefits of eating animals, as implied by Little Xuan's rebuttal to imagined advocates of eating fish to promote intelligence. In short, a straightforward argument that eating meat is bad for the environment is seen as insufficient: the science of vegetarianism must be joined to ethical arguments.

A comparison with another board book illustrates how vegetarianism is a special case that ties together scientific knowledge, environmental action, and Buddhism. Like the book on vegetarianism, *Water Is Life* (*Shui shi da shengming* 水是大生命) is shaped like a child: a smiling young boy cradles a drop of water on the cover. The book opens with a section presenting the importance of water for individual human life and environmental health in the tone and style of science education books. The latter half of the book turns to how children could conserve and reuse water. As with *I Love Fruits and Vegetables,* the Tzu Chi uniform is used to signal religious identity. Here, Taiwanese identity is also addressed, through discussion of average water use and how it compares to a geographically similar place like the Netherlands.[64] Five quotations from Zhengyan are included but are more general in tone than those for vegetarianism; all of Zhengyan's words here could be easily repurposed for other situations. Even as children serve as models for environmental behavior, water conservation does not have the same urgency as vegetarianism. Using less water takes place almost entirely outside the body—reusing water from handwashing for watering plants, for example—and so this environmental practice does not transform the individual in the same way. Vegetarianism, on the other hand, is a primary way to embody Buddhism.

Buddhist Scientists and Citizens

Tzu Chi's approach to science has been prompted by real-world experiences. Its origin story places medical inequalities at the center of Zhengyan's young organization, which later grew into a multifaceted medical enterprise. Their environmental mission has followed a similar path, prompted by a visible problem that led to greater environmental stewardship and engagement with the crisis of global warming. Although medical care and pro-environment practices can be treated through a Buddhist lens, these efforts may also be branded simply as "Tzu Chi," in keeping with their status as an international NGO.

The children's books discussed in this chapter have shown how Tzu Chi's interest in scientific knowledge, health, and the environment have extended into materials for young readers. Although all these books are clearly part of the Tzu Chi mission, they make apparent their Buddhist or Tzu Chi identity only when their message connects science to the reader's own body. In "The Multiple Intelligences Collection," children learn about plants and animals through stories that turn the natural world into lessons for human beings. The stories anthropomorphize animals, making them cute and giving them dialogue that depicts them in situations with human parallels. These connections are highlighted in sections devoted to interpersonal and intrapersonal intelligences, in which children are asked to apply lessons from animal stories in their own lives. The theory of different intelligences engages children to learn about the natural world in multiple ways, and assumes that knowledge will be integrated with personal behavior.

Through the anthropomorphizing of animals, young readers may also come to imagine their perspectives. This comes to the fore with insects that are too small to see, as with the mites at the center of *Dust Mite Dingding's Diary of Moving House*. Thinking about how a dust mite regards his family and his home can stretch a child's empathetic response. However, dust mites have a negative impact on humans, causing many allergies, and so the book recommends ways to get rid of them without explicitly stating that they should be killed. Learning about dust mites is fundamentally different from learning about rhinoceroses: one educational effort is for the avoidance of human suffering, and the other aims, obliquely, at animal conservation. Both fit within scientific or eco-edutainment more broadly, representing information Tzu Chi wants children to know. Picturebooks of this sort may be informed by Buddhist values, but these are not explicit in the works themselves.

Vegetarianism makes plain the connection between environmentalism and Buddhist identity: Scientific research on health and the environment can be deployed to support Buddhist ethical teachings about nonkilling and the care of animals. Further, nonkilling of animals has a greater and clearer urgency in the Buddhist moral universe than more abstract aims of conservation and environmental protection. The board book *I Love Fruits and Vegetables, I Love the Earth* connects environmentalism with nonkilling, and from the first-person pronoun used in the title to the children depicted in Tzu Chi uniforms, it situates vegetarianism within the formation of Buddhist identity and the shaping of global eco-citizens.

Conclusion

BUDDHIST PICTUREBOOKS GIVE FORM TO CHILDREN as religious and social actors, and families as spaces for cultivation. We have seen books that expand scriptural commentary or adapt monastic biographies, new stories about bodhisattvas in this world, and early science readers that explain animal behavior; these picturebooks have ranged from those that hew closely to Buddhist sources to those that are not ostensibly religious. Created by Buddhist authors and illustrators and published through Buddhist organizations, they are evidence of how children's literature functions with the complex mission of modern Taiwanese Buddhism. In the introduction I outlined three strands of the scholarly study of Buddhism to which this exploration of picturebooks and children's literature contributes: literature, family, and education. I would like to conclude by returning to each of these categories to consider what we have learned from Taiwanese Buddhist picturebooks and what future directions for research they might suggest.

Literature

The picturebooks explored here both engage with earlier Buddhist literature and *are* Buddhist literature, in a new form. *Picturebook Heart Sutra,* by Fo Guang Shan's founder Xingyun, is the most explicit about reinterpreting Buddhist scripture for young readers. I argued that this work is an innovative continuation of the commentarial tradition, which also draws on visual modes of communication through the illustrations. The *Heart Sutra* featured in Dharma Drum's *Bodhisattva Guanyin, Change, Change, Change!* as well, where a page of the scripture is reproduced with emoji-like illustrations inserted in the traditional-style text. Scriptures need not be explicitly mentioned to be part of these picturebooks: the importance of the *Medicine-Master Sutra* is reflected both in Dharma Drum's *Medicine-Master Buddha's Birthday*

Present and in Incense Light's *The Parking Dragon*. In the latter, the decorative ornament referenced in the book's title is inscribed with a phrase from the *Lotus Sutra*. Turning to stories about monks, canonical sources are in the background of retellings of Xuanzang's journey and of the story of Rāhula. Premodern Buddhist stories also inform the picturebook accounts of Ikkyū and the multiple manifestations of Guanyin.

Picturebooks about scriptures, monks, bodhisattvas, and buddhas undertake acts of translation and localization. As we saw in chapter 3, Shengyan, writing in the preface of *Code Words of the Great Teachers*, argues that the biographies of historical monks can be made relevant by updating their language. Buddhist values endure, but older language does not always make this clear; the argot of the *Biographies of Eminent Monks* needs to be rendered into the language of modern parenting and character education. The process of transforming premodern sources extends beyond language into stories and illustrations. In the same way that vocabulary needs to be revised to reflect modern expressions, so too do illustration styles: cute-ification, the use of bright colors, and dynamic depictions of Buddhist figures refresh the visual idiom of Buddhism. There is a long history of tales about the salvific efforts of Guanyin, and, localized into the story types of contemporary children's literature, the bodhisattva becomes one who saves children from monsters. Within these changes, continuity is still important: children should, for example, be able to recognize bodhisattvas after seeing them illustrated in picturebooks.

We have seen how Buddhist texts and ideas are presented to children with the expectation that they will meet them again and again. Bodhisattvas and buddhas are an example of this, as is the *Heart Sutra*. The stories Xingyun uses to explain this scripture recur in other Fo Guang Shan works, showing a repertoire of narratives that help people understand and apply Buddhism in different contexts. Children may also come across Buddhist figures and stories in other settings, such as finding Xuanzang in a textbook or in popular media. Picturebook encounters prepare them to understand secularized presentations in Buddhist ways. They also give children stories—narrative tools—that help them interpret the world around them.

Literature remakes Buddhism and it also facilitates the movement of Buddhism. Although we can read Taiwanese picturebooks as examples of localization, we might also ask how Buddhist children's literature (and other media) have a transnational dimension. Karen Derris's study of English-language picturebooks notes several dominant types: stories of the Buddha's life, *jātaka* tales, new narratives, and stories of mindfulness and meditation.[1] These overlap only partially with the types of picturebooks discussed here, yet translation and globalization mean that cultures of children's literature are permeable. Which picturebooks move, and where do they move to? Is there a Sinosphere of children's literature? Given that meditation is seldom a part of Taiwanese picturebooks, how do Western approaches to mindfulness circulate in Asia? These questions suggest future directions for the study of Buddhist children's literature.

Picturebooks also represent a special mode of reading—beyond simply comprehending the text, they ask readers to listen, view, touch, hold, and share. They may be read silently or aloud, offering a new way to think about how buddhas and bodhisattvas might speak, or how the Buddhist past might be voiced. Picturebooks necessitate attention to both text and illustration, with the visual aesthetics making a significant contribution to what the narrative conveys, and what emotions it elicits. Illustrations might also prompt readers to touch the book, and hold it, so that the reading experience is as much haptic as it is cognitive. Picturebooks have a dual audience, and are intended in part to be shared, cueing physical attunement and affective response. In short, picturebooks are lively texts—with bright colors, a sense of fun, and invitations to bodily engagement—and they remind us of the multidimensionality of Buddhist books in what they ask of readers. Although picturebooks have attributes that distinguish them from other forms of religious literature, they participate in the Buddhist tradition. We might ask whether the types of reading that picturebooks elicit are seen in materials for other audiences. To put it another way, picturebooks are a distinctly modern form of Buddhist literature—is there also a modern mode of Buddhist reading?

Families

One of the characteristic features of picturebooks is their address to dual audiences; they are intended to be consumed by families. They also *represent* families of many types. We have seen Shengyan's parents trying to make ends meet for a big family, a father negotiating single parenthood after the death of his wife in *The Parking Dragon,* a multigenerational all-female household in *The Boat of the Great Vow,* and the challenges families face when both parents have demanding jobs in *Medicine-Master Buddha's Birthday Present.* Buddhism is a part of family life in all of these, whether through Shengyan's later interpretations of his early years, older generations passing down traditions, or a pathway to independence for children. In depictions of modern families, children are not passive recipients of religious knowledge but are active in the process of religious formation, both through their questions and the actions that they take. In the case of *I Love Fruits and Vegetables, I Love the Earth,* those actions (keeping a vegetarian diet) may even influence family and friends. These representations of Buddhist children offer young readers new models, and contrast with the types of children often seen in earlier exemplar literature. Children as characters in these books also provide models for their parents, by showing childhoods that may differ from their own experiences. And, as parents read about these different families, they are provided with examples of how to talk to their own children.

The degree to which picturebooks are also aimed at adults is even clearer in the supporting materials, such as prefaces, that accompany the main narrative. Paratexts address parents and other adults explicitly, and they imply certain kinds of families. In the case of *Shengyan's Naughty Youth,* the preface explains why what seems like misbehavior might be better understood as creativity and free-thinking and should be encouraged. The notes in *My Buddhas and Bodhisattvas* supply parents with additional information, suggesting that they may be learning alongside their children. From the paratexts to the stories themselves, parents are offered opportunities to reflect on how adults and children interact. Shared reading meshes with parenting approaches in modern Taiwan, whether they emphasize skill acquisition or natural growth, and through picturebooks Buddhism has incorporated this practice into family education. In this book I have treated paratexts as supplements to picturebooks, and only touched briefly on other child-rearing advice, but resources like these merit further attention to understand how the role of parent is defined through religion.

Picturebooks help us see family roles in more complex ways, especially those that women take on. The traditional fourfold assembly (monks and nuns, laymen and laywomen) establishes binaries and, because monks have greater authority than nuns, assumes a gender hierarchy. We might consider how mothers-as-educators creates different dynamics—such as in *Whose Dream Is Longest?,* where the mother serves as the conduit for religious knowledge and practice. Mothers are also more likely to be reading to their children and have greater representation among authors and illustrators—both of these are creative, affective ways of taking ownership of the tradition that may be largely invisible from institutional perspectives. A focus on children also prompts us to consider growth and change not just as part of spiritual biographies but as part of religious sociality. In *Everyone's Mama* the little girl wanted to grow up to be like her mother and like Guanyin; her mother in turn may become a grandmother. Stories like *Shengyan's Naughty Youth* and *Whose Dream Is Longest?* feature siblings. Buddhism is gendered but also generational.

Education

What do families learn together through these picturebooks? Being a Buddhist could be described as requiring a set of competencies: First, there is textual competency—knowledge of the tradition's important scriptures and other literature. Second, ritual or practice competency might include recitation of those same scriptures or the names of the buddhas, other devotional practices, the ability to participate in rituals, and meditation. Third, being Buddhist implies an ethical competency—that one will keep a vegetarian diet, observe the appropriate precepts, and interact with others compassionately. The degree to which one masters these competencies varies by status, with fully ordained monks expected to have the highest level. These skills can be taught formally or informally.

Picturebooks are part of informal, iterative education, rather than a formal curriculum. As I argued in the introduction, we should see picturebooks as engaging in a recursive process of education, rather than one with a clear sequence and benchmarks such as we might find in a program that included examinations. In picturebooks the development of these three competencies happens in a range of ways: Rather than engage with primary texts themselves, young readers learn about stories of monks such as Xuanzang and Ikkyū. What they discover about ritual and practice is through preparatory activities such as tracing the text of the *Heart Sutra* or following rosary-like dots in *Bodhisattva Guanyin, Change, Change, Change!* They learn ethical competency in picturebooks like *I Love Fruits and Vegetables, I Love the Earth,* that prompt them to vegetarianism and environmental action.

Picturebooks in this study also develop what we might call attitudinal competency. This is the ability to see the world in Buddhist ways. As it cultivates perspective-taking and ethical imagination, literature is particularly suited to developing this skill. We see attitudinal competency at work in premodern miracle tales, in which unusual phenomena are interpreted as having Buddhist explanations. Exceptional events are more likely to be written down, but smaller-scale interpretative acts regularly happen in daily life. For example, *Picturebook Heart Sutra* used images and stories to show how everyday experiences could be understood through the philosophical lenses of this text, namely emptiness and illusion of form. Attitudinal competency is also at play in *Whose Dream Is Longest?* When the mother interprets her daughter's dream, she shows how to think about similar occurrences in a Buddhist way. Attitudinal competency connects and facilitates the other competencies, as we see in these two examples. To use the first example in relation to everyday experiences, building on a basic textual competency (the concepts of the *Heart Sutra*) leads to understanding what attitude to take (realizing the emptiness of material objects) and this in turn allows for appropriate ethical action (not stealing other's belongings, for example). In the case of *Whose Dream Is Longest?*, taking a Buddhist attitude toward dreams—rather than just noting their contents—leads to ritual action.

Affinity Work

This attitudinal competency is created through affinity work: connections to a Buddhist worldview are strengthened when its relevance can be seen at home or on the playground. Affinity work refers to those efforts within the noninstitutional space of the home to create and foster ties to Buddhist people, institutions, ideas, and practices so that later encounters feel natural or fated; affinity work is oriented toward the future through an iterative process. To better understand what affinity work is, let us return to the introduction of the *Illustrated Scripture of One Hundred Analogies* (discussed in chapter 2) to see how childhood connections play out over a lifetime. The author of the introduction, Zheng Shiyan, relates fond memories of being taken by his mother as a child to worship the Buddha at Leyin Temple 雷音寺 in Ilan, and the stories he heard there—and as it turns out, those stories were told by none other than Xingyun. Zheng explains that later in life he started reading the *Scripture of One Hundred Analogies* in vernacular (*baihua* 白話) translation, at which point he discovered that many of the stories he had heard when he was younger were drawn from this scripture. Yet further into adulthood, he finds himself arguing for the scripture's value for both adults and children. Zheng has had at least three encounters with the *Scripture of One Hundred Analogies,* each from a different perspective and leading over time to a deepened appreciation of the scripture's value and meaning. Zheng's mother provided the initial connection to the scripture, by bringing him to the temple, which led to a recognition the next time he encountered the text.

Zheng experienced a kind of proto-affinity work: both his mother and Xingyun acted in ways that would foster later appreciation for the stories of the *Scripture of One Hundred Analogies,* and they did so in relatively informal ways. Think about the ways in which a child encountering the picturebook *Scripture of One Hundred Analogies* has a different experience: he or she likely reads it at home, or perhaps in a library. A parent or grandparent might read the book aloud, and the child would have an opportunity to read it again at a different age. The parent or grandparent who brought the book home to the child likely recognized it as a Buddhist scripture or at the very least as a storybook with good moral lessons; the picturebook becomes part of ongoing instruction in character development. What differentiates this from Zheng's mid-century hearing of tales is that it happens within a noninstitutional space (the home rather than the temple) and that parents are central to connecting the child to Buddhism. The picturebook brings religion into family spaces.

Another characteristic of affinity work is conversation. By exploring Buddhist topics with their children—as facilitated through picturebooks—parents model how to integrate those ideas into everyday exchanges. In learning how to interpret the world through Buddhist lenses, children, as formed in these picturebooks, are also learning to interpret *themselves* as Buddhist. Part of understanding oneself as Buddhist comes through vow-making, which we saw as central to both to stories about Xuanzang and in Shengyan's self-narration. Vows are a way of prospectively organizing one's view of life.

Picturebooks represent affinity work as it happens in different settings. The Incense Light books show intergenerational conversations that bring in Buddhist ideas and texts. Shengyan's recounting of his own childhood illustrates how family life can inflect a career in Buddhist service. Stories about young monks like Rāhula suggest ways that affinity work might be read into accounts of the Buddha's own parenting. *My Buddhas and Bodhisattvas* shows how affinities can be formed with family-like interactions—birthday parties, games, picking up litter—with suprahuman figures. Children, too, can build affinities that lead to Buddhist action, as we see especially with the young vegetarians in *I Love Fruits and Vegetables, I Love the Earth.* Even Xingyun's commentary on the *Heart Sutra,* for all its talk of emptiness, offers stories that model the iterative, conversational style of education that creates both affinities to Buddhism and attitudinal competency.

Emotional responses and affective connections are a core part of affinity work; positive feelings help strengthen ties to people (family, religious figures) and institutions. Picturebooks prompt us to further explore the role that fun and pleasure play in Buddhist learning and practice. The experience of reading a picturebook has the potential to be pleasurable: sitting with someone else, looking at appealing illustrations, being invited to touch a page. The role aesthetics plays in affective response could be extended to other areas: How are the pleasures of the materiality present in other aspects of modern Buddhism? How do we account for the aesthetic enjoyment of Tzu Chi consumer packaging or a visit to Dharma Drum Mountain?

Although we can consider literature, family, and education separately, Buddhist picturebooks bring them together as *literature for family education.* Picturebooks present themselves as part of the social life of the family, affordances for parent-child interaction and the work of building affinities to Buddhism. Those interactions are intended to lead to learning, and how that learning takes place—as an aesthetic, bodily, affective experience—is as important as what is learned.

This study opened in a Buddhist bookstore, where I first encountered some of the picturebooks discussed here. The bookstore itself invites us to consider the places of Buddhism in the modern world. Reviewing the books discussed in this study we find Buddhism active outside monasteries and temples; institutional spaces are rarely depicted. *Code Words of the Great*

Teachers deals primarily with historical monks, and we might well expect their biographies to be set in temples and monasteries. Surveying the illustrations, however, we find that they largely focus on people. When Buddhist buildings are pictured, they are often represented by their parts: a bell, a bookshelf, a corridor, or a doorway. The edifice of Buddhism is less important than what goes on within its walls. Buddhism is what people *do*, rather than static spaces.

As I highlighted in the introduction, Robert Orsi characterizes lived religion as making worlds through religious idioms. The world-making in picturebook literature has most often been anchored in the social spaces for children—first domestic, and then moving outward. Consider the other spaces that appear in these picturebooks: Puxian helps a boy clean up his room in a multistory apartment building and then they collect litter in a crowded city. In a field in the countryside, a child steps on an eggplant and mistakes it for a frog. A little girl visits her parents working in a hospital, and readers visit a scientific laboratory to learn more about the newest coronavirus. A car and a kitchen are places for conversations about Buddhism and life. Conserving water in a preschool classroom is part of Buddhist practice. Such places may not be typically associated with Buddhism, but they are places a child might find themselves or could imagine being in; this is "Buddhism of the human realm" (*renjian fojiao*) for young readers. Modern Chinese Buddhism emphasizes the present world as a locus for religious action and intention, and picturebooks show how this approach to Buddhism translates into the everyday lives of families. This is a Buddhicizing of the ordinary, but not in a flattened way that makes everything Buddhist already. Rather, interpreting and behaving in Buddhist ways is an active effort. Placed alongside Buddhist picturebooks themselves, the different locations in which Buddhism takes place in these books should also prompt us to question how we as scholars have privileged certain modes of being Buddhist.

In the context of Taiwan, picturebooks also prompt us to think in more complex ways about the role of laypeople in traditions of Humanistic Buddhism (*renjian fojiao*). Picturebooks are clearly directed at lay audiences, but they also represent broader contemporary attitudes toward education. Huang Shiru writes that the popular assertion that "Buddhism is education" (*fojiao shi jiaoyu* 佛教是教育) entails a relation with contemporary education and consequently downplays ultimate or otherworldly spiritual concerns. This in turn has fostered an environment in which there are many possible routes to Buddhism.[2] The emphasis on education in Humanistic Buddhism not only opens up new paths but also offers new modes of participation: A monk or nun might be a teacher, but so might a parent, librarian, or even a child. Affinity work has allowed us to see the ways that connections to Buddhist traditions might be fostered first outside institutional settings, complicating the hierarchy between monastic and lay. Buddhist history (both modern and premodern) has usually been told almost exclusively from the monastic perspective. Recentering our scholarly endeavors reflects the changing relations between monastic and lay Buddhists in contemporary Taiwan.

Humanistic Buddhism has as a core ethical commitment to the betterment of this world. This has cosmological implications, in that Buddhalands or Pure Lands need not be understood as coterminous with other realms, but can be realized in the here and now. In picturebooks, we see this orientation conveyed through an emphasis on social and environmental action. Yet reading itself represents another form of ethical commitment. For parents, it means spending time with children, sharing attention, and imagining their perspectives. The paratexts show reading as a lifelong process that stitches together more and less experienced readers. Xingyun and Shengyan suggest that reading is not just a matter of text on a page but also a means of relating the past to the present. Reading scriptures and histories through modern perspectives allows the Buddhist tradition to be understood afresh; reading stories is a way to practice religious world-making.

Through what they teach children and how they represent them, picturebooks conceptualize childhoods and family life that are informed by Buddhism. The figure of the child is counterposed to that of the parent, articulating different stages of life, potentialities, and social roles. There are differences among Taiwanese organizations in how Buddhism is presented to young readers: Fo Guang Shan hews most closely to traditional categories in Chinese Buddhism, while Dharma Drum innovates narratives about buddhas, bodhisattvas, and monks. Incense Light stories revolve around open-ended conversations. Tzu Chi has a recognizable commitment to science and often publishes stories that understate their Buddhist or organizational origins. Yet given these differences in approach, Taiwanese Buddhist organizations treat children as part of modern Buddhism, capable of understanding and interpreting Buddhist teachings and bringing them to life in their social world. They do this by providing a literature that addresses them explicitly. Through picturebooks we also see the dynamism and multidimensionality of modern Buddhism, which includes busy parents, scientists and grandmothers, lonely kids and mischievous youngsters—all as Buddhists in the making.

Notes

INTRODUCTION

The first quote, an exchange between the poet Bai Juyi 白居易 (772–846) and the monk Niaoke Daolin 鳥窠道林 (741–824) is from *The Record of Chan Master Yun'e When He Resided at Faxing Temple in Suizhou, Huguang* 雲峨禪師住湖廣隨州法興寺語錄, J. 28, no. B203,182 b20–22; the second is in Marcus, *Show Me a Story!*, 17.

1 Of the hundreds of papers presented there, none had "child," "youth," or "young" in the title. Only one had "family" in the title; six paper titles had the word "woman" or "women." Only one panel was focused on Buddhist laity. "Program for The XVIth Congress of the International Association of Buddhist Studies," available at http://iabsinfo.net/conferences/past-conferences/ (accessed July 16, 2022).

2 Gould and McKay, "Introduction to Bad Buddhism."

3 Orsi, "Is the Study of Lived Religion Irrelevant to the World We Live in?," 172.

4 Hayot, "Bridge Essay," 2.

5 Donald and Zheng, "Chinese Modernisms."

6 McMahan, *The Making of Buddhist Modernism*, 42, 46.

7 McMahan, *The Making of Buddhist Modernism*, 59.

8 Gong, *Uneven Modernity: Literature, Film, and Intellectual Discourse in Postsocialist China*, 2.

9 Ackerman, "Household Religion, Family Religion, and Women's Religion," 127–128.

10 Mai, "The Guanyin Fertility Cult," 178.

11 Teiser, *The Scripture on the Ten Kings*, 10, 76. Murals in the caves at Dunhuang and elsewhere were another way of illustrating scriptures, with written cartouches providing the text. See also Mair's discussion of the relationship between *bianwen* and *bianxiang*, drawing on the scholarship of Paul Demiéville and Kanaoka Shōkō, in Mair, *T'ang Transformation Texts*, esp. 41 and 99.

12 Huang, "Early Buddhist Illustrated Prints," 139–140.

13 Berezkin, "Pictorial Versions of the Mulian Story," 104–105, 110.

14 Eisenstein, *The Printing Revolution*, and *The Printing Press as Agent of Change*.

15 For surveys of printing during this period see Brokaw and Chow, *Printing and Book Culture in Late Imperial China* and McDermott, *A Social History of the Chinese Book*.

16 Pomata, "Observation Rising," 48.

17 See Kiely, "Spreading the Dharma with the Mechanized Press," and Scott, "A Revolution of Ink."

18 These were Wuchang Buddhist Studies Academy (Wuchang Foxue yuan 武昌佛學院) in Wuhan, Minnan Buddhist Studies Academy (Minnan Foxue yuan 閩南佛

學院) in Xiamen, and the Sino-Tibetan Buddhist Studies Institute (Hanzang jiaoli yuan 漢藏教理院) in Chongqing. Taixu had studied at the Jetavana Hermitage, a short-lived academy set up by the Buddhist layman Yang Wenhui 楊文會 (Renshan 仁山, 1837–1911). Yang could be credited with the idea for new types of Buddhist educational institutions—on his contributions in this area, see Travagnin, "Concepts and Institutions," 94–97. One of the earliest accounts of Taixu's contributions is Welch, *The Buddhist Revival in China,* ch. 3. Taixu's reforms are analyzed in Pittman, *Toward a Modern Chinese Buddhism.* See also Ritzinger, *Anarchy in the Pure Land,* ch. 1 for Taixu's early years.

19 Lai, "The Wuchang Ideal," 56. See also Li, "The Practice of Buddhist Education" for a summary of these early academies in the context of contemporary institutions.

20 For an explanation of how the curriculum was divided up, see Travagnin, "Concepts and Institutions," 93.

21 McGuire, "Bringing Buddhism into the Classroom."

22 Borchert, *Educating Monks,* 108.

23 Kaplan, *Monastic Education in Korea,* 141.

24 Chandler, *Establishing a Pure Land,* 119. For the curriculum of the Fo Guang Shan Buddhist College, see Yao and Gombrich, *Chinese Buddhism Today,* 78–83.

25 BLIA is Fo Guang Shan's NGO incorporating both monastics and lay members. Chandler, *Establishing a Pure Land,* 127–129. See also sample illustrations from a test on pp. 128–130.

26 Starling, *Guardians of the Buddhist Home,* 3.

27 Starling, *Guardians of the Buddhist Home,* 18.

28 Starling, *Guardians of the Buddhist Home,* 47.

29 Starling, *Guardians of the Buddhist Home,* 13, 6.

30 Clarke, *Family Matters in Indian Buddhist Monasticisms,* 150.

31 Clarke, *Family Matters in Indian Buddhist Monasticisms,* 162.

32 Nikolajeva, "The Verbal and Visual," 85.

33 Cited in Nikolajeva and Scott, *How Picturebooks Work,* 11.

34 This number is a result of the constraints of modern printing presses, which work in sixteen-page signatures, but thirty-two pages has also come to be "generally regarded as the optimal number for a given picturebook work." Bird and Yokota, "Picturebooks and Illustrated Books," 285.

35 Nikolajeva and Scott, *How Picturebooks Work,* 1.

36 Hao, *Hao huiben ruhe hao?,* 95–99.

37 The Danish scholar Torben Gregersen proposes a four-fold typology of picturebooks: 1) "the exhibit book" or "picture dictionary," in which there is no narrative; 2) "the picture narrative," in which the pictures tell the story with minimal or no text; 3) "the picturebook," in which text and picture carry equal weight; and 4) "the illustrated book," in which the pictures are secondary to the text, which "can exist independently." Described in Nikolajeva and Scott, *How Picturebooks Work,* 6.

38 Kinney, "The Theme of the Precocious Child," 6. Kinney explores what early texts have to say about children and childhood in her *Representations of Childhood.*

39 Gubar, "The Hermeneutics of Recuperation," 299. See also her "Risky Business."

40 Knoepflmacher and Myers, "'Cross-Writing' and the Reconceptualization of Children's Literary Studies," vii.

41 Knoepflmacher and Myers, "'Cross-Writing' and the Reconceptualization of Children's Literary Studies," xi.

42 The term "paratext" was coined by French literary theorist Gerard Genette to refer to the "author's name, a title, a preface, illustrations" and other "accompanying productions" that "present" a text. Genette likens the paratext to a "threshold," as it bridges what is inside and outside the text. He also characterizes them

as a zone "of *transaction:* a privileged place of pragmatics and a strategy, of an influence . . . [that] is at the service of a better reception for the text and a more pertinent reading of it." Genette, *Paratexts,* 1–2.

43 DiLeonardo "The Female World of Cards and Holidays," 442–443.

44 Williams-Oerberg, "Buddhist Ritual as 'Connectionwork'," 489.

45 Williams-Oerberg, "Buddhist Ritual," 495, 497.

46 Literature distribution and discussion, along with devotional activities, have become common lay activities held in Buddhist spaces. Starting in the 2010s, lay Buddhists have also organized meetings in non-temple spaces, facilitated by social media and chat groups; this type of Buddhism is seen as often more authentic than what monastics offer in temples, which might be tainted by state influence or financial interests. Fisher, "From Temples to Teahouses," 44, 51–52.

47 Susana Narotzky defines abstract labor as "human energy and time necessary to reproduce the social totality as a meaningful whole, and this encompasses any collective effort in whatever form it is coordinated." Narotzky is quoted in Sharryn Kasmir, "The Anthropology of Labor," 14.

48 Verchery, "Both Like and Unlike," 4.

49 Eubanks, *Miracles of Book and Body,* 42–43; see also nn. 55–56 on 206–207.

50 Rossmanith et al., 18–19. I draw on Rossmanith's research throughout this paragraph.

PART I: BOOKS

CHAPTER 1: INVENTING BUDDHIST CHILDREN'S LITERATURE

1 David McMahan identifies finding "the locus of a meaningful life . . . not in another realm but in the way this life, everyday life, is lived" as key theme of discourses of modernity. McMahan, *The Making of Buddhist Modernism,* 13.

2 For detailed discussions of this term and its various usages see Pacey, "A Buddhism for the Human World," and Bingenheimer, "Some Remarks on the Usage of Renjian Fojiao." For a recent summary of its key features, see Travagnin, "Humanistic Buddhism."

3 Pittman, *Toward a Modern Chinese Buddhism,* esp. ch. 5.

4 See Ritzinger, *Anarchy in the Pure Land.*

5 Travagnin, "Genealogy and Taxonomy," 184.

6 For a thorough overview of Buddhism in Taiwan, see Jiang, *Taiwan Fojiao shi.* On how religion shapes identity in Taiwan more broadly, see the essays in Katz and Rubinstein, *Religion and the Formation of Taiwanese Identities.*

7 Laliberté, "The Five Worlds of Religious Establishment," 158.

8 To be distinguished from the similarly named Buddhist Association of China, Zhongguo Fojiao xiehui 中國佛教協會. On BAROC, see Jones, *Buddhism in Taiwan,* ch. 5.

9 When Yinshun was accused of being a Communist in 1954, based on his writings about Buddhist utopias, his coerced confession letter went both to the government and to BAROC. Kuo, *Religion and Democracy in Taiwan,* 16–19.

10 Charles B. Jones has called this a period of "pluralization." See Jones, *Buddhism in Taiwan,* ch. 6.

11 On the changing relationship between Buddhist clergy and lay Buddhists in the late twentieth century, see Huang, *Zhanhou Taiwan Fojiao de sengsu guanxi,* esp. 211–224.

12 This is not to say Buddhist organizations abjured all political activities; some advocates of *renjian fojiao* saw it as necessarily political, as Taixu had, and some Buddhist groups began to advocate for political parties or candidates, or for cross-strait relations. See Jiang, *Taiwan Fojiao bainianshi zhi yanjiu,* 448–456.

13 On BAROC and the changes in Buddhist organizations after the end of martial law, see Laliberté, *Politics of Buddhist Organizations,* chs. 2–3. On new media enterprises in Taiwanese Buddhism, see Travagnin, "Charting Religion and Media," 61.

14 Stefania Travagnin has written that "identity" is "a crucial analytical concept in the analysis of religious media in Taiwan." Travagnin, "Charting Religion and Media," 62. This stems in part from Taiwan's colonial history, during which period temples and other religious organizations provided a space for social action and identity formation. See Dawley, *Becoming Taiwanese,* ch. 4. Based on over two decades of tracking through the Election Study Center at National Chengchi University (https://esc.nccu.edu.tw/main.php), a growing percentage of the island's residents identify themselves as Taiwanese, not Chinese, especially among younger segments of the population.

15 Laliberté, "Religion and Politics," 332.

16 For comprehensive treatments of Tzu Chi, see Madsen, *Democracy's Dharma,* 16–50; Huang, *Charisma and Compassion;* Laliberté, *Politics of Buddhist Organizations,* 86–105; Yao, *Taiwan's Tzu Chi as Engaged Buddhism;* and Kan, *Chong du Taiwan Fojiao,* 342–392.

17 Pacey discusses Tzu Chi's relationship with various Christian organizations and figures in *Buddhist Responses,* 188–195.

18 On Fo Guang Shan, see Kan, *Chong du Taiwan Fojiao,* 277–341; Madsen, *Democracy's Dharma,* 51–84; Laliberté, *Politics of Buddhist Organizations,* 66–85; and Chandler, *Establishing a Pure Land on Earth.*

19 On Fagushan, see especially Kan, *Chong du Taiwan Fojiao,* 393–428, and Madsen, *Democracy's Dharma,* 85–103.

20 For a brief history of Zhongtai, see Kan, *Chong du Taiwan Fojiao,* 428–462.

21 Laliberté, *Politics of Buddhism,* 55.

22 Justin Ritzinger's recent work looks at a less prominent, working-class Buddhist organization. See Ritzinger, "Vernacular Modernism." For another study of lay Buddhists in Taiwan, see Guggenmos, *"I believe in Buddhism and Travelling."* See also Huang, *Zhanhou Taiwan Fojiao de sengsu guanxi.*

23 Zhengyan's brother Wang Duanzheng was instrumental in establishing Tzu Chi's media presence. Chen, "Building a Pure Land on Earth," 187. Chen discusses Tzu Chi's media strategies more broadly in this article but does not discuss those aimed specifically at children. For an overview of Fo Guang Shan media endeavors, see Yao and Gombrich, *Chinese Buddhism Today,* 64–67.

24 Zelizer, *Pricing the Priceless Child.*

25 Julia L. Mickenberg and Lynn Vallone, *The Oxford Handbook of Children's Literature,* 16. They draw on the work of Vivian Zelizer in her *Pricing the Priceless Child* to make the point about the shift from child labor to emotional value.

26 The "great clan" was fundamentally a patriarchal institution, and in contrast, the conjugal family was the form associated with the West. However, unlike Western nations, where the nuclear family carried with it an expectation of privacy and autonomy, in China reformers continued a tradition that understood the family unit within a moral economy that linked the individual to the state. Glosser, *Chinese Visions of Family and State,* 3–4, 21–22.

27 On fetal education see Stevens, "Hygienic Bodies and Public Mothers: The Rhetoric of Reproduction," as well as Richardson, "The Nation *in Utero.*" Although some reformers criticized fetal education as superstitious, it remained popular enough to be put to new uses. On a woman's role in maintaining the hygiene and social space of the home, see Schneider, *Keeping the Nation's House* and Af Sandberg, "Room for Improvement."

28 See Tillman, *Raising China's Revolutionaries* The stress on citizenship was a way of modernizing the socialization of children. Along with practical

skills, inculcating proper social behavior was prioritized in early texts on child-rearing. On the *Li ji* 禮記 as a source for this perspective, see Hsiung, *A Tender Voyage,* 106.

29 Zarrow, *Educating China,* 38, 86–87.

30 Cai, "Power, Politeness, and Print," esp. 42 and 53–54.

31 Fricke, Chang, and Yang, "Historical and Ethnographic Perspectives," 48.

32 Lan, "Compressed Modernity and Glocal Entanglement," 535–536.

33 Freedman, Chang, Sun, and Weinstein, "The Fertility Transition in Taiwan," 278; Branigan, "Taiwan offers baby bonus"; and Hsueh, "A Profile of the Taiwanese Family." See also Chu and Yu, *Understanding Chinese Families,* ch. 3. There has been a slight increase in the birthrate in recent years, but it is still well below replacement.

34 Cohen, *House United, House Divided,* xiii; Tang, *Urban Chinese Families.*

35 Television brought some of these tensions to rural communities. Wolf, *Women and the Family in Rural Taiwan,* 69.

36 For a brief survey of Taiwan's educational system, see Kagan, "Taiwan—Education System." Education through junior high school has been compulsory since 1968.

37 Thornton, "Theoretical Mechanisms of Family Change," 91.

38 Lan, "Compressed Modernity and Glocal Entanglement," 541–543.

39 Care provided by grandparents increased in the period from 1993 to 2007; by 2007 almost one in five grandparents were caring for grandchildren in some capacity. Early retirement, facilitated by National Health Insurance (NHI), seems to have had a positive effect. Tsai et al., "Evolution in Intergenerational Exchanges," 2–5. Grandparental involvement has a positive effect, especially for those families in which the grandparents and grandchildren live together for an extended period. Pong and Chen, "Co-resident Grandparents," 126–127.

40 Tamis-LeMonda et al., "Childrearing Values in Greece, Taiwan, and the United States," 187.

41 Lan, *Raising Global Families,* ch. 2, esp. 65.

42 Lan, *Raising Global Families,* 51. Lan here develops the idea of "pathway consumption" put forth by Allison Pugh, who explains it as spending not on consumer goods, but on "opportunities that shape children's trajectories" in a combination of "aspiration and hope." Pugh, *Longing and Belonging,* 178.

43 Lan, *Raising Global Families,* 52–59, esp. 58–59.

44 Lan, *Raising Global Families,* 98. This paragraph draws on ch. 3.

45 Religious affiliation seems to influence parental attitudes toward educational attainment, with Taiwanese Protestants having the highest aspirations for their children. Zhai and Woodberry, "Religion and Educational Ideals."

46 For one example of this kind of text, see Bai, *Shaping the Ideal Child,* 62–63.

47 Works in this vein include books like *A Program of Elementary Learning* (*Xiaoxue richeng* 小學日程), by Chen Hu 陳瑚 (1613–1675) and *Timely Teachings for Children* (*Mengyang shijiao* 蒙養詩教) by Hu Yuan 胡淵 (active sixteenth c.). Another work, *Stories from a Diary* (*Riji gushi* 日記故事), was an earlier text revised by a teacher in the sixteenth century; it was then illustrated with woodblock prints that occupied the upper portion of each page. Bai, *Shaping the Ideal Child,* 64–65.

48 On the uses of filial piety stories in medieval China, see Knapp, *Selfless Offspring.*

49 Chen, *The Sino-Japanese War and Youth Literature,* 15–16.

50 Boretti, "Purposeful Leisure," 890.

51 Bai, "Making Learning Enjoyable," 387. One example of early efforts at edutainment was the introduction of flashcards with pictures in the early twentieth century: the Commercial Press of Shanghai offered a set of flashcards with

colored images on one side and simple characters on the other. Bai, "Making Learning Enjoyable," 383, image on 386. On character recognition as a distinct step in acquiring literacy, see Yu, "Character Recognition."

52 Jones, *Developmental Fairy Tales,* 113–116. (Quoted phrase appears on p. 116).

53 Bi and Fang, "Childhoods: Childhoods in Chinese Children's Texts," 59.

54 Xu, "Imagination: Imaginations of the Nation," 70–71.

55 Xu, "Imagination: Imaginations of the Nation," 71–72.

56 See Peng and Chu, "Japan's Colonial Policies," for a study of primary education in the last decade of colonial rule.

57 Qiu, *Taiwan jindai ertong wenxue shi,* 49–54. Qiu covers this period in the history of Taiwanese children's literature in detail.

58 Qiu, *Taiwan jindai ertong wenxue shi,* ch. 3. On poetry for children in China during this period, see Shen, "Transcending the Nationalist Conception of Modernity."

59 The flourishing of children's literature during this period was connected with Taiwan's New Literature movement, modeled on the May Fourth movement. See Chang, "Taiwanese New Literature and the Colonial Context."

60 Lin, *Ertong wenxue lunji* 2, 206.

61 Lin, *Ertong wenxue lunji* 2, 212.

62 Wu, "Access to Books Matters," 685–686. See also the discussion of Leaf and Sattley's tour in Lin, *Ertong wenxue lunji* 2, 213.

63 Wu, "Access to Books Matters," 686–687.

64 Wu, "Postcoloniality, Globalization, and Transcultural Production," esp. 124–125.

65 Both these stories are discussed in Wei, "Shaping a Cultural Identity," 73–74. Wei provides a good overview of the development of picturebooks in postwar Taiwan.

66 Translated in Wu, "Postcoloniality, Globalization, and Transcultural Production," 125. Original passage in Hong, *Taiwan ertong wenxue shi,* 4–5.

67 Wu, "Postcoloniality, Globalization, and Transcultural Production," 125.

68 Wu, "Access to Books Matters," 684–685.

69 Lin, *Ertong wenxue lunji* 2, 219. Hong (1913–1987) was an entrepreneur who made his fortune in electronics. For an excellent survey of children's literature of the postwar period, focusing on themes of identity as shaped by nation, home, and place, see Wu, *Zhuti, xingbie, difang.*

70 Bradbury and Liu, "Everywhere a Children's Book," 242. Hsin Yi is an example of a publisher that centers on Taiwanese authors and illustrators, and emphasizes "child-centered philosophies of child development." Seitz, "Growth of Children's Book Publishing in Taiwan," 216.

71 Lin, *Ertong wenxue lunji* 2, 234.

72 Taylor, "The Children's Book Market," 36. The number of new titles in children's literature (7,718) was still behind that in comic books (8,920), popular among all ages.

73 Huang, "Go Beyond Borders," 52.

74 As with playing with their children, this seems to be a skill that many parenting guides assume mothers and fathers lack; in fact, expectations about what parents do with their children (and how they fail to meet this expectation) can be tied to the rise of "intensive parenting."

75 The authors recommend parents pre-read all books, going through a four-stage process: first, they should look at the cover, title page, publication data, and so forth to establish what kind of book it is. Next, parents should read through the book and look at the pictures, thinking about mood and tone. This is followed by considering how the words and images might be conveying different information, and how these two elements might be working together. Finally, parents should consider the abstract ideas conveyed by the illustrations. Xie

and Lu, *Baobao ting gushi,* 10, 74–76, 77–89. There is also pushback to this approach: one mother profiled in a 2019 parenting magazine talks about learning to let go of her anxiety that children should learn from reading together. Instead, she advocates reading without purpose (*mudi* 目的), and not being concerned if young children want to run around or don't want to read page by page. Huang, "Bu dai mudi de gongdu," 110–111.

76 In one demonstration, one mother read aloud to her children, followed by questions. Another combined guided reading with reading aloud, while a third mother covered up the words entirely and let their children tell a story based on the pictures. Zhang, *Kanjian huiben de liliang,* 172. This parenting discourse is aimed primarily at mothers. Phrases such as "parent-child" (*qinzi* 親子) and "fathers and mothers" (*fumu* 父母 or *babamama* 爸爸媽媽) are used frequently, but most of the authors of these type of guides are women who draw on their own experience as mothers. Reading picturebooks is primarily part of a mother's role.

77 Some authors want to look beyond the family. The author of *Using Picturebooks to Talk about Important Matters with Children,* Xing Jiahui 幸佳慧, sees children's books as deeply tied to civilization (*wenming* 文明) and as a source for global ethics. Xing, *Yong huiben gen haizi tan zhongyao de shi,* 8.

78 Katz, "Chen Hailiang's Vision of Buddhist Family Life."

79 For more on the *Three Character Classic,* see Bai, *Shaping the Ideal Child,* 27, 139; Liu, "The Classical Chinese Primer," 192.

80 Chen also quotes Yinguang: "The essential way of regulating the state and bringing peace to the world lies in education within the home, and mothers assume the better part of education within the home." For both these men, Buddhist education is to be undertaken by the women of a household. Chen, *Zaijia xuefo yaodian,* 321.

81 The prominent author Lu Xun admired the *Scripture of One Hundred Analogies,* and donated money to have one hundred copies of it printed. Even though he used a Buddhist press for this project, Lu Xun deleted the concluding sections that promoted Buddhist ideas. Later adaptations of the scripture include *New Explanations of the Scripture of One Hundred Analogies* (*Baiyu jing xinshi* 百喻經新釋), published in Shanghai in 1956, and *The Wealthy Old Man Builds a Three-Story House: Fables from India* (*Fuweng zao sancenglou: Indu yuyan* 富翁造三层楼：印度寓言), published in 1957. For studies of the original, consult Harbsmier, "Reading the *One Hundred Parables Sūtra,*" and Lo, "The Drama of Numskulls."

82 Zhou Huizhu writes that *Collected Illustrations for Protecting Life* has "long been considered the first illustrated book suitable for young and old alike." See Zhou, "Fojiao ertong duwu."

83 Feng later pledged to create a new volume every ten years, adding another ten paintings until he reached one hundred for the occasion of Hongyi's one hundredth birthday. Hongyi was both one of the most important monks of his time and an accomplished aesthete. Feng was an ambivalent Buddhist, taking from the tradition a kind of "philosophy of life" and a "deep feeling of sympathy for all (living) things." Harbsmeier, *The Cartoonist Feng Zikai,* 87. On Feng's life and art, see also Barmé, *An Artistic Exile.*

84 Christoph Harbsmeier points out the similarity between one of Feng's illustrations of a boy with an ox, and a Ming dynasty woodblock of the Buddhist oxherding series. Harbsmeier, *The Cartoonist Feng Zikai,* 114–115.

85 The first volume was published in 1928, in Shanghai, by Kaiming shudian 開明書店; it was republished the following year by Foxue shuju 佛學書局, also in Shanghai. Guangming she 光明社 is given as the publisher in 1930. The next volume, under the title *Further Collected Illustrations for Protecting Life* (*Xu husheng huaji* 續護生畫集), was published in 1940 by Kaiming and Foxue. The

two volumes were published together by the Chinese Society for the Protection of Animals 中國保護動物會 in 1946, based in Shanghai. In 1950, the third volume was published, by Dafalun shuju 大法輪書局, also in Shanghai. By 1960, attitudes toward Buddhism had changed on the mainland, and the fourth volume was published in Singapore, followed several years later in Taiwan. There are also undated versions from Hong Kong.

86 Hong, "Taiwan fojiao tuhuashu wojian wosi," 131–132.

87 For this section on Ci'en, I want to recognize the research assistance of Chris Rowe. Kaizheng was born into a farming family in Gaoxiong; his lay name was Huang Jinzhu 黃金柱. Exposed to Buddhism as a child, he worked at an emergency center after the end of Japanese colonial rule; this exposed him to the many types of human suffering. The head of the center was a devout Buddhist, and Kaizheng learned more about the religion from him, eventually leading to taking monastic vows. The early decades of his career were focused on founding and heading a series of temples, but after a back injury in 1969, Kaizheng turned his attention to cultural and educational activities. This summary of Kaizheng's career is drawn from his entry in the Digital Museum of Buddhism in Taiwan, part of the Digital Library and Museum of Buddhist Studies published online by the Research Center for Digital Humanities, National Taiwan University. See: http://buddhism.lib.ntu.edu.tw/museum/formosa/index-people.html, accessed January 21, 2021.

88 Lin, *Ertong wenxue lunji* 2, 225. See also the entry on Lin Shimin in *Foguang da cidian*.

89 Hong, "Taiwan fojiao tuhuashu wojian wosi," 131–132.

90 Hong, "Taiwan fojiao tuhuashu wojian wosi," 132–134.

91 Huang, "Go Beyond Borders," 55, 62–63. The government contributes to global promotion as well, with the Ministry of Culture highlighting translated Taiwanese literature, including picturebooks, on the "Books from Taiwan" website: https://en.taicca.tw/ (accessed July 20, 2022).

CHAPTER 2: ONCE I HAVE HEARD A STORY

1 Lopez, *The Heart Sutra Explained,* 7; Nattier, "The *Heart Sutra,*" 157. Although later Avalokiteśvara / Guanyin is most commonly represented as female, here the bodhisattva is male, and my pronoun use reflects this.

2 Muller and Wang, "Wu yun."

3 McRae, "Ch'an Commentaries on the *Heart Sutra,*" 87.

4 Lusthaus, "The *Heart Sutra* in Chinese Yogācāra," 60. Kuiji's commentary is titled *Appraisal of the Profundity of the Heart of the Perfection of Wisdom Scripture* (*Banruoboluomiduo xinjing youzan* 般若波羅密多心經幽贊, T. 33, no. 1710).

5 Lusthaus, "The *Heart Sutra* in Chinese Yogācāra," 73–74.

6 Cook, "Fa-tsang's Brief Commentary," 170–172, 178–181. Cook's translation of the commentary follows his explanatory introduction. Fazang's commentary is titled *A Brief Commentary on the Heart of the Perfection of Wisdom Scripture* (*Banruoboluomiduo xinjing lueshu* 般若波羅密多心經略疏, T. 33, no. 1712).

7 McRae, "Ch'an Commentaries on the *Heart Sutra,*" 91–98.

8 McRae, "Ch'an Commentaries on the *Heart Sutra,*" 101–102.

9 Excerpts of these commentaries, along with others, are included in a supplement to Xingyun and Nan, *Banruo lianhua chuchu kai.*

10 Xuanzang is a popular subject for stories for all ages, and the next chapter considers how this Tang monk has been represented in children's literature.

11 Nattier, "The *Heart Sutra,*" 194. The preceding paragraph offers a very brief summary of her detailed analysis of the texts.

12 Xingyun, *Huiben xinjing,* unpaginated (7).

13 Treating the water of the ocean as a metaphor for the mind appears in the *Laṅkāvatāra Sūtra*. There the storehouse consciousness (the deepest layer of consciousness) is the still water, while the activity of the lower consciousnesses is the waves. Another form of this metaphor appears in the *Awakening of Faith,* in which a pure or still mind is agitated by ignorance to form waves. The Huayan 華嚴 school took this metaphor further: Dushun 杜順 (557–640) used the interaction of water and waves to clarify the interrelationship between principle (*li* 理) and phenomena (*shi* 事). Another Huayan monk, Fazang, extended this to argue that phenomenal reality (waves) emerges out of Thusness (*zhenru* 真如), or the ultimate nature of things. Lai, "Chinese Buddhist Causation Theories," 250–251; Van Norden and Jones, "Huayan Buddhism"; Lai, "Ch'an Metaphors," 247–248.

14 For the former, see T. 8, no. 235, 752b28–9; for the latter see T. 14, no. 474, 521b2–7.

15 Xingyun, *Huiben xinjing,* unpaginated (9).

16 Xingyun, *Huiben xinjing,* unpaginated (11).

17 Appleton, "A Place for the Bodhisatta," 113. Appleton later demonstrates that nineteenth-century scholars of Buddhism saw them as sources for information about local culture, and without value as literature, sometimes denigrating them as not truly Buddhist (118–119). Katherine Bowie describes how local politics and social conditions have shaped presentations of the *Vessantra Jātaka* in twentieth-century Southeast Asia. Bowie, "The Historical Vicissitudes." On *jātaka* tales in contemporary Thailand, see McDaniel, "Superheroes and Slapstick," 294–295.

18 Appleton, "A Place for the Bodhisattva," 115.

19 The parallel with fairy tales is made by Carlson and Burk, "The ABC's of Enlightenment."

20 Derris, "Picturing Buddhism," 210. Along with their adaptability, these qualities made *jātakas* appealing source texts for Western authors and illustrators from the early decades of the twentieth century; Noor Inayat Khan's *Twenty Jātaka Tales,* published in 1939, is an example.

21 The preface is repeated in each of the twenty volumes. See, for example, Hong, *Bange tongqian.*

22 Huang, *Duoduo de yang,* unpaginated.

23 Desblache, "Animal Leaders and Helpers," 78.

24 In 1956, *A New Elucidation of the Scripture of One Hundred Analogies* was published in Shanghai. Editor Zheng Shifeng 鄭拾風 (1920–1996) notes that while it is a thoroughly Buddhist text, it is also one with the characteristics of a fable (*yuyan*); rewriting it to be simple and direct allows the text to have educational value in the present. Zheng also explains that these stories were first published with their illustrations in a manga monthly and are being republished because they were so well received. *A New Elucidation of the Scripture of One Hundred Analogies,* although in simple language, is not intended for children. Commentary after the stories suggest broader social and political readings—through the use of terminology such as "dogmatists" (*jiaotiao zhuyi zhe* 教條主義者) and five-year-plan (*wunian jihua* 五年計畫)—even as the illustrations are comic and with colorful appeal. Zheng, *Baiyujing xinshi,* unpaginated preface, 15–16, 25–26.

25 Xingyun, *Banruoxinjing de shenghuo guan,* 9.

26 This comment follows a story about an exchange between the eminent Song dynasty literatus and Buddhist layman Su Shi 蘇軾 (1037–1101) and his teacher, the Chan monk Foyin 佛印 (1032–1098). Su Shi, trying to be clever, tells his teacher his meditation posture makes him look like a pile of cow dung. To his disappointment, this fails to get a rise out of Foyin. Xingyun, *Banruoxinjing de shenghuo guan,* 78–79.

27 Closely paraphrased from Xingyun, *Huiben xinjing,* unpaginated (14).
28 A larger set of eighty-two fables titled *Yishi Yuyan* 意拾喻言 (1840)—with more fatalistic and pessimistic morals—was the collaborative effort of Robert Thom (1807–1846), an employee of a British trading company, and his Chinese language teacher, who appeared under an pseudonym. Tao, "Yishi yuyan," 2–20.
29 Xingyun, *Huiben xinjing,* unpaginated (16)
30 Ye, "Xingyun Dashi *Huiben xinjing,*" 111, 115. Bamboo is like the plantain tree, which also has a hollow center; the plantain or banana tree is one of the ten examples of other dependence in the *Vimalakīrti Sūtra.* See also Lopez, *Elaborations on Emptiness,* 144.
31 Ye, "Xingyun Dashi *Huiben xinjing,*" 111, 114.
32 Xingyun, *Huiben xinjing,* unpaginated (19).
33 The monk was renowned as a vinaya master, who believes that the toad (another difference) was full of eggs. Instead of being unable to eat, the monk dreams that one hundred frogs come to ask for his life. *Guzunsu yulu* 古尊宿語錄 j. 32, X 68, no. 1315, 207b12–20. Translated in Cleary, *Instant Zen,* 25–26.
34 For families in children's books as models for real families, see chapter 6.
35 As with previous sets of illustrations, there are visual parallels that link the pond in this story with the clearing in the reeds of the one previous.
36 Xingyun, *Huiben xinjing,* unpaginated (22).
37 In Chinese the mantra is 唵嘛呢叭彌吽, with the final character pronounced *hong* in modern Mandarin. The old woman has overlooked the mouth radical in the final character, and is reciting *niu* 牛, the word for cow.
38 Xingyun, *Huiben xinjing,* unpaginated (22).
39 Nan grew up with a rigorous education in the Classics and joined the military as a young man. In the early 1940s he left the military to pursue the study of Buddhism. He later fled to Taiwan with the Guomindang and taught there for half a century before returning to the Suzhou area late in life. Nan sets the story in Tibet and explains that the woman has lost both her husband and son, and so lives alone. Believing her misfortune and poverty are due to sin, she has been reciting for thirty years to expiate it. The visiting monk stops by her hut because it is radiating light and he assumes that a person of great attainment must live there. She is devastated when she learns she has been reciting incorrectly, but grateful that she still has time to change. The monk looks back after he leaves, and sees the hut is no longer aglow. After he tells the old woman she can recite as before, the hut glows once again. Ye, "Xingyun Dashi *Huiben xinjing,*" 74–76.
40 Foguang editorial team, *Sida pusa tuwenshu* 1, 12.
41 Ye, "Xingyun Dashi *Huiben xinjing,*" 78.
42 Xingyun, *Huiben xinjing,* unpaginated (25).
43 Stuart Chandler observes that "Fo Guang Shan as a place and Fo Guang Shan as institution are so closely associated with him that it is impossible to speak of either without reference to his activities, values, and ideals." Chandler, *Establishing a Pure Land on Earth,* 28.
44 Madsen, *Democracy's Dharma,* 65–66. For longer studies of Fo Guang Shan, see Madsen, *Democracy's Dharma,* 51–84; Laliberté, *Politics of Buddhist Organizations,* 66–85; and Chandler, *Establishing a Pure Land on Earth.*
45 Fu, *Chuan deng,* 39; Fu, *Handing Down the Light,* 36–37.
46 Fu, *Chuan deng,* 69–70; Fu, *Handing Down the Light,* 57–59.
47 Fu, *Chuan deng,* 112; Fu, *Handing Down the Light,* 95.
48 Work on the Fo Guang Buddhist Canon began in 1977 and is ongoing; Xingyun appointed nuns to carry out the work, a first in compilations of the Chinese Buddhist canon. Yikung, "The *Foguang Buddhist Canon,*" 207–208, 218. See Yao and Gombrich, *Chinese Buddhism Today,* 64, for the creation of literature as one of the four guidelines of Fo Guang Shan.

49 Quoted in Pacey, "Eminence and Edutainment," 80.
50 Xianghai's mission statement quotes Xingyun on the importance of reading as part of Buddhist formation. "Xianghai wenhua," accessed June 13, 2022 at https://gandhabooks.com/?page_id=886.
51 Although not a term Howard Gardner uses, EQ is linked to inter- and intrapersonal intelligences, part of the multiple intelligences discussed in chapter 6.
52 Xingyun, *Huiben xinjing,* unpaginated (1–2).
53 This movement is led by Wang Caigui 王財貴 (b. 1949), who has sought to bring classical Chinese, premodern texts, and traditional pedagogy into the contemporary age, framing his efforts in part as a response to a weak public education system. For explanations of how young people should study the classic texts, see Wang et al., *Dujing jiaoyu lilun yu shiwu,* and Wang, *Ertong dujing jiaoyu shuoming shouce.*
54 Hao, *Kongzi shuo,* back cover.
55 Landy, *How to Do Things with Fictions,* 10, 59.

CHAPTER 3: MODERNIZING XUANZANG

1 This description is based on Zheng, *Dashi mima A,* 112–119.
2 In this emphasis Huijiao follows Baochang. Kieschnick, "Buddhism: Biographies of Buddhist Monks," 541, 543
3 Huijiao used ten categories: translators, exegetes, wonderworkers, meditators, vinaya specialists, those who made bodily sacrifices, sutra-reciters, fundraisers, sutra teachers, and proselytizers. Wright, "Biography and Hagiography" argues that Huijiao wished to convince social elites who were familiar with the conventions of secular biographies. For a critique of Wright's distinction between elite and non-elite readers see Shinohara, "Biographies of Eminent Monks."
4 Kotyk, "Chinese State and Buddhist Historical Sources," 520. For a recent biography of the monk, see Brose, *Xuanzang.*
5 Kotyk, "Chinese State and Buddhist Historical Sources," 529.
6 Deeg, "Show Me the Land," 103.
7 Kotyk, "Chinese State and Buddhist Historical Sources," 530–531.
8 Dudbridge, *The Hsi-yu Chi,* ch. 2, cited in Wong, "The Making of a Saint," 71.
9 Zhang, *Xuanzang,* 1. This is an early reader, with minimal illustrations.
10 Moloughney, "*Monkey* and the Journey Back to Paradise," 224.
11 Although a fuller discussion of Xuanzang is beyond the scope of this chapter, Benjamin Brose has been exploring modern interpretations of the Tang monk. See his "Resurrecting Xuanzang."
12 Wong, "The Making of a Saint," 46.
13 Wong, "The Making of a Saint," 58.
14 Kim, "An Icon in Motion," 8.
15 Wong, "The Making of a Saint," 68–9.
16 Victor Mair has argued that many images of itinerant monks are plausibly "transformation performers" and cannot be pilgrims to India because the texts that they carry are in scroll form, whereas texts from India would have been in flat leaves, something artists at Dunhuang and other Silk Road sites certainly would have known. Mair, "The Origins of an Iconographical Form, 30–31.
17 Kim, "An Icon in Motion," 2, 13.
18 As Brose has noted, in the international sphere Xuanzang "has become the bearer of China's best intentions," akin to Confucius. Brose, *Xuanzang,* 255.
19 Guoli bianze guan, *Shenghuo yu lunli,* vol. 4, 64–70.
20 Guoli bianze guan, *Shenghuo yu lunli,* vol. 2, 70–74. Very few students will go on to be monks, but many more of them will be exchange students.
21 The Ming admiral Zheng He 鄭和 (1371–ca. 1433) would seem to be a better fit with the other three explorers featured.

22 Lin, *Wanli qujing lu,* unpaginated (26–27).
23 Lin, *Wanli qujing lu,* unpaginated (19).
24 Farrelly, "Buddhism and Books." In the mid-1990s Lin divorced his wife and married a much younger woman; this significantly damaged his reputation, and he attempted to rebuild his career in the People's Republic of China.
25 Lin, *Wanli qujing lu,* unpaginated (2). The text starts on the verso of the title page, so I have considered the title page to be page 1. The page numbers cited use this count.
26 In Zhipan's biography, however, this anecdote comes at the end, after Xuanzang has returned (T. 2035, 49: 295a4–7).
27 Lin, *Wanli qujing lu,* unpaginated (5). "Central plains" translates *zhongtu* 中土, which can also be translated as "China."
28 This series also includes a later volume of stories about the Buddha's ten closest disciples, a natural group. See Lin, *Shi da dizi.*
29 Lin, *Zhongguo weida de chujia ren,* 2.
30 This is the first line in the *Xiaojing.* Confucius asks Zengzi to be seated for his discourse on filiality.
31 Lin, *Zhongguo weida de chujia ren xia,* 4–5.
32 T. 2053: 221c1–7.
33 Levering, "The Precocious Child in Chinese Buddhism," 142. See the following chapter for a longer discussion of the childhood of monks.
34 Bai, *Shaping the Ideal Child,* 121. These models of exceptional childhood would seem to leave little room for play and silliness. See also Bakken, *The Exemplary Society,* for a discussion of how textual exemplars provide cultural scripts for imitation.
35 Lin, *Zhongguo weida de chujia ren xia,* 7.
36 Lin, *Zhongguo weida de chujia ren xia,* 19. Yan Di 炎帝 and Huang Di 黃帝 are mythical rulers that are considered the ancestors of Han people.
37 Fo Guang Shan has also published a fifty-one-volume series of the biographies of eminent monks in comic book form, under the title *Fojiao gaoseng manhua quanji* 佛教高僧漫畫全集. As these are intended for older readers, and are not in picturebook format, I will not consider this series here. Note, however, that it does not include a biography for Xuanzang.
38 Note that this set of eight schools is different from that of the eight schools of Buddhism in Nara, Japan.
39 Shih, "Modern Religious Tourism in Taiwan," 228. This set of stone statues sits near a set of statues of the eighteen arhats. None have color, distinguishing them from traditional statuary of religious figures.
40 The cover notes that they were in "adverse circumstances" (*nijing* 逆境), and an announcement of their publication lauds the monks for their "fearless spirit that embodied dedication and self-sacrifice in pursuit of the way." "Foguang wen hua *Si da pusa, Bazong zushi* tuwenshu" 佛光文化《四大菩薩》、《八宗祖師》圖文書, https://www.fgs.org.tw/news/news_content.aspx?news_no=20171027000002, accessed June 25, 2020.
41 Foguang, *Bazong zushi tuwenshu,* 13.
42 Foguang, *Bazong zushi tuwenshu,* 15–18.
43 T. 2053: 233c23–234b9; T. 2060: 449c10–c21; a translation of the former can be found in Li, *Biography of the Tripiṭaka Master,* 76–78. See also Brose, *Xuanzang,* 35.
44 Lin, *Zhongguo weida de chujia ren xia,* 7.
45 Lewis, *Sanctioned Violence,* 24.
46 For the former see Katz, *Divine Justice,* 53 and 74; examples of the latter are very numerous.
47 Fruh, "Promising's Neglected Siblings," 868.

48 Yu, "A New Chan (Zen) School in Taiwan."
49 Hao, "Nande yijian de yitao haoshu," 6.
50 "Not Just Kid Stuff," *Taiwan Today,* April 2, 2002, https://taiwantoday.tw/news.php?unit=20,29,35,45&post=24793, accessed January 8, 2019.
51 Hong Wenqiong believes that this is the primary aim of most Chinese-English Buddhist children's books. In this case, I believe that the vocabulary lists at the back suggest the opposite—that this is to assist English-language learning.
52 The importance of English as a language connecting Taiwan to the global economy is underscored by the decision in 2001 to begin English-language instruction in the primary grades. However, according to a study published in 2011, even this level of commitment to English-language acquisition was found wanting by parents: nearly three-quarters of fifth grade families surveyed also enrolled their children in extracurricular English lessons. Chen, "Parents' Perspectives," 206, 212.
53 The English translation in the book elides the doubling, in favor of "A Determined Explorer," which disconnects *jianqiang* from "adamant."
54 Zheng, *Dashi mima A,* 103.
55 Zheng, *Dashi mima A,* 104. Unless indicated otherwise, passages from the story are translations from the Chinese text. As here, often the Chinese text has more detail than the accompanying English translation.
56 T. 2053, 50: 223b–c3; translated in Li, *Biography of the Tripiṭaka Master,* 22–23.
57 Kotyk, "Chinese State and Buddhist Historical Sources," 530–531.
58 Zheng, *Dashi mima A,* 114.
59 Zheng, *Dashi mima A,* 116.
60 *Jueshi* can also be translated as "hunger strike," although that may be too modern in tone for the context. Zheng, *Dashi mima A,* 120.
61 T. 2053, 50: 225b11.
62 Stevenson, "A Vow for the Times," 2.
63 The earliest collections of monastic biographies were gender-specific (all monks or all nuns), but late imperial collections of Buddhist biographies sometimes mix men and women, clergy and laity; men usually dominated.
64 Heyu specializes in modernizations of the Classics, both Buddhist and Confucian. These two books are illustrated but intended for older children or teens. The preface talks about the importance of knowledge, and the need for models, and individual accounts hew closely to the format of standard biographies. Wu, *Lidai gaoseng jushi zhuan,* 2–3.
65 Shengyan, "Dashi de mima," 4. The brief preface appears on the same page in every volume of the series. Each volume includes multiple prefaces that serve both to offer endorsements of the work, as well as frame the objectives of these stories for parents. Other prefaces reflect different areas of expertise: there is one by an executive of a charitable foundation who is also a mother, the head of a major children's book publisher (considered above), and a psychologist.
66 I thank Wendy Swartz for her comments that helped me better formulate the significance of Shengyan's pairing of terms.
67 Shengyan, "Dashi de mima," 4.

PART II: KIDS

CHAPTER 4: NAUGHTY LITTLE MONKS

1 These vignettes are drawn from Shengyan, *Shengyan Fashi de wanpi tongnian.*
2 Warner, *Six Myths of Our Time,* 56.
3 Levering, "The Precocious Child in Chinese Buddhism," 142.
4 However, bad monks and nuns are a popular topic in late imperial literature meant for entertainment. See, for example, Wu, "Sex in the Cloister," and Goldman, "The Nun Who Wouldn't Be."

5 On "precocious 'Buddhist-ness'" see the discussion in Jensen, "Rhetorical Uses of the Exemplary Child Trope," 75–78.
6 Zheng, *Dashi mima E,* 99
7 Zheng, *Dashi mima D,* 13
8 Zheng, *Dashi mima F,* 87.
9 Zheng, *Dashi mima F,* 56.
10 Beauvais, *The Mighty Child,* 18.
11 As Beauvais puts it, "From the point of view of the adult, the child is always doing something wrong with their time." Beauvais, *The Mighty Child,* 63.
12 Murray, "The Childhood of Gods and Sages," 114–123.
13 As Sasson notes, "the very idea of childhood assumes a period of development and transformation that is not necessarily applicable to the Buddha's hagiography." Sasson, "The Buddha's 'Childhood'," 75.
14 Crosby, "The Inheritance of Rāhula," 108.
15 Crosby, "The Inheritance of Rāhula," 108.
16 Meeks, "Imagining Rāhula," 135–136.
17 Shayne Clarke describes vinaya as presenting an "'in-house' vision of what monks and nuns should and were thought to do." Clarke, *Family Matters,* 11.
18 T. 23, no. 1442, 760b16–761a1. A portion of the beginning section is translated in Anālayo, "The Buddha and His Son," 270. See also T. 1, no. 26, 436a13–b27.
19 Anālayo, "The Buddha and His Son," 271.
20 See discussion in Crosby, "The Inheritance of Rāhula," 114–115. She notes that one commentary has the Buddha telling Rāhula novices shouldn't indulge in animal stories, while also acknowledging their appeal.
21 "Sheijia de xiao haizi zhemme pi," in Zheng, *Dashi mima H,* 22. This series is bilingual and the difference between the Chinese and the English can be illuminating: here, the English specifies that it is the "inner self" that is polluted.
22 Blair, "When Sad is Good," 305.
23 For brief surveys of Ikkyū's life, see Fremerman, "Ikkyū," and Buswell and Lopez, *The Princeton Dictionary of Buddhism,* 371. More sustained treatments of his background and biography can be found in Arntzen, *Ikkyū and the Crazy Cloud Anthology,* 3–5, and Sanford, *Zen-Man Ikkyū,* 1–68.
24 Zheng, *Dashi mima A,* 35.
25 Curley, "Zen-Boy Ikkyū," esp. 339–341.
26 Kashiwagi, "Practices of Manabi in School," 129–130.
27 Nakano, "Who Initiates a Global Flow?," 234.
28 Nakano, "Shared Memories." Nakano observes that Asian parents tend to prefer American cartoons for their children, but teenagers gravitate toward Japanese characters. Nakano, "Who Initiates a Global Flow?," 232.
29 The Chinese title might be translated as "Leveling Up with Unmatched Cleverness" (機智無敵闖通關). See Curley, "Zen-Boy Ikkyū," for a discussion of these anecdotes in Japanese books for children.
30 Zheng, *Dashi mima A,* 38–39.
31 In the original tale, Ikkyū is supposed to be twelve or thirteen. Curley, "Zen-Boy Ikkyū," 335.
32 Barmé, *An Artistic Exile,* 138. See also Laureillard, "Regret of Spring."
33 Zheng, *Dashi mima A,* 56.
34 Chia, "Toward a Modern Buddhist Hagiography," 153–154.
35 The film, "The Biography of Guiding Teacher Yinshun" (Yinshun Daoshi zhuan 印順導師傳) has been posted multiple times to YouTube, and in some countries is available on Netflix.
36 Travagnin, "Dharma in Motion Pictures."
37 Levering, "The Precocious Child in Chinese Buddhism," 143–145.
38 Shengyan, *Shengyan fashi xuesi licheng,* 1–7.

39 Shengyan, *Guicheng,* 1–31.
40 Shengyan, *Shengyan Fashi de wanpi tongnian,* 14–15. This section is adapted from Shengyan, *Guicheng,* 17–18.
41 Shengyan, *Shengyan Fashi de wanpi tongnian,* 30–31.
42 Shengyan, *Shengyan Fashi de wanpi tongnian,* 5.
43 Shengyan, *Shengyan Fashi de wanpi tongnian,* 18.
44 For a discussion of playful or naughty behavior in children's literature produced by Christian missionaries, see Chen, *Children's Literature and Transnational Knowledge,* 168–175.
45 Shengyan, *Shengyan Fashi de wanpi tongnian,* 54. We might also read this as a cautionary note about the gap between media representations and reality.
46 Shengyan, *Shengyan Fashi de wanpi tongnian,* 56–59.
47 Shengyan, *Shengyan Fashi de wanpi tongnian,* 70.
48 Hillenbrand characterizes this as a tendency to slip into "retro schmaltz." Hillenbrand, "Nostalgia, Place, and Making Peace," 383.
49 Huang cites the work of Clay Routledge and his collaborators in "Old Trees as Memory Keepers," 210–211.
50 See the following chapter for a discussion of how cuteness works in depictions of Buddhist figures. Note that the illustration of Shengyan with a big head stands in contrast to his description of himself as small-headed. Shengyan, *Shengyan Fashi de wanpi tongnian,* 46.
51 Zhu, "Yuanlai Shengyan fashi ye hen wanpi!," 2. Zhu is a well-known Taiwanese illustrator, primarily for comics.
52 Nodelman, *The Hidden Adult,* 209.

CHAPTER 5: BEFRIENDING BODHISATTVAS

1 See discussion of Feng in chapter 1, 33–34.
2 Shi, *Dajia de mama* (unpaginated, 2).
3 Joosen, "'Look More Closely,' Said Mum," 148.
4 Yueguang pusa 月光菩薩 (Candraprabha) and Riguang pusa 日光菩薩 (Sūryaprabha) are often depicted on either side of Medicine-Master Buddha.
5 Ding, "Chaoji baomu da yi wang," 36.
6 Ngai, "The Cuteness of the Avant-Garde," 816; quoted in Ivy, "The Art of Cute Little Things," 14.
7 It may be especially for parents, as Daniel Harris writes: "The conventions of cuteness are the residue of unfulfilled wishes that crystallize in the gap between the daily realities of children and our quixotic and unobtainable notions of what they should, ideally, be. Cuteness is every parent's portable utopia, the rose-colored lenses that color and blur the profound drudgery of child-rearing with soft-focused sentimentality." Harris, *Cute, Quaint, Hungry, Romantic,* 15.
8 Kinsella, "Cuties in Japan," 241.
9 Kinsella explains that cuteness counteracts the de-personalization and social alienation of contemporary capitalist societies. "Cuties in Japan," 222.
10 Kinsella, "Cuties in Japan," 240, 224, 252.
11 Iwabuchi, *Recentering Globalization,* ch. 4, esp. 155–156.
12 Botz-Borstein argues that in Wong Kar-wai's films cute is a means to carve out "a dreamlike humanist space within the harsh reality of globalized capitalism" of Hong Kong. Botz-Bornstein, "Wong Kar-wai's Films and the Culture of the *Kawaii,*" 106.
13 Chuang, "The Power of Cuteness," 23, 26. The A-Bian 阿扁 character and dolls, based on politician Chen Shuibian 陳水扁 (b. 1950), are an example of how cute can be used in the pursuit of political power. Chen made a practice of attending public events in superhero and other costumes; this was perceived as evidence

of kindness and endeared him to the voting public. Stuffed dolls were first produced during Chen's campaign for mayor of Taibei in 1998 and were updated for his presidential campaigns in 2000 and 2004. People became fans of the products, incorporating them as part of their daily lives, which in turn worked to create a sense of collective identity. See Chuang, "Kawaii in Taiwanese Politics," 5–13. Chen Shuibian's later conviction for corruption puts his use of cute popular culture in a different light.

14 For a cute monk and his robot avatar in the People's Republic of China, see Bruntz, "Taking Tourism into Their Own Hands," and Travagnin, "From Online Buddha-Halls to Robot-Monks." Japan's initial late twentieth-century dominance of Asian popular culture offered an alternative to Euro-American culture. The circulation of mass media and consumer goods led to "integrated assemblages" that put different "events, processes, peoples, and identities within Asia" next to each other, creating new meanings out of varied contexts and relations. Ching, "Globalizing the Regional," 55–56.

15 For a discussion of these two books, see above, p. 71.

16 Dolls and figurines of non-Buddhist gods are readily available in Taiwan—in gift shops, as part of promotions—and they popularize in new ways old deities, inserting them into everyday consumer culture. For a discussion of these, see Silvio, "Pop Culture Icons."

17 Also called chebulic myrobalan (Terminalia chebula), this tree is found throughout South and Southeast Asia. It is identified in the introduction to the book but would be difficult to recognize by the illustration alone.

18 On the history of white-robed Guanyin, see Yü, *Kuan-yin,* 250–262.

19 Huang, *Guanyin Pusa, bian, bian, bian!,* 24–25.

20 Huang, *Guanyin Pusa, bian, bian, bian!,* 41–42. Fo Guang Shan, in its picture-book about Guanyin, combines this story with the closely related tale of Mr. Ma's wife, and has all the villagers engage in a sutra-memorization contest to win her hand in marriage. She dies before the marriage is consummated. On these stories, see also Yü, *Kuan-yin,* 419–434.

21 Zheng, "Xinshang *Mile Fo* de chahua zhi mei," 36–37.

22 Xu, "Play Happily Together with Bodhisattva Guanyin."

23 Suzanne Keen, cited in Mallan, "Empathy," 106.

24 Wyile, "First-Person Engaging Narration," 191.

25 Nodelman, "The Eye and I," 4–5, 10.

26 Nodelman, "The Eye and the I," 22–23, 29. Wyile makes a similar point in "First-Person Engaging Narration," 196–197.

27 Huang, *Guanyin Pusa, bian, bian, bian!,* 4–6.

28 Huang, *Guanyin Pusa, bian, bian, bian!,* 28–29.

29 The reader's guide for parents reinforces this, writing that the game was placed deliberately at the end, to cultivate cooperation and so that children can "study the compassionate spirit of Guanyin" 學習觀音菩薩的慈悲精神. Xu, "He Guanyin pusa yiqi youxi huanle!" 42.

30 As we will see in the following chapter, the sutra most closely associated with Medicine-Master Buddha is popular in Taiwan and has had particular meaning for those suffering from illness.

31 The Buddha's hand is not visible, but their figures are depicted as overlapping with the Buddha just behind her. If he is touching her, their positions convey physical intimacy.

32 Reader's guides of this sort appear in the majority of Taiwanese picturebooks but have been criticized as patronizing to parents and limiting how a book might be understood. For an overview of the debate over *daodu,* see Yu, "Huiben daodu, CUT bu CUT?"

33 Xu, "He Guanyin pusa yiqi youxi huanle!," 37.

34 McGuire, "Playing with Karma," 16. See also McGuire, "Permeable Boundaries Between Ritual and Play."

35 On the Indian game, see Topsfield, "The Indian Game of Snakes and Ladders," and "Snakes and Ladders in India."

36 Bernstein, "Dances with Things," 70

37 Bernstein, "Dances with Things," 75.

38 Guerra, *Slantwise Moves,* 10–11.

39 Travagnin, "Master Yinshun and the Pure Land Thought," 315–321. We will also see this connection in the books discussed in chapter 7.

40 In Chen, *Maitreya Buddha and the Weird Circus* the main characters are animals in need of rescue, and in Huang, *Bodhisattva Wenshu's Super-responsibilty* the focal character is a king in a fantastical realm.

41 Winnicott, *Playing and Reality,* 7.

42 Winnicott, *Playing and Reality,* 5–13.

43 Winnicott, *Playing and Reality,* 7.

44 In Taiwan, continuing to use transitional objects in adolescence has been linked to social isolation. Stagg and Li, "Transitional Object Use," 168.

45 Silvio, *Puppets, Gods, and Brands,* 120.

46 This is not necessarily to imply that the buddhas and bodhisattvas are not real—this question can be set aside—but since they are not constant physical presences must entail some mental acts.

47 Going further, Galbraith has argued that picturebooks that do not include adults "present the adult world as fundamentally hostile to children." Galbraith, "Goodnight Nobody," 174, quoted in Chou, "Co-Sleeping and the Importation of Picturebooks," 26.

48 Although language and communities may cause children to develop an understanding of other minds at somewhat different rates, meta-analysis has shown that the developmental path is roughly the same. Wellman, Cross, and Watson, "Meta-Analysis of Theory-of-Mind Development," 678–679.

49 Barrett, Richert, and Driesenga, "God's Beliefs versus Mother's," esp. 59–60.

50 See discussion in Knight et al., "Children's Attribution of Belief to Humans and God."

51 On testimony as a source of belief about objects that cannot be sensed, see Harris and Richert, "William James."

52 Nelson, "Language Pathways into the Community of Minds," 42. For a general treatment of very young children and other minds, see Reddy, *How Infants Know Minds.*

53 Luhrmann, *How God Becomes Real,* 30.

54 Clegg et al., "Gods, Germs, and Evolution," 102.

55 Taken as a symbol of human ignorance and craving, it is also not surprising that Guanyin knows what motivates these.

56 Sara Schwebel argues that "what we can access and analyze . . . is the way in which adults consciously and unconsciously shape children's interactions with books by the choices they make in writing, publishing, designing, editing, prizing, adopting, and teaching." Schwebel, "The Limits of Agency," 288.

57 As Richard Flynn puts it, to treat children as having agency and as "active participants" in their own lives "does not underestimate the power that adult and institutional discourses have." Flynn, "What Are We Talking about When We Talk about Agency?," 258. For a recent survey of the theoretical issues around the agency of the child, see Esser, ed., *Reconceptualizing Agency and Childhood,* especially section 1.

58 "I suggest that hairpins thus manifested women's desire to overcome the distinction between worhsipped as an object and the worshipper as subject. Their shared female identity, in the case of Guanyin, was a necessary

condition for this mimetic behavior." Li, *Becoming Guanyin,* 143. This chapter discusses the role of hairpins and other jewelry in women's devotional activities.

PART III: WORLDS

CHAPTER 6: HOW TO BE A BUDDHIST FAMILY

1 Note that I follow Yü Chün-fang's translation of their name; Cheng Wei-yi and Elise DeVido both use "Luminary."

2 Reimer, "Home," 106–107.

3 For a discussion of this body of texts, see Choo, "That 'Fatty Lump'," 207–211.

4 Studies of both Mulian and Miaoshan are numerous. See, for example, Dudbridge, *The Legend of Miaoshan*; Idema, *Personal Salvation and Filial Piety*; Johnson, *Ritual Opera*; and Berezkin, *Many Faces of Mulian.*

5 Cheng, "Luminary Buddhist Nuns," 43; DeVido, *Taiwan's Buddhist Nuns,* 82.

6 In addition to chapter 3 of Yü, *Passing the Light,* see also the discussions of Wuyin in Cheng, "Luminary Buddhist Nuns," esp. 43–48, and in DeVido, *Taiwan's Buddhist Nuns,* ch. 5. Other important Taiwanese nuns are described in Eichman, "Prominent Nuns."

7 Yü, *Passing the Light,* 46.

8 Yü, *Passing the Light,* 150.

9 Yü, *Passing the Light,* 170.

10 Yü, *Passing the Light,* 152–153.

11 For a list of essay topics and translations of selected essays, see Yü, *Passing the Light,* 171–185.

12 DeVido, *Taiwan's Buddhist Nuns,* 84.

13 Liao, "Buda yuan," 63–64.

14 *Zijue jueta* 自覺覺他 is an expression that refers to the work of bodhisattvas to enlighten others after becoming awakened themselves, but also evokes a non-Buddhist sense of being self-aware and conscious of others.

15 Liao, "Buda yuan," 65.

16 In contrast to most of the books discussed, these are not commercial books and cannot be purchased; they are marked as "not for sale" (*fei maipin* 非賣品) on the page with publication data. This places them within a category of freely distributed texts that are part of propagation or merit-making.

17 Hong, "Taiwan fojiao tuhuashu wojian wosi," 137–138.

18 Zhu, *Tingche long,* 7, 11.

19 Zhu, *Tingche long,* 31, 33.

20 Nikolajeva and Scott, *How Picturebooks Work,* 67–69.

21 Morley, *Home Territories,* 47, quoted in Reimer, "Home," 108.

22 T. 450, 14: 405a29–b4.

23 Travagnin, "Master Yinshun and the Pure Land Thought," 316, 320–321. Yinshun drew parallels between Medicine-Master Buddha's vows and Sun Yatsen's principles of the people (minzu zhuyi 民族主義), making the Buddha an especially important model for transforming China or Taiwan. Travagnin notes that Medicine-Master Buddha is very popular in Taiwan, in part due to Yinshun's continued influence. Her summary of Yinshun's treatment of Medicine-Master Buddha's Pure Land spans pp. 315–321.

24 See, for example, Liao, "'Yaoshi jing' dui xiandai anning liaohu guan zhi qishi," on how the scripture might be used in the context of hospice care; Yang, "Ciji yu 'Yaoshi jing' de yinyuan"; and a special section of *Rencheng Fokan* 人乘佛刊 32 no. 2: 13–35. Accessed at https://docs.google.com/file/d/0B-304Qf8aev1YWlxdkp5cVBSQjA/preview.

25 T. 262, 9: 19a27–c9.

26 Later interpreters of the passage took "one form" to refer to the universal mind with which all sentient beings are endowed, and the "one flavor" to refer to the teachings. The term is explained in Muller, "Yi xiang yi wei." See *Wanshan tonggui* 萬善同歸, T. 2017, 48: 959b.
27 Zhu, *Huifei de baibu xie,* 32
28 Jones, "Buddha One," esp. 266–272 and 276–278.
29 Carr, "'Mind-Monkey' Metaphors," 154–159.
30 Zhu, *Shei de meng chang?,* 23.
31 Lin, *You xifan jile shijie,* 5–10.
32 See the introduction for a discussion of Pei-chia Lan's work on this topic.
33 See Heller, "*Peaceful Piggy*'s Paratext" for a discussion of how these texts are framed in translation.
34 Cai, *Baotiao niu de xinqing guanzi,* 35
35 Xiao, *Qinzi kuaile Chan,* 56–58. Other essays also feature conversations with her child that serve as catalysts to insights.
36 Robert A. Orsi, "Is the Study of Lived Religion Irrelevant?" See also Ammerman, *Sacred Stories, Spiritual Tribes,* and McGuire, *Lived Religion,* both of which discuss how parenting fits into lived religion.
37 Kathryn Lofton, *Consuming Religion*, 163
38 Ji, "The Origins of Secular Public Space," 62.
39 Ji, "The Origins of Secular Public Space," 63 and 76ff.
40 Lan, *Raising Global Families,* 52–59, esp. 58–59.
41 If a rabbit's diet lacks sufficient fiber, their incisors may overgrow, necessitating trimming by a veterinarian.
42 Zhu, *Dayuan chuan,* unpaginated (12–17). Because there is printing on the verso of the title page, I have counted pages with the title page as the first page.
43 This alters the original, changing *fei* 非 into *wu* 無. T. 235, 8: 752b18–19.
44 See T. 235, 8: 752b18–19, 749c22–23 and 752b28–29. The first quotation captures the gist but not the exact words of the text.
45 Zhu, *Dayuan chuan,* unpaginated (29).
46 It seems that what is meant here are the animals in the ocean, but it could also be people who had been lost at sea.
47 Happening on a religious statue or shrine is common when hiking in Taiwan, and in a postface the author writes that it reflects her own experience. Fang, *Yinghuochong qu xuyuan,* unpaginated.
48 Starling, *Guardians of the Buddha's Home,* 39.
49 Starling, *Guardians of the Buddha's Home,* 43.

CHAPTER 7: MAKING SCIENCE BUDDHIST

1 These are from Chen, *Youqu de zhiwu;* Weng, *Chenman dingding banjia ji;* and Jingsi renwen chuban tuandui, *Wo ai shuguo, wo ai diqiu.*
2 Hammerstrom, *The Science of Chinese Buddhism,* 8. Hammerstrom's work explores the varied ways early twentieth-century Buddhist thinkers addressed science.
3 Scott, "Buddhism and Biomedicine in Republican China," 89. See also Scott's translations on the following pages for illustration of these themes.
4 On environmentalism in Taiwan more generally, see Weller, *Discovering Nature.*
5 For comprehensive treatments of Tzu Chi, see Madsen, *Democracy's Dharma,* 16–50; Huang, *Charisma and Compassion;* Laliberté, *Politics of Buddhist Organizations,* 86–105; and Yao, *Taiwan's Tzu Chi as Engaged Buddhism.* On Tzu Chi's environmentalism, especially as it relates to gender and families, see Ho, *Ecofamilism,* ch. 2.
6 Bingenheimer, "Some Remarks on the Usage of Renjian Fojiao," 151.

7 Pacey discusses Tzu Chi's relationship with various Christian organizations and figures in *Buddhist Responses,* 188–195.

8 Madsen, *Democracy's Dharma,* 19, 35; see also Huang, *Charisma and Compassion,* ch. 6.

9 Huang, "Scientific and Sacramental," 74.

10 Huang, "Scientific and Sacramental," 74.

11 Huang, "Scientific and Sacramental," 77.

12 Huang, "Scientific and Sacramental," 81–82. In the case of cadaver donation, the Silent Mentor program has worked to transform a routine part of medical training into an opportunity for the cultivation of humanistic medicine and compassionate care. See Santibañez et al., "The Tzu Chi Silent Mentor Program," and the discussion in Huang, "Scientific and Sacramental," 84–87. This program has attracted international interest as a different model of medical education. See also Požun and Klemenc, "A Visit to the Tzu Chi General Hospital."

13 Dillard, Dutta, and Sun, "Culture-Centered Engagement."

14 There are a large number of scholarly publications by professors based at the Tzu Chi College of Medicine attesting to the active research agenda there.

15 Huang, *Charisma and Compassion,* ch. 6.

16 Huang, "Scientific and Sacramental," 77.

17 Greene, "Tzu Chi's Environmental Bodhisattvas," 25–29.

18 Lee and Han, "Recycling Bodhisattva," 317.

19 See explanation under the subheading "Sizhong huanbao" 四種環保 on the webpage titled "Fagushan de gongshi" 法鼓山的共識: https://www.ddm.org.tw/xchome?xsmsid=0K333816916533380810. Shengyan follows a Buddhist tradition that sees all life as interconnected, and nonsentient beings as having the potential for buddhahood; see Nicolaisen, "The Intersection of Sentient Beings," 301. Jens Reinke notes that that Shengyan's message varies whether speaking to Buddhists or non-Buddhists. For the former he emphasizes spiritual purification followed by environmental action; for the latter, he hopes that protecting the environment will lead to spiritual engagement. Reinke, "Innovation and Continuity," 191.

20 Recognizing that different forms of life may be in conflict with each other, Zhaohui (Chao-hwei) has argued that priority should be given to those beings that are closer to attaining buddhahood. Human beings and animals of higher sentience may merit different consideration than animals of lesser sentience, but they also have a greater degree of responsibility for caring for other beings. Nicolaisen, "Protecting Life in Taiwan," 622–623.

21 Chen, *Youqu de zhiwu,* 61–71.

22 Chen, *Youqu de zhiwu,* 72.

23 Gardner, *Frames of Mind.*

24 Interestingly, all these intelligences are identified in English. The ones noted here appear on pp. 21, 49, 72, 75, and 89.

25 Chen, *Youqu de zhiwu,* 74.

26 This book is intended for emerging or young readers: it is richly illustrated in color with approximately a paragraph of text per page, and *zhuyin fuhao* is used to provide pronunciation for the characters.

27 Not all the stories in this volume have narratives related to conservation. One story concerns a squirrel who is told by a rabbit that her tail is too big, and after it is magically shortened, she realizes how necessary it was for her activities as a squirrel. Another story is about a little bird who is playing with a crocodile, and wonders about the reptile's tears. The first of these has a theme common to children's literature—self-acceptance and the value of differences—and the second is an attempt to explain a strange phenomenon in entertaining terms.

28 Zeng, *Dongwu de xiao mimi,* 3.
29 Zeng, "Rang haizi zai duoyuan kongjianzhong ziyou fazhan," 3.
30 Freestone and O'Toole, "The Impact of Childhood Reading."
31 Larsson, "The Cosmopolitanization of Childhood," 202–203.
32 The episode, titled "Barbecuing Mid-Autumn Festival" (Kaojiao de zhongqiu jie 烤焦的中秋節) was added to the Da Ai YouTube channel on September 25, 2015. See https://www.youtube.com/watch?v=BThXsPpo5VI, accessed July 7, 2022.
33 Weng, *Chenman dingding banjia ji,* 30–31.
34 Heirman, "How to Deal with Dangerous and Annoying Animals," 5.
35 The series is divided into subseries on commonly seen illnesses and insects.
36 Lin and Xu, "Qinzi gongdu yipu," https://tcdata.tzuchi-org.tw/asset/detail/W_TC001_97396.
37 The little boy mentioned was one of few children at the event; adults outnumbered children five to one. Lin and Xu, "Qinzi gongdu yipu," https://tcdata.tzuchi-org.tw/asset/detail/W_TC001_97396.
38 This raises interesting questions about whether destroying the virus would count as killing a living thing. The narrative, like others in this series, emphasizes prevention, and the development of a vaccine.
39 Liu, *Xin guanbingdu dajiemi,* 23.
40 It is labeled as intended for ages 5 through 9 on the back cover.
41 Liu, *Xin guanbingdu dajiemi,* 48.
42 Liu, *Xin guanbingdu dajiemi,* 48.
43 Taidong County Government, "Ciji zeng 23 xiao 3000 ben yipu tongshu," https://www.taitung.gov.tw/News_Content.aspx?n=13370&s=51558.
44 Jingsi, *Wo ai shuguo,* unpaginated (13). Here and below, I have counted the first page as the verso of the cover, since there are no intervening pages.
45 Madsen, *Democracy's Dharma,* 18.
46 Adam Chau writes that the organization is invested in "not only providing public goods but more importantly trying to bring into being a good public (defined in its own terms) composed of Ciji-interpellated religious subjects." See his discussion of the term *Cijiren* and the subjectivity it cultivates in his "Religious Subjectification," 105–106.
47 Jingsi, *Wo ai shuguo,* unpaginated (1–2).
48 Manufacturing and transportation are far larger contributors to global warming, but the production of meat and dairy accounts for 14.5 percent of greenhouse gas emissions, according to a report from the United Nations Food and Agriculture organization. Cited in Dunne, "What is the climate impact?"
49 Jingsi, *Wo ai shuguo,* unpaginated (9–10).
50 Jingsi, *Wo ai shuguo,* unpaginated (20).
51 Verchery, "Both Like and Unlike," 4.
52 Interestingly, the common term for protein—which references egg whites—is not used here.
53 Early scriptural support for vegetarianism can be found in the *Nirvana Sutra* (*Dabanniepan jing* 大般涅槃經) and the *Laṅkāvatāra Sūtra* (*Lengqie jing* 楞伽經). Examples of prominent lay Buddhists who advocated for vegetarianism include the literatus Buddhist Shen Yue 沈約 (441–513), who argued that it aligned with Mencius's ideal of humaneness (*ren* 仁). Mather, "The Bonze's Begging Bowl," 421–423. Zhou Yong 周顒 (d. 488) was another elite advocate of vegetarianism. See Pu, *Ethical Treatment of Animals,* 76.
54 The edict is discussed in Pu, *Ethical Treatment of Animals,* 86–92.
55 T. 24, no. 1484, 1005b10–14.
56 Eric Greene concludes that Buddhists used vegetarianism to contrast themselves with others. Greene, "A Reassessment of the Early History," 40–41.

57 Jensen, "Rhetorical Uses of the Exemplary Child Trope," 79.
58 Chen, *Zaijia xuefo yaodian,* 305.
59 Lin, *You xifan jile shijie,* 70–75.
60 Ambros, "*Partaking of Life.*"
61 Similar media offerings and restaurants are affiliated with Dharma Drum and Fo Guang Shan as well. For a study of vegetarianism in Fajie Fojiao Zonghui 法界佛教總會, see Verchery, "Both Like and Unlike."
62 The rabbit returns the gesture, suggesting that animals should be understood both as Buddhist and as capable of communicating in human ways.
63 Jingsi, *Wo ai shuguo,* unpaginated (13–16)
64 Although the phrase used is "geographical environment" (*dili huanjing* 地理環境), perhaps the comparison is based more on size.

CONCLUSION

1 Derris, "Picturing Buddhism."
2 Huang, *Zhanhou Taiwan Fojiao de sengsu guanxi,* 239–240.

Bibliography

CHILDREN'S BOOKS

Alderfer, Lauren. *Mindful Monkey, Happy Panda*. Illustrated by Kerry Lee MacLean. Boston: Wisdom, 2011.

Cai Mengxuan 蔡孟璇, trans. *Baotiao niu de xinqing guanzi* 暴跳牛的心情罐子 (The mind-Jar of the furious cow). By Kerry Lee MacLean. Taibei: Fagu wenhua, 2013.

——. *Heping xiaozhu xue chanxiu* 和平小豬學禪修 (Peaceful Piggy studies Chan cultivation). By Kerry Lee MacLean. Taibei: Fagu wenhua, 2013.

——. *Tanxin hou he kuaile xiongmao* 貪心猴和快樂熊貓 (Greedy monkey and happy panda). By Lauren Alderfer. Taibei: Fagu wenhua, 2013.

Chen Chen 陳辰. *Dizang pusa de shenqi baozang* 地藏菩薩的神奇寶藏 (Bodhisattva Dizang's magical treasure). Illustrated by Gao Yingxue 高鶯雪. Taibei: Fagu wenhua, 2010.

——. *Mile Fo yu guaiguai maxituan* 彌勒佛與怪怪馬戲團 (Maitreya Buddha and the weird circus). Illustrated by Jun Yi 君宜. Taibei: Fagu wenhua, 2010.

——. *Puxian pusa da zhan laji guaishou* 普賢菩薩大戰垃圾怪獸 (Bodhisattva Puxian wages a battle against the garbage monster). Illustrated by Wansui shaonü 萬歲少女. Taibei: Fagu wenhua, 2010.

——. *Yaoshi Fo de shengri liwu* 藥師佛的生日禮物 (Medicine-Master Buddha's birthday present). Illustrated by Juzi 菊子. Taibei: Fagu wenhua, 2010.

Chen Junhua 陳俊華. *Shenxian de jia* 神仙的家 (Home of the immortals). Illustrated by Chen Junhua 陳俊華. Taoyuan: Taoyuan Government, 2013.

Chen Li 陳琛, trans. *My Melody Du Lunyu My Melody* 讀論語 (My Melody reads the *Analects*). By Asahibunko henshubu 朝日文庫編輯部. Taibei: Jianduan Publishing, 2019.

Chen Lihong 陳麗虹. *Youqu de zhiwu* 有趣的植物. (Interesting plants). Illustrated by Lin Huizhen 林慧貞. Taibei: Tzu Chi Culture and Communication Foundation, 2010.

Chen Yingfan 陳盈帆. *Guimen kai* 鬼門開 (The ghost gate opens). Taibei: Lianjing, 2013.

Chen Zhenyu 陳振瑜, Su Yiru 蘇憶如, and Luo Chuanqiao 羅傳樵. *Nasierding shuo gushi: Isilan wenhua yu shenghuo* 納斯爾丁說故事：伊斯蘭文化與生活 (Nasreedin tells stories: Islamic culture and life). Taibei: Guoli Taiwan bowuguan, 2014.

Cihui 慈惠. *Zui meili de qinggan* 最美麗的情感 (The most beautiful feeling). Illustrated by Tao Yishan 陶一山. Hao ertong gushi 1 好兒童故事 (Stories for good children) 1. Taibei: Xianghai chuban, 2010.

Cirong 慈容, publisher. *Xiao shami xihuan kan renjian* 小沙彌喜歡看人間 (The little śrāmaṇera likes to watch the world) 3. Taibei: Renjian dianshi, 2010.

Cui Lijun 崔麗君. *Shei zai qiao men* 誰在敲門 (Who's knocking at the door?). Taibei: Hsin Yi Publications, 1999.

Fang Suzhen 方素珍. *Zhiyao chi bange/ xiao huanggou zhong mantou* 只要吃半個/ 小黃狗種饅頭 (I only want to eat half/ The yellow dog plants steamed buns). Illustrated by Huang Shuying 黃淑英. *Baiyujing tuhuashu* 百喻經圖畫書 12 (Illustrated scripture of one hundred analogies). Taibei: Foguang, 1995.

——. *Yinghuochong qu xuyuan* 螢火蟲去許願 (Firefly makes a vow). Illustrated by Wu Jiaqing 吳嘉倩. Taibei: Weijing guoji, 2007.

Foguang bianji xiaozu 佛光編輯小組 (Foguang editorial team). *Bazong zushi tuwenshu* 1–2 八宗祖師圖文書 1–2 (The patriarchs of the eight lineages illustrated). Gaoxiong: Foguang wenhua, 2017.

——. *Sida pusa tuwenshu* 1–2 四大菩薩圖文書 1–2 (The four great bodhisattvas illustrated). Gaoxiong: Foguang wenhua, 2017.

Guoli bianyi guan 國立編譯館 (National Institute for Translation and Compilation). *Shenghuo yu lunli,* vol. 4 生活與倫理第四冊 (Life and ethics, vol. 4). Taibei: Guoli bianze guan, 1975.

——. *Shenghuo yu lunli,* vol. 2 生活與倫理第二冊 (Life and ethics, vol. 2). Taibei: Guoli bianze guan, 1998.

Haha shutao youjiaobu bianji 哈哈書套幼教部編輯 (Haha Book Youth Education Editors). *Fumu enzhong nanbao jing* 父母恩重難報經 (The scripture of the vast kindness of parents that is difficult to repay). Tainan: Heyu, 1994.

Hanlin 翰林 Publishing. *Guomin xiaoxue shenghuo keben* 國民小學生活課本 (National primary school life textbook). Taibei: Hanlin Publishing, 2008.

Hao Guangcai 郝廣才. *Xiao Shi Fo* 小石佛 (Little stone Buddha). Illustrated by Giuliano Ferri 朱里安諾. Taibei: Grimm, 2019.

——. *Kongzi shuo: Lunyu congxiaodong* 孔子說: 論語從小懂 (Kongzi says: Understanding the *Analects* from childhood). Taibei: Grimm, 2020.

Hong Zhiming 洪志明. *Bange tongqian/Shuizhong laoye* 半個銅錢/水中撈月 (Half a copper coin / fishing for the moon). Illustrated by Hong Yinan 洪義男. *Baiyujing tuhuashu* 百喻經圖畫書 2 (Illustrated scripture of one hundred analogies). Taibei: Foguang, 1995.

Huang Huimin 黃慧敏. *Tanzi qu lunai* 郯子取鹿奶 (Tanzi collects deer milk). Illustrated by Liu Bole 劉伯樂. Tainan: Shiyi wenhua, 2006.

Huang Shuping 黃淑萍. *Duoduo de yang / zhi yao gai sanlou* 多多的羊 / 只要蓋三樓. (Lots of sheep / I only want to build the third floor). Illustrated by Wu Xiaofang. 巫筱芳. Taibei: Foguang chuban she, 1995.

Huang Yuhui 黃鈺惠. *Amituofo da maoxian* 阿彌陀佛大冒險 (Amitābha Buddha's big adventure). Illustrated by Jun Yi 君宜. Taibei: Fagu wenhua, 2009.

——. *Guanyin pusa, bian, bian, bian!* 觀音菩薩變變變! (Bodhisattva Guanyin, change, change, change). Illustrated by Cai Yalan 蔡雅蘭. Taibei: Fagu wenhua, 2009.

——. *Wenshu pusa chaoji renwu* 文殊菩薩超級任務 (Bodhisattva Wenshu's super-assignment). Illustrated by Wang Ruixian 王瑞嫻. Taibei: Fagu wenhua, 2009.

——. *Xidaduo bu jian le* 悉達多不見了! (Siddhartha disappears!). Illustrated by Zhang Zhensong 張振松. Taibei: Fagu wenhua, 2009.

Jingsi renwen chuban tuandui 靜思人文出版團隊 (Still Thoughts Culture Publishing team). *Shui shi da shengming* 水是大生命 (Water is life). Illustrated by Jiang Jiaqing 江佳菁. Taibei: Still Thoughts Culture Publishing, 2015.

——. *Wo ai shuguo, wo ai diqiu* 我愛蔬果，我愛地球 (I love fruits and vegetables, I love the earth). Illustrated by Jiang Jiaqing 江佳菁. Taibei: Still Thoughts Culture Publishing, 2016.

Lai Zhiming 賴志銘. *Yinyue xiao jingling* 音樂小精靈 (Little music prodigy). Illustrated by Yongzi 泳子. Taibei: Tzu Chi Chuanbo renwen zhiye jijinhui, 2011.

Li Guangfu 李光福 and BO2. *Tudi gonggong yao huijia* 土地公公要回家 (Grandpa Earth God wants to go home). Xinbei: Kanxuan wenjiao shiye, 2016.

Liao Bingkun 廖炳焜 and Wang Shuman 王書曼. *Huo shao cuo* 火燒厝 (Burning the house). Taibei: Baba wenhua, 2016.

Lin Liang 林良. *Touniu de ren / Houzi reng douzi* 偷牛的人/猴子扔豆子 (The ox-thief/ The monkey who threw away beans). Illustrated by Cao Junyan 曹俊彥 *Baiyujing tuhuashu* 百喻經圖畫書 11 (Illustrated scripture of one hundred analogies). Taibei: Foguang, 1995.

Lin Qingxuan 林清玄. *Wanli qujing lu: Xuanzang* 萬里取經路：玄奘 (A road of a thousand miles in search of scriptures: Xuanzang). Illustrated by Robert Ingpen 羅伯英潘. Taibei: Grimm, 2000.

Lin Rongzi 林榮梓, ed. *Guomin xiaoxue shehui keben* 國民小學社會課本 (National primary school society textbook). Taizhong: Renlin wenhua, 2004.

Liu Rugui 劉如桂. *Suliaodai liulang ji* 塑料袋流浪記 (Record of the wanderings of a plastic bag). Illustrated by Liu Rugui 劉如桂. Taibei: Fagu wenhua, 2014.

Lin Ruiguan 林瑞冠 and Zhe Ye 哲也, trans. *Xiao Ji baobei: Mingjiu renpoqie de xiaopengyou kaixin Chan* 小吉寶貝: 明就仁波切的小朋友開心禪 (Darling little Ji: Mingyur Rinpoche's happy Chan for little friends), by Yongey Mingyur Rinpoche and Torey Hayden (original title: *Ziji: The Puppy Who Learned to Meditate*). Banqiao: Zhongsheng wenhua, 2011.

Lin Shimin 林世敏. *You xifang jile shijie* 遊西方極樂世界 (A trip to the western world of extreme happiness). Gaoxiong: Ci'en chubanshe, 1978.

——. *Zhongguo weida de chujiaren* 中國偉大的出價家人 (China's great monks), vols. 1–2. Gaoxiong: Ci'en chubanshe, 1980.

——. *Shi da dizi* 十大弟子 (Ten great disciples). Gaoxiong: Ci'en chubanshe, 1981.

Liu Yijun 劉怡均. *Xin guanbingdu dajiemi* 新冠病毒大解密! (The new coronavirus declassified!). Taibei: Ciji chuanbo renwen zhiye jijinhui, 2020.

Ma Jingxian 馬景賢 and Chen Shengqun 陳昇群. *Mulian jiumu* 目連救母 (Mulian saves his mother). Taibei: Guoyu ribao she, 2012.

Renlin wenhua 仁林文化, ed. *Guomin xiaoxue shehui* 國民小學社會 (National primary school society). Taibei: Renlin wenhua, 2006.

Shen, Yueqing 沈月清, ed. *Guomin xiaoxue shenghuo keben* 國民小學生活課本 (National primary school life textbook). Taizhong: Renlin wenhua, 2004.

Shengyan 聖嚴. *Shengyan Fashi de wanpi tongnian* 聖嚴法師的頑皮童年 (Master Shengyan's naughty youth). Taibei: Fagu wenhua, 2009.

Shi Changdeng 釋常燈 . *Zui ku de xiao niao* 最酷的小鳥 (The coolest little bird). Taibei: Fagu wenhua, 2013.

Shi Demao 釋德懋. *Yingong daoshi shuo gushi: chang yu duan* 印公導師說故事:長與短 (Master Yinshun tells stories: Long and short). Illustrated by Lin Qianru 林倩如. Taibei: Jingsi renwen, 2006.

Shi Guofan 釋果梵. *Dajia de mama* 大家的媽媽 (Everyone's mama). Reprint. Taibei: Fagu wenhua, 1999.

Shi Guoxiang 釋果祥. *Wode shifu* 我的師父 (My teacher). Taibei: Fagu wenhua, 2013.

Shi Jianju 釋見鑴, illustrator. *Foshuo: ba darenjue jing* 佛說: 八大人覺經 (The Buddha speaks: the eight great enlightenment sutras). Jiayi: Xiangguang shuxiang, 2004.

Shi Yanru 石晏如. *Tudigong zhuo micang* 土地公捉迷藏 (The earth god plays hide and seek). Illustrated by Zhang Zhensong 張振松. Gaoxiong: Aizhi tushu, 2013.

Wang Jianxuan 王建煊. *Zou guangming de lu* 走光明的路 (Walking the road of light). Illustrated by Xu Yanhong 許燕紅. Taibei: Gelin wenhua, 2011.

Wang Wenhua 王文華 and Chen Huli 陳狐狸. *Cao Cao diao xiaqule* 曹操掉下去了 (Cao Cao fell down). Taibei: Baba wenhua, 2013.

Wang Zaozao 王早早. *Ande zhongzi* 安的種子 (An's seed). Illustrated by Huang Li 黃麗. Taibei: Shangyi wenhua, 2010.

Weng Chunying 翁純瑩. *Chenman dingding banjia ji* 塵蟎丁丁搬家記 (Dust mite Dingding's diary of moving house). Illustrated by Xi Zhuwei 洗豬尾. Taibei: Ciji chuanbo renwen zhiye jijinhui, 2018.

Wu Chongde 吳重德. *Lidai gaoseng jushi de gushi* 歷代高僧居士的故事 1–2 (Stories of the great monks and laymen of history). Tainan: Heyu chuban she, 2001.

Wu Liping 吳立萍. *Wangle youshou de nühai* 忘了右手的女孩 (Little girl with the forgotten right hand). Illustrated by Yongzi 泳子. Taibei: Tzu Chi Chuanbo renwen zhiye jijinhui, 2011.

Xie Wuzhang 謝武彰. *Xiao hei hou* 小黑猴 (Little black monkey). Illustrated by Shi Lirong 石麗蓉. Taibei: Xiaoxiong chubanshe, 2011.

Xingyun 星雲. *Huiben xinjing* 繪本心經 (Picturebook Heart Sutra). Illustrated by Giuliano Ferri (Zhuliannuo 朱里安諾). Taibei: Grimm, 2009.

——. *Renjian tonghua* 人間童話 (Fairy tales of the human realm). Illustrated by Juenian 覺念. Taibei: Renjian dianshi, 2010.

Xu He 徐荷. *Qiyi de muji* 奇異的木屐 (The special clogs). Taibei: Tianxia yuanjian, 2004.

Xu Ximan 徐錫滿. *Rexue xiao yewen* 熱血的小葉問 (Fierce little Yip Man). Illustrated by Xiao Jun 曉君. Taibei: Tzu Chi Chuanbo renwen zhiye jijinhui, 2012.

Yang Shuqing 楊淑清. *Shangdi baobei* 上帝寶貝 (God's precious one). Illustrated by Huang Meilian 黃美廉. Taibei: Tianyun, 2004.

Ye Marn 冶夢. *Manhua Fotuo de wan'an gushi* 漫畫佛陀的晚安故事 1 (Manga Buddhist bedtime stories), trans. Chen Haiyuan 陳海源 and Xu Shuangqiu 許雙秋. Xin Taibei: Gougou tushu, 2017.

Ye Yongshao 葉永韶. *Dashenwang: Tanxun Toucheng miren de guwenfeng* 大神尪：探尋頭城迷人的古文風 (Great god puppets: In search of Toucheng's enchanting old traditions). Yilan: Yilan zhengfu wenhua ju, 2014.

Yu Liang 余亮, author and illustrator. *Deleisha: Zuimei de heping tianshi* 德蕾莎：最美的和平天使 (Teresa: The most beautiful angel of peace). Taoyuan: Hongcan lianqiye, 2006.

Zeng Weihui 曾維惠. *Dongwu de xiao mimi* 動物的小秘密 (Little secrets of animals). Illustrated by Li Houji 李後佶. Taibei: Tzu Chi Culture and Communication Foundation, 2010.

Zhang Lingling 張玲玲. *Mazu Goes Home* 馬祖回娘家. Illustrated by Wang Jiazhu 王家珠. Taibei: Liyan tushu, 2013.

Zhang Qingshi 張青史, ed. *Yongyuan de zhizhe: Fotuo* 永遠的智者: 佛陀 (Eternal wisdom: Buddha). Yonghe: Yangming, 1999.

Zhang Qiongling 張瓊齡. *Toby de jubao he Toby* 的聚寶盒 (Toby's treasure chest). Illustrated by Huang Yingjie 黃瑩潔. Taibei: Tzu Chi chuanbo renwen zhiye jijinhui, 2013.

Zhang Shuqiong 張淑瓊. *Chuanguo zhenyan de luotuo: jianqiaoqijie de gushi* 穿過針眼的駱駝：劍橋七傑的故事 (The camel that passes through the eye of a needle: The story of the Cambridge Seven). Taibei: Jidu jiao yuzhouguang quanren guanhuai jigou, 2006.

Zhang Xiuyu 張秀毓. *Mazu chun youqu* 媽祖春遊趣 (Mazu's spring lark). Taizhong: Taizhongshi zhengfu wenhuaju, 2015.

Zhang Yiping 章衣萍. *Xuanzang* 玄奘. Shanghai: Ertong shuju, 1935, rpt. 1947. https://taiwanebook.ncl.edu.tw/zh-tw/book/NCL-003121590.

Zheng Lier 鄭栗兒. *Dashi mima A* 大師密碼A (Code words of the great teachers A). Illustrated by Liu Jianzhi 劉建志. Taibei: Fagu wenhua, 2006.

——. *Dashi mima B* 大師密碼B (Code words of the great teachers B). Illustrated by Guoxiang 果祥. Taibei: Fagu wenhua, 2006.

——. *Dashi mima D* 大師密碼D (Code words of the great teachers D). Illustrated by Su Lika 蘇力卡. Taibei: Fagu wenhua, 2006.

——. *Dashi mima E* 大師密碼E (Code words of the great teachers E). Illustrated by Liu Xiaoqi 劉小琦. Taibei: Fagu wenhua, 2006.

——. *Dashi mima F* 大師密碼F (Code words of the great teachers F). Illustrated by Gao Yingxue 高鶯雪. Taibei: Fagu wenhua, 2006.

——. *Dashi mima G* 大師密碼G (Code words of the great teachers G). Illustrated by Jian Hanping 簡漢平. Taibei: Fagu wenhua, 2006.

——. *Dashi mima H* 大師密碼H (Code words of the great teachers H). Illustrated by Juzi 菊子. Taibei: Fagu wenhua, 2006.

——. *Dashi mima I* 大師密碼I (Code words of the great teachers I). Illustrated by Zhou Ruiping 周瑞萍. Taibei: Fagu wenhua, 2006.

——. *Dashi mima L* 大師密碼L (Code words of the great teachers L). Illustrated by Juzi 菊子. Taibei: Fagu wenhua, 2006.

——. *Dashi mima M* 大師密碼M (Code words of the great teachers M). Illustrated by Zhong Shuting 鍾淑婷. Taibei: Fagu wenhua, 2006.

——. *Dashi mima S* 大師密碼S (Code words of the great teachers S). Illustrated by Huang Yiwei 黃宜葳. Taibei: Fagu wenhua, 2006.

——. *Dashi mima V* 大師密碼V (Code words of the great teachers V). Illustrated by Sun Jingling 孫靜玲. Taibei: Fagu wenhua, 2006.

——. *Dashi mima X* 大師密碼X (Code words of the great teachers X). Illustrated by Lin Zongxian 林宗賢. Taibei: Fagu wenhua, 2006.

——. *Dashi mima Z* 大師密碼Z (Code words of the great teachers Z). Illustrated by Wang Zimian 王子麵. Taibei: Fagu wenhua, 2006.

Zheng Shifeng 鄭拾風. *Baiyujing xinshi* 百喻經新釋 (A new elucidation of the scripture of one hundred analogies). Illustrated by Zhang Leping 張樂平. Shanghai: Shanghai renmin meishu, 1956.

Zhengyan 證嚴. *Tiantang yu diyu* 天堂與地獄 (Heaven and hell). Illustrated by Lin Qianru 林倩如. Taibei: Tzu Chi wenhua, 2005.

——. *Xiao houzi* 小猴子 (Little monkey). Illustrated by Lin Yuling 林玉玲. Taibei: Tianxia yuanjian and Jingsi wenhua, 2005.

——. *Zhuanshi de laoniu* 轉世的老牛 (The reincarnated old ox). Illustrated by Lin Qianru 林倩如. Taibei: Tzu Chi wenhua, 2005.

——. *Chengshi de shangren* 誠實的商人 (The honest merchant). Illustrated by Liu Jianzhi 劉建志. Taibei: Jingsi wenhua, 2008.

Zhu Yan 朱顏. *Huazhi chunman* 華枝春滿 (Flowering branches and the fullness of spring). Illustrated by Zhuang Xiaoxian 莊孝先. Jiayi: Xiangguang shuxiang, 2011.

——. *Huifei de baibu xie* 會飛的百布鞋 (Flying shoes of one hundred fabrics). Illustrated by Liu Tongxuan 劉彤渲. Jiayi: Xiangguang shuxiang, 2011.

——. *Sheide meng chang?* 誰的夢長?(Whose dream is longest?). Illustrated by Bao Dashan 包大山. Jiayi: Xiangguang shuxiang, 2011.

——. *Tingche long* 停車龍 (Parking dragon). Illustrated by Zhuang Xiaoxian 莊孝先. Jiayi: Xiangguang shuxiang, 2011.

——. *Erchong zou* 二重奏 (Duet). Illustrated by Lin Qianyi 林倩誼. Jiayi: Xiangguang shuxiang, 2014.

——. *Dayuan chuan* 大願船 (The boat of the great vow). Jiayi: Xiangguang shuxiang, 2014.

Zheng, Wen. *Star and Cloud: Venerable Master Hsing Yun*. Translated by Madelon Wheeler-Gibb. Hacienda Heights, CA: Buddha's Light Publishing, 2003.

Other Sources

Ackerman, Susan. "Household Religion, Family Religion, and Women's Religion in Ancient Israel." In *Household and Family Religion in Antiquity,* edited by John Bodel and Saul M. Olyan, 127–158. Malden, MA, and Oxford: Blackwell, 2008.

Af Sandberg, Maria. "Room for Improvement: The Ideal of the Educational Home in *The Ladies' Journal.*" In *Women and the Periodical Press in China's Long Twentieth Century: A Space of Their Own?,* edited by Michel Hockx, Joan Judge, and Barbara Mittler, 192–211. Cambridge: Cambridge University Press, 2018.

Ambros, Barbara. "*Partaking of Life:* Buddhism, Meat-Eating, and Sacrificial Discourses of Gratitude in Contemporary Japan." *Religions* 10 (2019), doi:10.3390/rel10040279.

Ammerman, Nancy Tatom. *Sacred Stories, Spiritual Tribes: Finding Religion in Everyday Life.* Oxford: Oxford University Press, 2014.

Anālayo. "The Buddha and His Son." *Mindfulness* 12 (2021): 269–274.

Appleton, Naomi. "A Place for the Bodhisattva: The Local and the Universal in Jātaka Stories." *Acta Orientalia Vilnensia* 8, no. 1 (2007): 109–122.

Arntzen, Sonja. *Ikkyū and the Crazy Cloud Anthology: A Zen Poet of Medieval Japan.* Tokyo: University of Tokyo Press.

Bai, Limin. *Shaping the Ideal Child: Children at Their Primers in Late Imperial China.* Hong Kong: The Chinese University Press, 2005.

——. "Making Learning Enjoyable: Picture Character-Cards as 'Educational Play Items' in Early Twentieth-Century China." *The Journal of the History of Childhood and Youth* 11, no. 3 (Fall 2018): 383–402.

Bakken, Børge. *The Exemplary Society: Human Improvement, Social Control, and the Dangers of Modernity in China.* Studies on Contemporary China. Oxford and New York: Oxford University Press, 2000.

Barmé, Geremie. *An Artistic Exile: A Life of Feng Zikai (1898–1975).* Berkeley and Los Angeles: University of California Press, 2002.

Barrett, Justin L., Rebekah A. Richert, and Amanda Driesenga. "God's Beliefs versus Mother's: The Development of Nonhuman Agent Concepts." *Child Development* 72, no. 1 (January–February 2001): 50–65.

Beauvais, Clémentine. *The Mighty Child: Time and Power in Children's Literature.* Amsterdam and Philadelphia: John Benjamins Publishing Company, 2015.

Berezkin, Rostislav. "Pictorial Versions of the Mulian Story in East Asia (Tenth–Seventeenth Centuries): On the Connections of Religious Painting and Storytelling." *Fudan Journal of Humanities and Social Sciences* 8, no. 1 (2015): 95–120.

——. *Many Faces of Mulian: The Precious Scrolls of Late Imperial China.* Seattle: University of Washington Press, 2017.

Bernstein, Robin. "Dances with Things: Material Culture and the Performance of Race." *Social Text* 27, no. 4 (2009): 67–94.

Bi, Lijun, and Xiangshu Fang. "Childhoods: Childhoods in Chinese Children's Texts—Continuous Reconfiguration for Political Needs." In *(Re)imagining the World: Children's Literature's Response to Changing Times,* edited by Yan Wu, Kerry Mallan, and Roderick McGillis, 55–68. Berlin: Springer, 2013.

Bingenheimer, Marcus. "Some Remarks on the Usage of Renjian Fojiao and The Contribution of Venerable Yinshun to Chinese Buddhist Modernism." In *Development and Practice of Humanitarian Buddhism: Interdisciplinary Perspectives,* edited by Mutsu Hsu, Jinhua Chen, and Lori Meeks, 141–161. Hualien: Tzu Chi University Press, 2007.

Bird, Elizabeth, and Junko Yokota. "Picturebooks and Illustrated Books." In *The Routledge Companion to Picturebooks,* edited by Bettina Kümmerling-Meibauer, 281–290. London and New York: Routledge, 2018.

Blair, Heather. "When Sad Is Good: Affect among Friends in and out of Japanese Picturebooks." In *Practices and Objects in India, China, and Japan,* edited by Barbara Schuler, 297–326. Leiden and Boston: Brill, 2017.

Borchert, Thomas. *Educating Monks: Minority Buddhism on China's Southwest Border.* Honolulu: University of Hawaiʻi Press, 2017.

Boretti, Valentina. "Purposeful Leisure: Aspects of Toy Discourse in Republican China." *The Princeton University Library Chronicle* 68, no. 3 (Spring 2007): 881–908.

Botz-Bornstein, Thorsten. "Wong Kar-wai's Films and the Culture of the *Kawaii.*" *SubStance* 37, no. 2 (2008): 94–109.

Bowie, Katherine A. "The Historical Vicissitudes of the *Vessantara Jataka* in Mainland Southeast Asia." *Journal of Southeast Asian Studies* 49, no. 1 (February 2018): 34–62.

Bradbury, Steve, and Fiona Feng-hsin Liu. "Everywhere a Children's Book: The View from Taiwan." *The Horn Book* 79, no. 2 (March–April 2003): 239–248.

Branigan, Tania. "Taiwan offers baby bonus to fix plummeting birth rate." *The Guardian,* January 23, 2012. Accessed April 17, 2019, at https://www.theguardian.com/world/2012/jan/23/taiwan-low-birth-rate.

Brokaw, Cynthia J., and Kai-wing Chow, eds. *Printing and Book Culture in Late Imperial China.* Berkeley: University of California Press, 2005.

Brose, Benjamin. "Resurrecting Xuanzang: The Modern Travels of a Medieval Monk." In *Buddhists and Buddhism in the History of 20th Century China,* edited by Jan Kiely and J. Brooks Jessup, 143–176. New York: Columbia University Press, 2016.

———. *Xuanzang: China's Legendary Pilgrim and Translator.* Boulder, CO: Shambala Publications, 2021.

Bruntz, Courtney. "Taking Tourism into Their Own Hands: Monastic Communities and Temple Transformations in China." In *Buddhist Tourism in Asia,* edited by Courtney Bruntz and Brooke Schedneck, 144–160. Honolulu: University of Hawaiʻi Press, 2020.

Buswell, Robert E., Jr., and Donald S. Lopez, Jr. *The Princeton Dictionary of Buddhism.* Princeton: Princeton University Press, 2014.

Cai, Danni. "Power, Politeness, and Print: Children's Letter Writing in Republican China." *Journal of the History of Childhood and Youth* 13, no. 1 (Winter 2020): 38–62.

Carlson, Gyokuku, and Domyo Burk. "The ABC's of Enlightenment." *Tricycle: The Buddhist Review* (Fall 2008). https://tricycle.org/magazine/the-abcs-enlightenment/.

Carr, Michael. "'Mind-Monkey' Metaphors in Chinese and Japanese Dictionaries." *International Journal of Lexicography* 6, no. 3 (1993): 149–180.

Chandler, Stuart. *Establishing a Pure Land on Earth: The Foguang Buddhist Persepctive on Modernization and Globalization*. Honolulu: University of Hawai'i Press, 2004.

Chang, Sung-sheng Yvonne. "Taiwan New Literature and the Colonial Context: A Historical Survey." In *Taiwan: A New History,* edited by Murray A. Rubinstein, 261–274. Armonk, NY: Routledge, 1999.

Chau, Adam Yuet. "Religious Subjectification: The Practice of Cherishing Written Characters and Being a Ciji (Tzu Chi) Person." In *Chinese Popular Religion: Linking Fieldwork and Theory: Papers from the Fourth International Conference on Sinology,* 75–113. Taipei: Academia Sinica, 2013.

Chen, Ai-hua. "Parents' Perspectives on the Effects of the Primary EFL Education Policy in Taiwan." *Current Issues in Language Planning* 12, no. 2 (2011): 205–224.

Chen, Chiung Hwang. "Building a Pure Land on Earth: Ciji's Media Cultural Discourse." *Journal of Media and Religion* 6, no. 3 (2007): 181–199.

Chen Hailiang 陳海量. *Zaijia xuefo yaodian* 在家學佛要典 (Essentials of studying Buddhism at home). Hong Kong: Zhonghua fo jiao tu shu guan, 1965.

Chen, Minjie. *The Sino-Japanese War and Youth Literature: Friends and Foes on the Battlefield*. London: Routledge, 2016.

Chen, Shih-Wen Sue. *Children's Literature and Transnational Knowledge in Modern China: Education, Religion, and Childhood*. Singapore: Palgrave Macmillan, 2019.

Cheng, Wei-yi. "Luminary Buddhist Nuns in Contemporary Taiwan: A Quiet Feminist Movement." *Journal of Buddhist Ethics* 10 (2003): 39–56.

Chia, Jack Meng-Tat. "Toward a Modern Buddhist Hagiography: Telling the Life of Hsing Yun in Popular Media." *Asian Ethnology* 74, no. 1 (2015): 141–165.

Ching, Leo T. S. "Globalizing the Regional, Regionalizing the Global: Mass Culture and Asianism in the Age of Late Capital." *Public Culture* 12, no. 1 (Winter 2000): 233–257.

Choo, Jessey. "That 'Fatty Lump': Discourses on the Fetus, Fetal Development, and Filial Piety in Early Imperial China." *Nan Nü: Men, Women and Gender in Early and Imperial China* 14, no. 2 (2012): 177–221.

Chou, Wan-Hsiang. "Co-Sleeping and the Importation of Picture Books About Bedtime." *Children's Literature in Education* 40 (2009): 19–32.

Chu, C. Y. Cyrus, and Ruoh-Rong Yu. *Understanding Chinese Families: A Comparative Study of Taiwan and Southeast China*. Oxford and New York: Oxford University Press, 2009.

Chuang, Tzu-i. "The Power of Cuteness." *Stanford Journal of East Asian Affairs* 5, no. 2 (2005): 21–28.

Chuang, Yin C. "Kawaii in Taiwan Politics." *International Journal of Asia Pacific Studies* 7, no. 3 (September 2011): 1–17.

Clarke, Shayne. *Family Matters in Indian Buddhist Monasticisms*. Honolulu: University of Hawai'i Press, 2014.

Cleary, Thomas. *Instant Zen: Waking Up in the Present*. Berkeley, CA: North Atlantic Books, 1994.

Clegg, Jennifer M., Yixin K. Cui, Paul L. Harris, and Kathleen H. Corriveau. "God, Germs, and Evolution: Belief in Unobservable and Scientific Entities in the U.S. and China." *Integrative Psychological and Behavioral Science* 53 (2019): 93–106.

Cohen, Myron L. *House United, House Divided: The Chinese Family in Taiwan*. New York and London: Columbia University Press, 1976.

Cook, Francis H. "Fa-tsang's Brief Commentary on the *Prajñāpāramitā-hṛdaya-sūtra*." In *Mahāyāna Buddhist Meditation: Theory and Practice,* edited by Minoru Kiyota with Elvin W. Jones, 167–206. Honolulu: University of Hawai'i Press, 1978.

Crosby, Kate. "The Inheritance of Rāhula: Abandoned Child, Boy Monk, Ideal Son and Trainee." In *Little Buddhas: Children and Childhoods in Buddhist Texts and Traditions,* edited by Vanessa R. Sasson, 97–123. Oxford and New York: Oxford University Press, 2013.

Curley, Melissa Anne-Marie. "Zen-Boy Ikkyū." In *Little Buddhas: Children and Childhoods in Buddhist Texts and Traditions,* edited by Vanessa R. Sasson, 326–346. Oxford and New York: Oxford University Press, 2013.

Dawley, Evan N. *Becoming Taiwanese: Ethnogenesis in a Colonial City, 1880s–1950s.* Cambridge, MA, and London: Harvard East Asia Center 2019.

Deeg, Max. "'Show Me the Land Where the Buddha Dwelled . . .' Xuanzang's 玄奘 'Record of the Western Regions' (Xiyu ji 西域記): A Misunderstood Text?" *China Report* 48, nos. 1–2 (2012): 89–113.

Derris, Karen. "Picturing Buddhism: Nurturing Buddhist Worldviews through Children's Books." In *Little Buddhas: Children and Childhoods in Buddhist Texts and Traditions,* edited by Vanessa R. Sasson, 206–226. Oxford and New York: Oxford University Press, 2013.

Desblache, Lucile. "Animal Leaders and Helpers: From the Classical Tales of Charles Perrault to the Postmodern Fables of Angela Carter and Patrick Chamoiseau." *Journal of Romance Studies* 11, no. 2 (2011): 75–88.

DeVido, Elise Anne. *Taiwan's Buddhist Nuns.* Albany: State University of New York Press, 2010.

DiLeonardo, Micaela. "The Female World of Cards and Holidays: Women, Families, and the Work of Kinship." *Signs* 12, no. 3 (Spring 1987): 440–453.

Dillard, Sydney J., Mohan Dutta, and Wei-San Sun. "Culture-Centered Engagement With Delivery of Health Services: Co-Constructing Meanings of Health in the Tzu Chi Foundation Through Buddhist Philosophy." *Health Communication* 29, no. 2 (2014): 147–156.

Ding Min 丁敏. "Chaoji baomu dayiwang" 超級保母大醫王 (Super-nanny medicine king). In Chen Chen, *Yaoshi Fo de shengri liwu* 藥師佛的生日禮物 (Medicine-Master Buddha's birthday present), 36–39. Illustrated by Juzi 菊子. Taibei: Fagu wenhua, 2010.

Donald, Stephanie Hemelryk, and Yi Zheng. "Chinese Modernisms." In *The Oxford Handbook of Modernisms,* edited by Peter Brooker et al. Oxford Academic online edition, 2012. https://doi-org/10.1093/oxfordhb/9780199545445.013.0055.

Dudbridge, Glen. *The Hsi-yu Chi: A Study of Antecedents to the Sixteenth Century Chinese Novel.* Cambridge: Cambridge University Press, 1970.

——. *The Legend of Miaoshan.* Rev. ed. Oxford and New York: Oxford University Press, 2004.

Dunne, Daisy. "Interactive: What is the climate impact of eating meat and dairy?" CarbonBrief. Published September 14, 2020. Accessed March 15, 2021. https://interactive.carbonbrief.org/what-is-the-climate-impact-of-eating-meat-and-dairy/.

Eichman, Jennifer. "Prominent Nuns: Influential Taiwanese Voices." *CrossCurrents* 61, no. 3 (September 2011): 345–373.

Eisenstein, Elizabeth L. *The Printing Press as an Agent of Change: Communications and Cultural Transformations in Early Modern Europe,* vols. I and II. Cambridge: Cambridge University Press, 1980.

——. *The Printing Revolution in Early Modern Europe.* Cambridge: Cambridge University Press, 1993.

Esser, Florian, Meike S. Baader, Tanja Betz, and Beatrice Hungerland, eds. *Reconceptualizing Agency and Childhood: New Perspectives in Childhood Studies.* London and New York: Routledge, 2016.

Eubanks, Charlotte. *Miracles of Book and Body: Buddhist Textual Culture and Medieval Japan.* Berkeley: University of California Press, 2011.

"Fagushan de gongshi" 法鼓山的共識 (The shared understanding of Dharma Drum Mountain). Accessed November 25, 2022. https://www.ddm.org.tw/xchome?xsmsid=0K333816916533380810.

Farrelly, Paul J. "Buddhism and Books: Lin Ching-hsuan's Cross-Strait Careers." *Taiwan Insight,* University of Nottingham, Taiwan Studies Programme, March 20, 2019. Accessed January 13, 2021. https://taiwaninsight.org/2019/03/20/buddhism-and-books-lin-ching-hsuans-cross-strait-careers/.

Fisher, Gareth. "From Temples to Teahouses: Exploring the Evolution of Lay Buddhism in Post-Mao China." *Review of Religion and Chinese Society* 7 (2020): 34–61.

Flynn, Richard. "What Are We Talking about When We Talk about Agency?" *Jeunesse: Young People, Texts, Cultures* 8 no. 1 (Summer 2016): 254–265.

Foguang da cidian 佛光大辭典 (Foguang dictionary). Taibei: Foguang, 1995.

Freedman, R., M. C. Chang, T. H. Sun, and M. Weinstein. "The Fertility Transition in Taiwan." In *Social Change and the Family in Taiwan,* edited by Arland Thornton and Hui-Sheng Lin, 264–304. Chicago and London: University of Chicago Press, 1994.

Freestone, Margaret, and John Mitchell O'Toole. "The Impact of Childhood Reading on the Development of Environmental Values." *Environmental Education Research* 22, no. 4 (2016): 504–517.

Fremerman, Sarah. "Ikkyū." In *Encylopedia of Buddhism,* vol. 1, edited by Robert E. Buswell, Jr., 351–352. New York: Macmillan Reference, USA, 2004.

Fricke, Tom E., Jui-Shan Chang, and Li-Shou Yang. 1994. "Historical and Ethnographic Perspectives on the Chinese Family." In *Social Change and the Family in Taiwan,* edited by Arland Thornton and Hui-Sheng Lin, 22–48. Chicago: University of Chicago Press, 1994.

Fruh, Kyle. "Promising's Neglected Siblings: Oaths, Vows, and Promissory Obligation." *Pacific Philosophical Quarterly* 100 (2019): 858–880.

Fu, Zhiying 符芝英, *Chuan deng: Xingyun Dashi zhuan* 傳燈：星雲大師傳 (Transmission of the lamp: The biography of Master Xingyun). Taibei: Tianxia wenhua, 1995.

——. *Handing Down the Light: The Biography of the Venerable Master Hsing Yun,* translated by Amy Lui-Ma. Hacienda Heights, CA: Buddha's Light Publishing, 2004.

Galbraith, Mary. "'Goodnight Nobody' Revisited: Using an Attachment Perspective to Study Picture Books about Bedtime." *Children's Literature Association Quarterly* 23, no. 4 (Winter 1998): 172–180.

Gardner, Howard. *Frames of Mind: The Theory of Multiple Intelligences.* 3rd ed. New York: Basic Books, 2011.

Genette, Gerard. *Paratexts: Thresholds of Interpretation,* translated by Jane E. Lewin. Cambridge: Cambridge University Press, 1997.

Glosser, Susan L. *Chinese Visions of Family and State, 1915–1953.* Berkeley and Los Angeles: University of California Press, 2003.

Goldman, Andrea S. "The Nun Who Wouldn't Be: Representations of Female Desire in Two Performance Genres of 'Si Fan.'" *Late Imperial China* 22, no. 1 (June 2001): 71–138.

Gong, Haomin. *Uneven Modernity: Literature, Film, and Intellectual Discourse in Postsocialist China.* Honolulu: University of Hawai'i Press, 2011.

Gould, Hannah, and Melyn McKay. "An Introduction to Bad Buddhism." *Journal of Global Buddhism* 21 (2020): 141–151.

Greene, Eric M. "A Reassessment of the Early History of Chinese Buddhist Vegetarianism." *Asia Major,* 3rd ser., 29, no. 1 (2016): 1–43.

Greene, Kathryn Therese. "Tzu Chi's Environmental Bodhisattvas: Confronting Environmental Crisis through Humanistic Buddhist Action." MA Thesis, University of Oslo, 2020.

Gubar, Marah. "Risky Business: Talking About Children in Children's Literature Criticism." *Children's Literature Association Quarterly* 38, no. 4 (Winter 2013): 450–457.

——. "The Hermeneutics of Recuperation: What a Kinship-Model Approach to Children's Agency Could Do for Children's Literature and Childhood Studies." *Jeunesse: Young People, Texts, Cultures* 8, no. 1 (Summer 2016): 291–310.

Guerra, Douglas A. *Slantwise Moves: Games, Literature, and Social Invention in Nineteenth-Century America.* Philadelphia: University of Pennsylvania Press, 2018.

Guggenmos, Esther-Maria. *"I Believe in Buddhism and Travelling": Denoting Oneself a Lay Buddhist in Contemporary Urban Taiwan.* Würzburg: Ergon-Verlag, 2017.

Hammerstrom, Erik J. *The Science of Chinese Buddhism: Early Twentieth-Century Engagements.* New York: Columbia University Press, 2015.

Hao Guangcai 郝廣才. *Hao huiben ruhe hao* 好繪本如何好 (What makes a good picturebook?). Taibei: Grimm, 2006.

——."Nande yijian de yitao haoshu" 難得一見一套好書 (A rarely seen set of good books). In *Dashi mima A* 大師密碼A, by Zheng Lier 鄭栗兒. Taibei: Fagu wenhua, 2006.

Harbsmeier, Christoph. *The Cartoonist Feng Zikai: Social Realism with a Buddhist Face.* Oxford: Oxford University Press, 1985.

——. "Reading the *One Hundred Parables Sūtra:* The Dialogue Preface and the *Gāthā* Postface." In *Zen Buddhist Rhetoric in China, Korea, and Japan,* edited by Christoph Anderl, 163–204. Leiden: Brill, 2011.

Harris, Daniel. *Cute, Quaint, Hungry and Romantic: The Aesthetics of Consumerism.* Boston: Da Capo Press, 2001.

Harris, Paul L., and Rebekah A. Richert. "William James, 'The World of Sense' and Trust in Testimony." *Mind & Language* 23, no. 5 (November 2008): 536–551.

Hayot, Eric. "Bridge Essay: The Emergence of Modernity." In *A Companion to World Literature,* edited by Ken Seigneurie. https://doi.org/10.1002/9781118635193.ctwl0118.

Heirman, Ann. "How to Deal with Dangerous and Annoying Animals: A Vinaya Perspective." *Religions* 10 (2019): 1–18. doi:10.3390/rel10020113.

Heller, Natasha. "*Peaceful Piggy*'s Paratext: Meditation for Children and Cross-Cultural Translation." *Bookbird: A Journal of International Children's Literature* 59, no. 2 (June 2021): 92–95.

Hillenbrand, Margaret. "Nostalgia, Place, and Making Peace with Modernity in East Asia." *Postcolonial Studies* 13, no. 4 (2010): 383–401.

Ho, Wan-Li. *Ecofamilism: Women, Religion, and Environmental Protection in Taiwan.* St. Petersburg, FL: Three Pines Press, 2016.

Hong, Wenqiong 洪文瓊. *Taiwan ertong wenxue shi* 臺灣兒童文學史 (A history of children's literature in Taiwan). Taibei: Chuanwen wenhua, 1994.

——. "Taiwan Fojiao tuhuashu wojian wosi" 臺灣佛教圖畫書我見我思 (My thoughts and views on Taiwanese Buddhist picturebooks). *Fojiao tushuguan guankan* 佛教圖書館館刊 59 (2005): 128–144.

Hsiung, Ping-chen. *A Tender Voyage: Children and Childhood in Late Imperial China.* Stanford: Stanford University Press, 2005.

Hsueh, James C. T. "A Profile of the Taiwanese Family." Institute for Family Studies, February 20, 2017. Accessed April 17, 2019. https://ifstudies.org/blog/a-profile-of-the-taiwanese-family.

Huang, C. Julia. *Charisma and Compassion: Cheng Yen and the Buddhist Tzu Chi Movement.* Cambridge, MA: Harvard University Press, 2009.

Huang, C. Julia. "Scientific and Sacramental: Engaged Buddhism and the Sacrilization of Medical Science in Tzu Chi (Ciji)." *Journal of Global Buddhism* 18 (2017): 72–90.

Huang, Hui-Ling. "Go Beyond Borders with Picture Books: A Case Study of a Taiwanese Children's Book Publisher." *Publishing Research Quarterly* 35 (2019): 52–67.

——. "Old Trees as Memory Keepers in Taiwanese Children's Books: Nostalgia as a Search for the Meanings of Change." *Children's Literature in Education* 51, no. 2 (2020): 207–227.

Huang, Shiru 黃詩茹. *Zhanhou Taiwan Fojiao de sengsu guanxi* 戰後台灣佛教的僧俗關係 (Lay-monastic relation in post-war Taiwanese Buddhism). Taibei: Academia Historica, 2010.

Huang, Shih-shan Susan. "Early Buddhist Illustrated Prints in Hangzhou." In *Knowledge and Text Production in an Age of Print: China, 900–1400,* edited by Lucille Chia and Hilde De Weerdt, 136–165. Leiden: Brill, 2011.

Huang Yijing 黃怡菁. "Bu dai mudi de gongdu" 不帶目的的共讀 (Shared reading without a purpose). *Qinzi tianxia* 親子天下 106 (May 2019): 110–111.

Idema, Wilt L. *Personal Salvation and Filial Piety: Two Precious Scroll Narratives of Guanyin and Her Acolytes.* Honolulu: University of Hawai'i Press, 2008.

Ivy, Marilyn. "The Art of Cute Little Things: Nara Yoshitomo's Parapolitics." *Mechademia* 5 (2010): 3–29.

Iwabuchi, Koichi. *Recentering Globalization: Popular Culture and Japanese Transnationalism.* Durham, NC: Duke University Press, 2002.

Jensen, Christopher. "Rhetorical Uses of the Exemplary Child Trope in the *Biographies of Eminent Monks* and *Biographies of Nuns.*" *Studies in Chinese Religions* 7, no. 1 (2021): 63–111.

Ji, Zhe. "The Origins of Secular Public Space: Religion, Education, and Politics in Modern China." In *A Secular Age Beyond the West: Religion, Law and the State in Asia, the Middle East and North Africa,* edited by Mirjam Künkler, John Madeley, and Shylashri Shankar, 61–85. Cambridge: Cambridge University Press, 2018.

Jiang, Canteng 江燦騰. *Taiwan Fojiao bainianshi zhi yanjiu* 台灣佛教百年史之研究 (Research on one hundred years of Buddhism in Taiwan). Taibei: Nantian shuju, 1996.

——. *Taiwan Fojiao shi* 臺灣佛教史 (History of Buddhism in Taiwan). Taibei: Wunan tushu chuban, 2009.

Johnson, David K., ed. *Ritual Opera, Operatic Ritual: "Mu-lien Rescues His Mother" in Chinese Popular Culture.* Berkeley: University of California Press, 1987.

Jones, Andrew F. *Developmental Fairy Tales: Evolutionary Thinking and Modern Chinese Culture.* Cambridge, MA: Harvard University Press, 2011.

Jones, Charles Brewer. *Buddhism in Taiwan: Religion and the State,* 1660–1990. Honolulu: University of Hawai'i Press, 1999.

——. "Buddha One: A One-day Buddha-Recitation Retreat in Contemporary Taiwan." In *Approaching the Land of Bliss: Religious Practice in the Cult of Amitābha,* edited by Richard K. Payne and Kenneth K. Tanaka, 264–280. Kuroda Institute, University of Hawai'i Press, 2004.

Joosen, Vanessa. "'Look More Closely, Said Mum': Mothers in Anthony Browne's Picture Books." *Children's Literature in Education* 46 (2015): 145–159.

Kagan, Richard C. "Taiwan—Education System." In *Encyclopedia of Modern Asia,* edited by David Levinson and Karen Christensen. New York: Charles Scribner's Sons, 2002.

Kan Zhengzong 闞正宗. *Chong du Taiwan Fojiao: Zhanhou Taiwan Fojiao* 重讀台灣佛教：戰後台灣佛教 (Re-reading Taiwanese Buddhism: Post-war Taiwanese Buddhism). Taibei: Daqian, 2004.

Kaplan, Uri. *Monastic Education in Korea: Teaching Monks about Buddhism in the Modern Age.* Honolulu: University of Hawai'i Press, 2020.

Kashiwagi, Yasunori. "Practices of Manabi in School." In *Manabi and Japanese Schooling Beyond Learning in the Era of Globalisation,* edited by Masamichi Ueno, Yasunori Kashiwagi, Kayo Fujii, Tomoya Saito, and Taku Murayama, 125–139. London: Routledge, 2020.

Kasmir, Sharryn. "The Anthropology of Labor." In *Oxford Research Encyclopedias.* Published online April 20, 2020. https://doi.org/10.1093/acrefore/9780190854584.013.97.

Katz, Paul R. *Divine Justice: Religion and the Development of Chinese Legal Culture.* London and New York: Routledge, 2009

——. "Chen Hailiang's Vision of Buddhist Family Life: A Preliminary Study." *Journal of Chinese Religions* 47, no. 1 (May 2019): 33–60.

Katz, Paul R., and Murray Rubinstein, eds. *Religion and the Formation of Taiwanese Identities.* New York: Palgrave Macmillan, 2003.

Kiely, Jan. "Spreading the Dharma with the Mechanized Press: New Buddhist Print Cultures in the Modern Chinese Print Revolution, 1866–1949." In *From Woodblocks to the Internet: Chinese Publishing and Print Culture in Transition, Circa 1800 to 2008,* edited by Cynthia Brokaw and Christopher A. Reed, 185–210. Leiden: Brill, 2010.

Kieschnick, John. "Buddhism: Biographies of Buddhist Monks." In *The Oxford History of Historical Writing,* edited by Daniel Woolf, vol. 1: *Beginnings to A.D. 600,* edited by Andrew Feldherr and Grant Hardy, 535–552. Oxford and New York: Oxford University Press, 2011.

Kim, Haewon. "An Icon in Motion: Rethinking the Iconography of Itinerant Monk Paintings from Dunhuang." *Religions* 11 (2020): 1–28.

Kinney, Anne Behnke. "The Theme of the Precocious Child in Early Chinese Literature." *T'oung Pao,* 2nd ser., 81, no. 1/3 (1995): 1–24.

——. *Representations of Childhood and Youth in Early China.* Stanford: Stanford University Press, 2004.

Kinsella, Sharon. "Cuties in Japan." In *Women, Media, and Consumption in Japan,* edited by Brian Moeran and Lise Scov, 220–254. London: Routledge, 1995.

Knapp, Keith Nathaniel. *Selfless Offspring: Filial Children and Social Order in Medieval China.* Honolulu: University of Hawai'i Press, 2005.

Knight, Nicola, Paulo Sousa, Justin L. Barrett, and Scott Atran. "Children's Attributions of Belief to Humans and God: Cross-Cultural Evidence." *Cognitive Science* 28 (2004): 117–126.

Knoepflmacher, U. C., and Mitzi Myers. "'Cross-Writing' and the Reconceptualizing of Children's Literary Studies." *Children's Literature* 25 (1997): vii–xvii.

Kotyk, Jeffrey. "Chinese State and Buddhist Historical Sources on Xuanzang: Historicity and the *Daci'en si sanzang fashi zhuan* 大慈恩寺三藏法師傳." *T'oung Pao* 105 (2019): 513–544.

Kuo, Cheng-tian. *Religion and Democracy in Taiwan.* Albany: State University of New York Press, 2008.

Lai, Rongdao. "The Wuchang Ideal: Buddhist Education and Identity Production in Republican China." *Studies in Chinese Religions* 3, no. 1 (2017): 55–70.

Lai, Whalen. "Chinese Buddhist Causation Theories: An Analysis of the Sinitic Mahāyāna Understanding of Pratitya-samutpāda." *Philosophy East and West* 27, no. 3 (July 1977): 241–264.

——. "Ch'an Metaphors: Wave, Water, Mirror, Lamp." *Philosophy East and West* 29, no. 3 (July 1979): 243–253.

Laliberté, André. *Politics of Buddhist Organizations in Taiwan, 1989–2003: Safeguarding the Faith, Building a Pure Land, Helping the Poor.* London and New York: RoutledgeCurzon, 2004.

——. "The Five Worlds of Religious Establishment in Taiwan." In *Varieties of Religious Establishment,* edited by Lori G. Beaman and Winnifred Fallers Sullivan, 147–162. London: Taylor & Francis Group, 2013.

——. "Religion and Politics." In *Routledge Handbook of Contemporary Taiwan,* edited by Gunter Schubert, 326–341. London: Routledge, 2016.

Lan, Pei-Chia. "Compressed Modernity and Glocal Entanglement: The Contested Transformation of Parenting Discourses in Postwar Taiwan." *Current Sociology* 62, no. 4 (2014): 531–549.

——. *Raising Global Families: Parenting, Immigration, and Class in Taiwan and the US.* Stanford: Stanford University Press, 2018.

Landy, Joshua. *How to Do Things with Fictions.* Oxford and New York: Oxford University Press, 2012.

Larsson, Bengt. "The Cosmopolitanization of Childhood: Eco-Knowledge in Children's Eco-Edutainment Books." *Young* 20, no. 2 (2012): 199–218.

Laureillard, Marie. "Regret of Spring: The Child According to Feng Zikai." *Oriens Extremus* 53 (2014): 47–60.

Lee, Chengpang, and Lin Han. "Recycling Bodhisattva: The Tzu-Chi Movement's Response to Global Climate Change." *Social Compass* 62, no. 3 (2015): 311–325.

Levering, Miriam. "The Precocious Child in Chinese Buddhism." In *Little Buddhas: Children and Childhood in Buddhist Texts and Transitions,* edited by Vanessa R. Sasson, 124–156. Oxford and New York: Oxford University Press, 2013.

Lewis, Mark Edward. *Sanctioned Violence in Early China.* Albany: State University of New York Press, 1990.

Li, Rongxi. *A Biography of the Tripiṭaka Master of the Great Ci'en Monastery of the Great Tang Dynasty.* Berkeley, CA: Bukkyō Dendō Kyōkai and Numata Center for Buddhist Translation and Research, 1995.

Li, Silong. "The Practice of Buddhist Education in Modern China." *Chinese Studies in History* 46, no. 3 (2013): 59–78.

Li, Yuhang. *Becoming Guanyin: Artistic Devotion of Buddhist Women in Late Imperial China.* New York: Columbia University Press, 2020.

Liao Peijun 廖珮均. "*Yaoshi jing* dui xiandai anning liaohu guan zhi qishi—yi ruai binghuan wei duixiang zhi yanjiu" 《藥師經》對現代安寧療護觀之啟示—以乳癌病患為對象之研究 (How the *Medicine Master Sūtra* illuminates palliative care perspectives—taking breast cancer as an example). MA Thesis, Huafan University, 2008.

Liao Qianrou 廖謙媃. "'Buda yuan' ertong foxue kecheng jiaoxue sheji yu jiaoju gaijie" 「佈達園」兒童佛學課程教學設計與教具概介 (Introduction to the design and teaching aids in "Buddha garden" Buddhist education for children). *Fojiao tushuguan guangkan* 佛教圖書館館刊 67 (2010): 63–85.

Lin Wenbao 林文寶. *Ertong wenxue lunji* 2 兒童文學論集二 (Collected essays on children's literature, vol. 2). Taibei: Wanjuan lou, 2017.

Lin Zhengyu 林正宇 and Xu Yating 許雅婷. "Qinzi gongdu yipu shouhu jiankang" 親子共讀醫普守護健康 (Parent-child shared reading of medical texts to protect health). *Ciji shuwei dianzang ziyuan wang* 慈濟數位典藏資源網. February 1, 2019. https://tcdata.tzuchi-org.tw/asset/detail/W_TC001_97396.

Liu, James T. C. "The Classical Chinese Primer: Its Three-Character Style and Authorship." *Journal of the American Oriental Society* 105, no. 2 (June 1985): 191–196.

Lo, Yuet Keung. "The Drama of Numskulls: Structure, Texture, and Functions of the Scripture of One Hundred Parables." *Early Medieval China* 12 (2006): 69–90.

Lofton, Kathryn. *Consuming Religion.* Chicago: University of Chicago Press, 2017.

Lopez, Donald S., Jr. *The Heart Sūtra Explained: Indian and Tibetan Commentaries.* Albany: State University of New York Press, 1988.

——. *Elaborations on Emptiness: Uses of the* Heart Sūtra. Princeton: Princeton University Press, 1996.

Lurhrmann, T. H. *How God Becomes Real: Kindling the Presence of Invisible Others*. Princeton and Oxford: Princeton University Press, 2020.

Lusthaus, Dan. "The *Heart Sūtra* in Chinese Yogācāra: Some Comparative Comments on the *Heart Sūtra* Commentaries of Wŏnch'ŭk and K'uei-chi." *International Journal of Buddhist Thought & Culture* 3 (2003): 59–103.

Madsen, Richard. *Democracy's Dharma: Religious Renaissance and Political Development in Taiwan*. Berkeley and Los Angeles: University of California Press, 2007.

Mai, Cuong T. "The Guanyin Fertility Cult and Family Religion in Late Imperial China: Repertoires across Domains in the Practice of Popular Religion." *Journal of the American Academy of Religion* 87, no. 1 (March 2019): 156–190.

Mair, Victor H. "The Origins of an Iconographical Form of the Pilgrim Hsüan-tsang." *T'ang Studies* 4 (1986): 29–41.

——. *T'ang Transformation Texts: A Study of the Buddhist Contributions to the Rise of Vernacular Fiction and Drama in China*. Cambridge, MA: Council on East Asian Studies, Harvard University, 1989.

Mallan, Kerry. "Empathy: Narrative Empathy and Children's Literature." In *(Re)imagining the World: Children's Literature's Response to Changing Times*, edited by Yan Wu, Kerry Mallan, and Roderick McGillis, 105–114. Berlin: Springer, 2013.

Marcus, Leonard S., comp. and ed. *Show Me a Story! Why Picture Books Matter: Conversations with 21 of the World's Most Celebrated Illustrators*. Somerville, MA: Candlewick Press, 2012.

Mather, Richard B. "The Bonze's Begging Bowl: Eating Practices in Buddhist Monasteries of Medieval India and China." *Journal of the American Oriental Society* 101, no. 4 (October–December 1981): 417–424.

McDaniel, Justin. "Superheroes and Slapstick: New Media and the Teaching of Buddhist Children in Thailand." In *Little Buddhas: Children and Childhoods in Buddhist Texts and Traditions*, edited by Vanessa R. Sasson, 290–304. Oxford and New York: Oxford University Press, 2013.

McDermott, Joseph P. *A Social History of the Chinese Book: Books and Literati Culture in Late Imperial China*. Hong Kong: Hong Kong University Press, 2006.

McGuire, Beverley Foulks. "Bringing Buddhism into the Classroom: Jiang Qian's 江謙 (1876–1942) Vision for Education in Republican China." *Journal of Chinese Religions* 39 (2011): 33–54.

——. "Playing with Karma: A Buddhist Board Game." *Material Religion* 10, no. 1 (2014): 4–29.

——. "Permeable Boundaries Between Ritual and Play: Religious and Ludic Possibilities in a Chinese Buddhist Board Game." *Journal of Chinese Buddhist Studies* 35 (2022): 109–151.

McGuire, Meredith B. *Lived Religion: Faith and Practice in Everyday Life*. Oxford: Oxford University Press, 2008.

McMahan, David L. *The Making of Buddhist Modernism*. Oxford: Oxford University Press, 2009.

McRae, John R. "Ch'an Commentaries on the *Heart Sutra:* Preliminary Inferences on the Permutation of Chinese Buddhism." *Journal of the International Association of Buddhist Studies* 11, no. 2 (1988): 87–115.

Meeks, Lori. "Imagining Rāhula in Medieval Japan: The 'Raun kōshiki.'" *Japanese Journal of Buddhist Studies* 43, no. 1 (2016): 131–151.

Mickenberg, Julia L., and Lynn Vallone, eds. *The Oxford Handbook of Children's Literature*. Oxford and New York: Oxford University Press, 2011.

Moloughney, Brian. "*Monkey* and the Journey Back to Paradise." *Script & Print* 29, no. 1–4 (2005): 221–233.

Morley, David. *Home Territories: Media, Mobility and Identity*. Abingdon, Oxon, and New York: Routledge, 2000.

Muller, Charles. "Yi xiang yi wei" 一相一味. *Digital Dictionary of Buddhism*. http://www.buddhism-dict.net/cgi-bin/xpr-ddb.pl?q=%E4%B8%80%E7%9B%B8%E4%B8%80%E5%91%B3.

Muller, Charles, and Lu Wang. "Wu yun" 五蘊. *Digital Dictionary of Buddhism*. http://www.buddhism-dict.net/cgi-bin/xpr-ddb.pl?4e.xml+id(%27b4e94-860a%27).

Murray, Julia K. "The Childhood of Gods and Sages." In *Children in Chinese Art,* edited by Ann Barrott Wicks, 108–132. Honolulu: University of Hawai'i Press, 2002.

Nakano, Yoshiko. "Who Initiates a Global Flow? Japanese Popular Culture in Asia." *Visual Communication* 1, no. 2 (June 2002): 229–253.

——. "Shared Memories: Japanese Pop Culture in China." In *Soft Power Superpowers: Cultural and National Assets of Japan and the United States,* edited by Watanabe Yasushi and David McConnell, 111–127. Armonk, NY: M. E. Sharpe, 2008.

Nattier, Jan. "The *Heart Sūtra:* A Chinese Apocryphal Text?" *Journal of the International Association of Buddhist Studies* 15, no. 2 (1992): 153–223.

Nelson, Katherine. "Language Pathways into the Community of Minds." In *Why Language Matters for Theory of Mind,* edited by Janet Wilde Astington and Jodie A. Baird, 26–49. Oxford and New York: Oxford University Press, 2005.

Ngai, Sianne. "The Cuteness of the Avant-Garde." *Critical Inquiry* 31, no. 4 (Summer 2005): 811–847.

Nicolaisen, Jeffrey. "The Intersection of Sentient Beings and Species, Traditional and Modern, in the Practices and Doctrine of Dharma Drum Mountain." In *Chinese Environmental Humanities: Practices of Environing at the Margins,* edited by Chia-Ju Chang, 289–308. Cham, Switzerland: Springer International Publishing AG, 2019.

——. "Protecting Life in Taiwan: Can the Rights of Nature Protect All Sentient Beings?" *ISLE: Interdisciplinary Studies in Literature and Environment* 27, no. 3 (2020): 613–632.

Nikolajeva, Maria. "The Verbal and the Visual: The Picturebook as Medium." In *Children's Literature as Communication: The ChiLPA Project,* edited by Roger D. Sell, 85–108. Amsterdam and Philadelphia: John Benjamins Publishing Company, 2002.

Nikolajeva, Maria, and Carole Scott. *How Picturebooks Work*. New York and London: Garland Publishing, 2001.

Nodelman, Perry. "The Eye and the I: Identification and First-Person Narratives in Picture Books." *Children's Literature* 19 (1991): 1–30.

——. *The Hidden Adult: Defining Children's Literature*. Baltimore: Johns Hopkins University Press, 2008.

"Not Just Kid Stuff." *Taiwan Today*. April 2, 2002. Accessed January 8, 2019. https://taiwantoday.tw/news.php?unit=20,29,35,45&post=24793.

Orsi, Robert A. "Is the Study of Lived Religion Irrelevant to the World We Live in? Special Presidential Plenary Address, Society for the Scientific Study of Religion, Salt Lake City, November 2, 2002." *Journal for the Scientific Study of Religion* 42, no. 2 (2003): 169–174.

Pacey, Scott. "A Buddhism for the Human World: Interpretations of *Renjian Fojiao* in Contemporary Taiwan," *Asian Studies Review* 29, no. 1 (2005): 61–77.

——. "Eminence and Edutainment: Xingyun and Daoxin as Television Celebrities." In *Religion and Media in China: Insights and Case Studies from the Mainland,*

Taiwan, and Hong Kong, edited by Stefania Travagnin, 71–89. New York and Oxon: Routledge, 2017.

——. *Buddhist Responses to Christianity in Postwar Taiwan: Awakening the World.* Amsterdam: Amsterdam University Press, 2020.

Peng, Huan-Sheng, and Jo-Ying Chu. "Japan's Colonial Policies—from National Assimilation to the Kominka Movement: A Comparative Study of Primary Education in Taiwan and Korea (1937–1945)." *Paedagogica Historica* 53, no. 4 (2017): 441–459. https://doi.org/10.1080/00309230.2016.1276201.

Pittman, Don A. *Toward a Modern Chinese Buddhism: Taixu's Reforms.* Honolulu: University of Hawai'i Press, 2001.

Pomata, Gianna. "Observation Rising: Birth of an Epistemic Genre, 1500–1650." In *Histories of Scientific Observation,* edited by Lorraine Daston and Elizabeth Lunbeck, 45–80. Chicago: University of Chicago Press, 2011.

Pong, Suet-ling, and Vivien W. Chen. "Co-resident Grandparents and Grandchildren's Academic Performance in Taiwan." *Journal of Comparative Family Studies* 41, no. 1 (Winter 2010): 111–129.

Požun, Peter, and Darinka Klemenc. "A Visit to the Buddhist Tzu Chi General Hospital in Hualien, Taiwan." *Nursing Ethics* 13, no. 1 (2006): 87–90.

Pu, Chengzhong. *Ethical Treatment of Animals in Early Chinese Buddhism: Beliefs and Practices.* Newcastle upon Tyne: Cambridge Scholars Publishing, 2014.

Pugh, Allison J. *Longing and Belonging: Parents, Children, and Consumer Culture.* Berkeley and Los Angeles: University of California Press, 2009.

Qiu Gerong 邱各容. *Taiwan Jindai ertong wenxue shi* 臺灣近代兒童文學史 (A history of modern children's literature in Taiwan). Taibei: Xiuwei (Showwe), 2013.

Reddy, Vasudevi. *How Infants Know Minds.* Cambridge, MA: Harvard University Press, 2010.

Reimer, Mavis. "Home." In *Keywords for Children's Literature,* edited by Philip Nel and Lissa Paul, 106–108. New York and London: New York University Press, 2011.

Reinke, Jens. "Innovation and Continuity in the Pure Lands: Pure Land Discourses and Practices at the Taiwanese Buddhist Order Dharma Drum Mountain." *Journal of Chinese Buddhist Studies* 30 (2017): 169–210.

Research Center for Digital Humanities, National Taiwan University. "Digital Library and Museum of Buddhist Studies." 1995. Accessed January 22, 2021. http://doi:10.6681/NTURCDH.DB_DLMBS/Collection.

Richardson, Nicole. "The Nation *in Utero:* Translating the Science of Fetal Education in Republican China." *Frontiers of History in China* 7, no. 1 (March 2012): 4–31.

Ritzinger, Justin R. *Anarchy in the Pure Land: Reinventing the Cult of Maitreya in Modern Chinese Buddhism.* Oxford: Oxford University Press, 2017.

——. "Vernacular Modernism: Humanistic Buddhism from Below in Bade, Taiwan." *Journal of Chinese Religions* 51, no. 1 (June 2023): 137–159.

Rossmanith, Nicole, Alan Costall, Andreas F. Reichelt, Beatriz López, and Vasudevi Reddy. "Jointly Structuring Triadic Spaces of Meaning and Action: Book Sharing from 3 Months On." *Frontier in Psychology* 5 (December 2014): article 1390.

Sanford, James. *Zen-Master Ikkyū.* Chico, CA: Scholar's Press, 1981.

Santibañez, Scott, Debra Boudreaux, Guo-Fang Tseng, and Kimberly Konkel. "The Tzu Chi Silent Mentor Program: Application of Buddhist Ethics to Teach Student Physicians Empathy, Compassion, and Self-Sacrifice." *Journal of Religion and Health* 55 (2016): 1483–1494.

Sasson, Vanessa R. "The Buddha's 'Childhood': The Foundation for the Great Departure." In *Little Buddhas: Children and Childhoods in Buddhist Texts and Traditions,* edited by Vanessa R. Sasson, 75–96. Oxford and New York: Oxford University Press, 2013.

Schneider, Helen M. *Keeping the Nation's House: Domestic Management and the Making of Modern China*. Vancouver: University of British Columbia Press, 2012.

Schwebel, Sara L. "The Limits of Agency for Children's Literature Scholars." *Jeunesse: Young People, Texts, Cultures* 8, no. 1 (Summer 2016): 278–290.

Scott, Gregory Adam. "A Revolution of Ink: Chinese Buddhist Periodicals in the Early Republic." In *Recovering Buddhism in Modern China,* edited by Jan Kiely and J. Brooks Jessup, 111–140. New York: Columbia University Press, 2016.

——. "Buddhism and Biomedicine in Republican China: Taixu's 'Buddhism and Science' (1923) and Ding Fubao's *Essentials of Buddhist Studies* (1920)." In *Buddhism and Medicine: An Anthology of Modern and Contemporary Sources,* edited by C. Pierce Salguero, 86–93. New York: Columbia University Press, 2020.

Seitz, Emily. "Growth of Children's Book Publishing in Taiwan." *International Journal of the Book* 4, no. 4 (2007): 213–220.

Shen, Lisa Chu. "Transcending the Nationalist Conception of Modernity: Poetic Children's Literature in Early Twentieth-Century China." *Children's Literature in Education* 49 (2018): 396–412.

Shengyan 聖嚴. *Guicheng* 歸程 (The road back). Tainan: Kaiyuan si, 1968.

——. *Shengyan fashi xuesi licheng* 聖嚴法師學思歷程 (Dharma Master Shengyan: Learning to think). Taibei: Zhongzheng shuju, 1993.

——. "Dashi de mima, chenggong de tezhi" 大師的密碼，成功的特質 (Code words of the great teachers, the special qualities of success). In *Dashi mima A* 大師密碼A, by Zheng Lier 鄭栗兒. Taibei: Fagu wenhua, 2006.

Shih, Miao Guang. "Modern Religious Tourism in Taiwan: A Case Study of Fo Guang Shan Buddha Memorial Center." *Renjian Fojiao xue bao: yishu* 人間佛教學報：藝術 3 (2016): 218–237.

Shinohara, Koichi. "Biographies of Eminent Monks in a Comparative Perspective: The Function of the Holy in Medieval Chinese Buddhism." *Chung-Hwa Buddhist Journal* 7 (1994): 477–500.

Silvio, Teri. "Pop Culture Icons: Religious Inflections of the Character Toy in Taiwan." *Mechademia* 3 (2008): 200–220.

——. *Puppets, Gods, and Brands: Theorizing the Age of Animation from Taiwan*. Honolulu: University of Hawai'i Press, 2019.

Stagg, Steven D., and Yi Chih Li. "Transitional Object Use, Attachment, and Help-seeking Behaviour in Taiwanese Adolescents." *Asian Journal of Social Psychology* 22, no. 2 (June 2019): 163–171.

Starling, Jessica. *Guardians of the Buddha's Home: Domestic Religion in Contemporary Jōdo Shinshū*. Honolulu: University of Hawai'i Press, 2019.

Stevens, Sarah E. "Hygienic Bodies and Public Mothers: The Rhetoric of Reproduction, Fetal Education, and Childhood in Republican China." In *Mapping Meanings: The Field of New Learning in Late Qing China,* edited by Michael Lackner and Natascha Vittinghoff, 559–683. Leiden: Brill, 2004

Stevenson, Dan. "A Vow for the Times: Sheng-yen and His Mission to 'Realize Human Potential' Through 'Conjoined Pursuit of Learning and Practice.'" In *Hoofprint of the Ox: Principles of the Chan Buddhist Path as Taught by a Modern Chinese Master,* edited by Sheng-yen Chang, 1–13. Oxford and New York: Oxford University Press, 2001.

Taidong County Government. "Ciji zeng 23 xiao 3000 ben yipu tongshu," 慈濟贈23校3000本醫普童書 (Tzu Chi gives 3000 children's medical books to 23 schools). October 2, 2018. https://www.taitung.gov.tw/News_Content.aspx?n=13370&s=51558.

Tamis-LeMonda, Catherine S., Shuyuan Wang, Eugenia Koutsouvanou, and Martina Albright. "Childrearing Values in Greece, Taiwan, and the United States." *Parenting: Science and Practice* 2, no. 3 (July–September 2002): 185–208.

Tang, Mei-chun. *Urban Chinese Families: An Anthropological Field Study in Taipei City, Taiwan*. Taipei: National Taiwan University Press, 1978.

Tao, Ching-sin. "Yishi Yuyan: Aesop's Fables in Late Qing China." *Translation Quarterly* 56 (2010): 1–55.

Taylor, Sally. "The Children's Book Market in Taiwan." *Publishers Weekly* 246 (July 12, 1999): 36–40.

Teiser, Stephen F. *The Scripture on the Ten Kings and the Making of Purgatory in Medieval Chinese Buddhism*. Honolulu: University of Hawai'i Press, 1994.

Thornton, Arland, T. Fricke, L. S. Yang, and J. S. Chang. "Theoretical Mechanisms of Family Change." In *Social Change and the Family in Taiwan*, edited by Arland Thornton and Hui-Sheng Lin, 88–115. Chicago and London: University of Chicago Press, 1994.

Thornton, Arland, L. S. Yang, and T. Fricke. "Weakening the Linkage between the Ancestors, the Living, and Future Generations." In *Social Change and the Family in Taiwan*, edited by Arland Thornton and Hui-Sheng Lin, 359–395. Chicago and London: University of Chicago Press, 1994.

Tillman, Margaret Mih. *Raising China's Revolutionaries: Modernizing Childhood for Cosmopolitan Nationalists and Liberated Comrades, 1920s–1950s*. New York: Columbia University Press, 2018.

Topsfield, Andrew. "The Indian Game of Snakes and Ladders." *Artibus Asiae* 46, no. 3 (1985): 203–226.

——. "Snakes and Ladders in India: Some Further Discoveries." *Artibus Asiae* 66, no. 1 (2006): 143–179.

Travagnin, Stefania. "Master Yinshun and the Pure Land Thought: A Doctrinal Gap Between Indian Buddhism and Chinese Buddhism." *Acta Orientalia Academiae Scientiarum Hungaricae* 57, no. 3 (2004): 271–328.

——. "Concepts and Institutions for a New Buddhist Education: Reforming the Saṃgha Between and Within State Agencies." *East Asian History* 38 (2014): 89–102.

——. "Charting Religion and Media in Taiwan: Media Expressions of Faith as (Pluri) Identity Markers in the Democratization Era." In *Religion and Media in China: Insights and Case Studies from the Mainland, Taiwan, and Hong Kong*, edited by Stefania Travagnin, 53–68. New York and Oxon: Routledge, 2017.

——. "Dharma in Motion Pictures: Buddhist Cartoons and Documentaries in Contemporary Taiwan." In *Religion and Media in China: Insights and Case Studies from the Mainland, Taiwan, and Hong Kong*, edited by Stefania Travagnin, 225–240. New York and Oxon: Routledge, 2017.

——. "Genealogy and Taxonomy of the 'Twentieth-century Renjian Fojiao 人間佛教': Mapping a famen 法門 from Mainland China and Taiwan to Europe." *Journal of Humanistic Buddhism* 人間佛教學報 9 (2017): 180–197.

——. "From Online Buddha Halls to Robot-Monks: New Developments in the Long-term Interaction between Buddhism, Media, and Technology in Contemporary China." *Review of Religion and Chinese Society* 7, no. 1 (2020): 120–148.

——. "Humanistic Buddhism (Rensheng Fojiao 人生佛教 / Renjian Fojiao 人間佛教)." In *Oxford Research Encyclopedia of Religion*. November 22, 2022. Accessed June 5, 2023. https://doi.org/10.1093/acrefore/9780199340378.013.635.

Tsai, Feng-jen, Sandrine Motamed, Nadia Elia, and André C. Rougemont. "Evolution in Intergenerational Exchanges Between Elderly People and Their Grandchildren in Taiwan; Data from a Multiple Round Cross-Sectional Study from 1993 to 2007." *BMC Public Health* 11 (2011): 639. http://www.biomedcentral.com/1471–2458/11/639.

Van Norden, Bryan, and Nicholaos Jones. "Huayan Buddhism." In *The Stanford Encyclopedia of Philosophy* (Winter 2019 ed.), edited by Edward N. Zalta. https://plato.stanford.edu/archives/win2019/entries/buddhism-huayan/.

Verchery, Lina. "Both Like and Unlike: Rebirth, Olfaction, and the Transspecies Imagination in Modern Chinese Buddhism." *Religions* 10, no. 6 (2019): 364. https://doi.org/10.3390/rel10060364.

Wang Caigui 王財貴. *Ertong dujing jiaoyu shuoming shouce* 兒童讀經教育說明手冊 (Instruction manual for children's education in reading the Classics). Taibei: Guoli Taizhong Shifan xueyuan yuwen jiaoxue yanjiu zhongxin, 1996.

Wang Caigui 王財貴, Ma Xingyi 馬行誼, Zhou Bixiang 周碧香, Shi Zhifang 施枝芳, Li Zhiying 李芝瑩, and Cheng Yaohua 陳珧華. *Dujing jiaoyu lilun yu shiwu* 讀經教育理論與實務 [The theory and practice of education in reading the Classics]. 2nd ed. Taibei: Hungyeh, 2015.

Warner, Marina. *Six Myths of Our Time: Little Angels, Little Monsters, Beautiful Beasts, and More*. New York: Vintage Books, 1995.

Wei Shu-chu. "Shaping a Cultural Identity: The Picture Book and Cartoons in Taiwan, 1945–1980." In *Illustrating Asia: Comics, Humor Magazines and Picture Books,* edited by John A. Lent, 64–80. Honolulu: University of Hawai'i Press, 2001.

Welch, Holmes. *The Buddhist Revival in China*. Cambridge, MA: Harvard University Press, 1968.

Weller, Robert P. *Discovering Nature: Globalization and Environmental Culture in China and Taiwan*. Cambridge: Cambridge University Press, 2006.

Wellman, Henry M., David Cross, and Julanne Watson. "Meta-Analysis of Theory-of-Mind Development: The Truth about False Belief." *Child Development* 72, no. 3 (May/June 2001): 655–684.

Williams-Oerberg, Elizabeth. "Buddhist Ritual as 'Connectionwork': Aesthetics and Technologies of Mediating Religious Belonging." *Numen* 68 (2021): 488–512.

Winnicott, D.W. *Playing and Reality*. London and New York: Routledge Classics, 2005.

Wolf, Margery. *Women and the Family in Rural Taiwan*. Stanford: Stanford University Press, 1972.

Wong, Dorothy C. "The Making of a Saint: Images of Xuanzang in East Asia." *Early Medieval China* 8 (2002): 43–95.

Wright, Arthur F. "Biography and Hagiography: Hui-chiao's *Lives of Eminent Monks*." In *Studies in Chinese Buddhism,* edited by Robert M. Somers, 73–111. New Haven, CT: Yale University Press, 1990.

Wu, Andrea Mei-ying 吳玫瑛. *Zhuti, xingbie, difang lunshu yu (hou) xiandai tongnian xiangxiang: zhanhou Taiwan shaonian xiaoshuo zhuanlun* 主題，性別，地方論述與（後）現代童年想像：戰後台灣少年小說專論 (Discourses of subject, gender, place, and (post)modern childhood in postwar Taiwanese juvenile fiction). Tainan: Chengda chuban she, 2017.

——. "Postcoloniality, Globalization, and Transcultural Production of Children's Literature in Postwar Taiwan." In *The Routledge Companion to International Children's Literature,* edited by John Stephens, Celia Abicalil Belmiro, Alice Curry, Li Lifang, and Yasmine S. Motawy, 123–134. London and New York: Routledge, 2018.

——. "Access to Books Matters: Cultural Ambassadors and the Editorial Task Force." *The Reading Teacher* 72, no. 6 (March 2019): 683–688.

Wu, Junqing. "Sex in the Cloister: Behind the Image of the 'Criminal Monk' in Ming Courtroom Tales." *T'oung Pao* 105, no. 5–6 (2020): 545–586. doi: https://doi.org/10.1163/15685322-10556P02.

Wyile, Andrea Schwenke. "First-Person Engaging Narration in the Picture Book: Verbal and Pictorial Variations." *Children's Literature in Education* 32, no. 3 (September 2001): 191–202.

Xiao Ya 曉亞. *Qinzi kuaile Chan* 親子快樂禪. Taibei: Fagu wenhua, 2014.

Xie Mingfang 謝明芳 and Lu Yifang 盧怡方. *Baobao ting gushi: gongdu haohao wan, yong huiben qidong haizi de yueduli* 寶寶聽故事：共讀好好玩，用繪本啟動孩子

的閱讀力 (Little darlings listen to stories: Shared reading is fun, using picture books to activate your child's strength in reading). Taibei: Xinshou fumu, 2015.

Xing Jiahui 幸佳慧. *Yong huiben gen haizi tan zhongyao de shi* 用繪本跟孩子談重要的事 (Using picture books to talk about important matters with children). Taibei: Ruhe, 2014.

Xingyun 星雲. *Banruoxinjing de shenghuo guan* 般若心經的生活觀 (The life-outlook of the *Prajña Heart Sūtra*). Taibei: Youlu wenhua, 2010.

Xingyun 星雲 and Nan Huaijin 南懷瑾. *Banruo lianhua chuchu kai: Ting Foxue dashi jiang xinjing* 般若莲花处处开：听佛学大师讲心经 (The lotus of prajñā opens everywhere: Listen to great teachers of Buddhism lecture on the *Heart Sūtra*). Beijing: Zhongguo huaqiao chuban, 2010.

Xu Suxia 徐素霞. "He Guanyin pusa yiqi youxi huanle!" 和觀音菩薩一起遊戲歡樂! (Play happily together with Bodhisattva Guanyin!). In Huang Yuhui 黃鈺惠, *Guanyin pusa bian bian bian* 觀音菩薩變變變 (Bodhisattva Guanyin, change, change, change). Taibei: Fagu wenhua, 2009.

Xu, Xu. "Imagination: Imaginations of the Nation—Childhood and Children's Literature in Modern China." In *(Re)imagining the World: Children's Literature's Response to Changing Times,* edited by Yan Wu, Kerry Mallan, and Roderick McGillis, 69–80. Berlin: Springer, 2013.

Yang Xiumian 楊秀娩. "Ciji yu *Yaoshi jing* de yinyuan" 慈濟與《藥師經》的因緣 (The relationship between Ciji and the *Medicine Master Sūtra*). MA Thesis, Ciji University, 2014.

Yao, Yushuang. *Taiwan's Tzu Chi as Engaged Buddhism: Origins, Organization, Appeal and Social Impact.* Boston: Global Oriental, 2012.

Yao, Yu-shuang, and Richard Gombrich. *Chinese Buddhism Today: Conservatism, Modernism, Syncretism and Enjoying Life on the Buddha's Light Mountain.* Sheffield, UK, and Bristol, CT: Equinox Publishing, 2022.

Ye Jingyi 葉靜宜. "Xingyun dashi *Huiben xingjing* tuwen quanshi yanjiu" 星雲大師《繪本心經》圖文詮釋研究 (Commentary and research on Master Xingyun's *Picturebook Heart Sūtra*). MA Thesis, Nanhua University, 2007.

Yikung. "The *Foguang Buddhist Canon:* The Unique and Creative Classification of Buddhist Works." *Studies in Chinese Religions* 2, no. 2 (2016): 202–219.

Yü, Chün-fang. *Kuan-yin: The Chinese Transformation of Avalokiteśvara.* New York: Columbia University Press, 2001.

——. *Passing the Light: The Incense Community and Buddhist Nuns in Contemporary Taiwan.* Honolulu: University of Hawai'i Press, 2016.

Yu, Jimmy. "A New Chan (Zen) School in Taiwan: Dharma Drum Lineage of Chan Buddhism." *Oxford Handbooks Online: Religion,* 2014. Accessed July 19, 2021. Doi: 10.1093/oxfordhb/9780199935420.013.006.

Yu, Li. "Character Recognition: A New Method of Learning to Read in Late Imperial China." *Late Imperial China* 33, no. 2 (December 2012): 1–39.

Yu Li. 玉立. "Huiben daodu, CUT bu CUT?" 繪本導讀，CUT不CUT?" (Should readers' guides in picturebooks be cut?"). *Xiaodahuixun* di22qi 小大會訊第22期, Huiben huayuan 繪本花園. Accessed July 30, 2020. https://www.ylib.com/kids/info2-LB.asp?DNO=66.

Zarrow, Peter. *Educating China: Knowledge, Society, and Textbooks in a Modernizing World, 1902–1937.* Cambridge: Cambridge University Press, 2015.

Zelizer, Viviana. *Pricing the Priceless Child: The Changing Social Value of Children.* Reprint. Princeton: Princeton University Press, 1994.

Zeng Weihui 曾維惠. "Rang haizi zai duoyuan kongjianzhong ziyou fazhan," 讓孩子在多元空間中自由發展 (Let children freely develop in a multiple dimensions). In Zeng Weihui, *Zhiduoxing xuetang* 智多星學堂 [Mastermind school]. Taibei: Tzu Chi chuanbo renwen zhiye jijinhui, 2009.

Zhai, Jiexia Elisa, and Robert D. Woodberry. "Religion and Educational Ideals in Contemporary Taiwan." *Journal for the Scientific Study of Religion* 50, no. 2 (2011): 307–327.

Zhang Jiazhen 張嘉真. *Kanjian huiben di liliang: cong huiben gushi daodu zhidao haizi zai xiang sheme* 看見繪本的力量：從繪本故事導讀知道孩子在想什麼 (Seeing the power of picturebooks: From the guided reading of picture-book stories know what your child is thinking). Taibei: Wunan, 2017.

Zheng Mingjin 鄭明進. "Xinshang *Mile Fo* de chahua zhi mei" 欣賞《彌勒佛》的插畫之美 (An appreciation of the beauty of the illustrations in *Maitreya Buddha*). In *Mile Fo yu guaiguai maxituan* 彌勒佛與怪怪馬戲團, by Chen Chen 陳辰, 36–37. Taibei: Fagu wenhua, 2010.

Zhou Huizhu 周慧珠. "Fojiao ertong duwu—jiaomu chenyou yuren chenshao yuedu qingsong xinling shengeng" 佛教兒童讀物——矯木趁幼 育人趁少 閱讀輕鬆 心靈深耕 (Buddhist reading material for children—straighten wood when green, educate people when young , and through relaxed reading plow deep the soul). *Renjian fobao* 人見佛報 (The Merit Times), May 27, 2012. Accessed January 21, 2021. https://www.merit-times.com.tw/NewsPage.aspx?unid=262929.

Zhu Deyong 朱德庸. "Yuanlai Shengyan fashi ye hen wanpi!" 原來聖嚴法師也很頑皮！(From the start Master Shenyan was very naughty!). In *Shengyan Fashi de wanpi tongnian* 聖嚴法師的頑皮童年 (Master Shengyan's naughty youth), by Shengyan 聖嚴, 2–4. Taibei: Fagu wenhua, 2009.

Index

Note: Page numbers in **bold** refer to illustrative matter

About the Author

Natasha Heller is associate professor in the Department of Religious Studies at the University of Virginia. She is the author of *Illusory Abiding: The Cultural Construction of the Chan Monk Zhongfeng Mingben (1263–1323)* (Harvard University Asia Center, 2014). Her recent work has also appeared in the *Journal of the American Academy of Religion, Brill's Encyclopedia of Buddhism, Bookbird: A Journal of International Children's Literature,* and *Education About Asia*, along with several edited volumes. She is currently working on a book about trees in the history of Chinese Buddhism.